Our Racist Legacy: Will The Church Resolve The Conflict?

Our Racist Legacy:

Will The Church Resolve The Conflict?

By Ivan A. Beals

The Church and the World Series, Volume IX

Cross Cultural Publications, Inc.

CrossRoads Books

The Church and The World Series, Volume IX

This series is dedicated to the scholarly investigation of Christianity's interaction with the non-Christian world. This includes the Church's initial encounters with the civilizations of the ancient world, its influence on the various tribal nationalities of medieval times and its missionary impact in modern times. It also includes Christianity's ideological and institutional impacts on the secular worlds of science, technology, politics, economics and the arts. It is hoped that this series will encourage scholars to research and publish monographs on themes in some of these areas in which scholarship is particularly deficient.
General Editor: Cyriac K. Pullapilly, St. Mary's College, Notre Dame; Consulting Editor: George H. Williams, Harvard University.

Published by **CROSS CULTURAL PUBLICATIONS, INC.**
CROSS ROADS BOOKS
Post Office Box 506
Notre Dame, Indiana, 46556, U.S.A.
Phone: (219) 273-6526, 1-800-561-6526
FAX: (219) 273-5973

ISBN: 0-940121-36-0
Library of Congress Catalog Card Number: 96-85046

Dedicated to the glory of God and to the encouragement
of peacemakers

Acknowledgements

I am specially indebted to Drs. Jorge M.S. Barros and W.E. McCumber
for their critical evaluation of the manuscript. Also, Mrs. Patty Hall,
Mrs. Kris Prince, Mrs. Linda Phelps, Mr. Tony DePina were computer
and secretarial assistants.

Cover design, Isaac Abundis

Contents

Foreword

I did not write this book. Had I done so, I would be immeasurably proud.

Having read this important Judeo-Christian work on the role of the Church in uprooting the deep division between the races, I am convinced that it has great value to a church population which has become far too silent on issues of diversity and racial tolerance.

While the title of this book, *Our Racist Legacy*, might offend some, racism, like alcoholism, cannot be cured until or unless we, the body of Christ, are willing to declare, "I stand in awe of my own racism."

The insightful author, The Reverend Dr. Ivan Beals, reminds us that the Church of Jesus Christ has had a long and ugly history of worshipping at the altar of the *"status quo* of white supremacy. . . ." This fact leaves us with a rather obvious and painful conclusion: the Christian Church has historically been possessed with a devil called racism. This is one of the worst kinds of devils for it seeks to separate the family of God on the sinfully presumptive grounds that God made an error at creation.

There are refreshing, if not redemptive moments in the author's description of the period of Jacksonian Democracy which "Launched an anti-slavery impulse." According to Beals, just about every religious body in the United States had its chance to serve as a lantern during the darkness of the 300 years of chattel slavery. Some, like the Pennsylvania Quakers, were daring in their opposition to slavery. Albeit tardy, a number of other religious groups eventually added their voices to the abolitionist movement. To be sure, the Church never quite became "the light of the world."

Today, the Church remains in the shadows on the issue of race. It has often been said 11:00, Sunday morning, is the most segregated hour of the week in America.

It will be impossible for the Church of Jesus Christ to assume its rightful place as the headlight of society while she fumbles and stumbles through the darkness of exclusion and bigotry herself. Paul cautioned us through his first letter to the church in Corinth, "For God is not the author of confusion, but of peace, as in all churches of the saints" (1 Corinthians 14:33, KJV).

Reverend Beals and I still have hope that the Church will triumph and will, one day, usher in the kingdom of everlasting righteousness and harmony among the family of God. Racism, as powerful as its legacy, will not extinguish the bright light of the Church. It is our great honor, it is our high heritage to ripen our faith to see that kingdom, and to see it even in this shameful hour of church-owned and-operated Jim Crowism. I believe this to be true for it was from the lips of the Son of God, the King of kings, the one preordained and blessed Potentate, Lord of lords who uttered these words: "Upon this rock I will build my church; and the gates of hell shall not prevail against it."

No, the racist legacy of the Church will not continue. The Light of the world, His Church, will become brighter as it illumines the souls of the intolerant. But if this light be extinguished with continued disobedience, God will light another.

EMANUEL CLEAVER II
Mayor
Kansas City, Missouri

Author's Preface

I was born and raised a WASP—a White Anglo-Saxon Protestant.

Living in Sioux City, Iowa, the first half of this 20th century, I eventually learned that subtle racism mingled with the Northern tradition against slavery. Despite my family religious teaching, racial prejudice cropped up in my childhood. Going beyond what society and the church practiced saying and doing, my parents rebuked such prejudice. I clearly recall some blatant and oft-times silent attitudes and actions against blacks throughout my school years, secular work, and 23 years of pastoring churches.

In 1985, veiwing the increasing issues of racism, I became impressed with the chronic impact of the Civil War on American churches and all society. My interest occurred at the 120th year of my great-grandfather's discharge from the Union Army. I found copies of some letters he sent home during the struggle. The pall of that conflict saturated his words. I asked myself: What were Christians saying and churches doing at that time? In what ways did Christian teaching affect the effort to free the slaves and support the Reconstruction years? How have present race relationships been affected by the past?

This study is not to tag any church denomination as a scapegoat. Neither is it to mock the noble, though often ineffective, attempts of some to abolish slavery and correct the racial injustice. Both secular society and the Church, once slavery became approved, stood exposed to a double-edged sword. The enticing master-slave lifestyle dealt heartache to both parties involved. Individuals, and the Church as a whole, held bitter attitudes, which soured past relationships and pollute the present situation. This corruption can only be purged by divine love.

The writer faces Christians with the thorny truth of racism in American churches, North and South. Though this treatise offers no easy solutions, the complacency to current problems becomes challenged. It is as much a personal spiritual summons as a charge to social change. The growth of other ethnic cultures within America require a whole turning from Christian action tainted with white supremacy. Any partial, *status quo* approach weakens the gospel's reconciling effect.

Neither our words nor our actions can convey, "Get outa here!" to blacks, or any other ethnics. We must begin as Christians, having the love of Christ, to build bridges of honest acceptance to all persons. Such love could produce equal justice for all. The Christian Church must fully admit in word and deed that God is no respecter of persons—or skin color.

What can and will be done to calm the turmoil of injustice, which has been rising for centuries? Since the abolition of slavery, the earthworks of civil rights laws have stemmed the tide some, but proper racial attitudes cannot be legislated. The Church must lead the way in changing people's attitudes. Will it begin with me—and you? Only Christ the Master, working through us, can calm this raging sea of conflict springing from the Civil War.

Introduction

Layers of treacherous racism surge beneath the surface of our society, spawned centuries ago. The historical Anglo-Saxon surmise of white supremacy still disrupts people relations now. The issue stems not from any human or racial defect, as some might suppose, but rather from differences of culture and color of skin. The focus of prejudice has long been on the African-American.

Black African slavery became an institution common to most of the New World colonies, jointly created by the maritime powers of Europe. These nations shared beliefs and associations regarding slavery, which they derived from the Scripture, classical works, and various types of servitude. Their cultural heritage framed and defined the issues for the American dissensions, which climaxed in the late 18th and 19th centuries, and extend till now.

How could enlightened Christian civilization explain slavery so as to accept it? Many Christians viewed slavery as a necessary but primitive stage in developing human institutions. An enforced social discipline such as bondage on savages might serve a dynamic purpose at an early stage of civilization. This agreed with the orthodox Biblicists who viewed the slavery approved by the Old Testament as precursory to universal freedom and justice as the final human destiny.

American colonists, and national citizens, moved from a "Christian" context to view African slavery as a means to progress in white civilization. The freedom offered to those in bondage was primarily deliverance from "the chains of sin." Yet converting blacks to Christianity never became the gateway to social freedom. It was used as a humane means of keeping them in their place.

The myth of white supremacy was made real primarily by the suppression of black Africans. People justified that inhumanity by claiming that bondage promoted their general progress and provided a means of their salvation. The idea of separate races, perceived by the contrast of skin color, supported the false notion that blacks were meant to be servants. Sadly, the Christian Church closed its eyes to the big lie, and courted the evil.

The Christian Church at first offered little protest against African slavery, often being party to it. This reproach sullies the valiant history of the Church in America. Efforts to assure group religious freedom did not include liberty for all people. Flawed religious beliefs combined with economic greed, induced even loyal churchmen to excuse heinous acts against black humanity.

Certain religious views fostered approval of human bondage. Between the 5th and 16th centuries, Christian scholars like Augustine and John Calvin proclaimed that God's saving grace was only to the elect—those predestined to be saved. This concept acclaimed the whites as elect—the blacks were not. The 18th century revolt by American white Protestants and Catholics for release from British rule only forged shackles for the slaves.

American Christianity's roots can often be traced to Puritan beliefs and pietism. The pre- and Revolutionary War eras have been called the fountainhead of Christian thought in this country. Many present religious concepts do stem from that period. Yet the more recent source feeding the stream of Christian beliefs and practice is the Civil War. That crisis and ensuing racial trauma is the present watershed of religious ideas and actions. Before the Civil War, the evils of slavery in America increased for over 200 years.

Slavery became a massive social institution which strained many of the colonies, and it split a number of church denominations. Even so, the South, with its distinct "racial plight," refused to consider emancipation of slaves. They valued the slave establishment above the union. By 1860 the nation's uneasy conscience became aroused. In the North a crusade swelled to combat the stands of indefinite compromise or peaceable secession.

The tragic course of events leading to the Civil War climaxed in the most traumatic experience Americans have endured on their soil. From the bloody test of arms a new nation emerged, purged and scarred, stripped of innocence, and facing the task of reconstruction. Over a century and a quarter later, that mission remains unfinished. The ongoing ordeal is the crucial, sacrificial venture of the nation—and its churches. Many do not understand this rugged "cross" carried by a free people— both black and white.

Ever since Abraham Lincoln freed the slaves, bitter racial strife has grown. This flow still pollutes every region and all society. Some probing questions arise: How strongly did Christians (North and South) condemn slavery? How has the Christian Church handled the racial problems resulting from freeing the slaves? To what extent have white Christians helped blacks regain human dignity? Will church people now meet the challenge to resolve the conflict and reconstruct a peace ruined by wrong moral choices? A sacrificial price in effort must be paid to right the wrongs.

With the war's triumphant end, gaining their freedom, Negroes tried to claim and experience what the Emancipation Proclamation promised. At first, the Constitution, legislatures, and courts fulfilled their assigned roles. Yet in a few years, an imposed white racial bias denied the lawful rights of blacks. Their crucial struggle for equal human rights continues now. Thus racial peace is being held hostage by this prejudice.

The socio-religious problems flowing from the slavery issue have increased throughout the generations. Though the Civil War halted the purchase and keeping of slaves, we still wallow in the "backwater" problems of that flood. Old swamps of corrupt human relations remain caustic from neglect. Although slavery ceased, racial bias remains— sometimes strident, or at times subtle. The current generation is challenged afresh not to refight the Civil War, but to clear a new plane of acceptance and reconciliation.

The Christian Church in America has met racism with a cautious gaze to avert the complex issue. The Church has been content with the *status quo* of white supremacy, and remained silent. The witness of early American churches—Anglican, Baptist, Catholic, Dutch Reformed, Lutheran, Methodist, Moravian, Presbyterian, Puritan (Congregational), and Quaker (Friends)—is soiled by the blood of slaves on their hands. That guilty stain was set both by selfish actions in support of, and by failures to halt the bondage.

Any history of America must relate the havoc of slavery and non-emancipation. Indeed, the black churches, in connection with the white churches, record the unique African-American heritage from the early 19th century revivals to the present time. American civilization is faced with making the harmful commitments that processed from medieval Christianity and Puritan ideas. Also, the impact of Social Darwinianism in the late 19th century persists.

Since the beginnings of these United States the Christian Church has largely assumed white supremacy. A racist legacy also stems from the dogmatic greed that allowed and advanced African slavery. This mindset fostered attitudes that persist in viewing Negroes as less-than-human. These concepts gained support from accepted religious, political, scientific, and economical bases. Such ideas prompted actions to pass laws and erect barriers that deprived a people, though freed, from having equal human rights.

This present generation's guilt is not over 390-year-old sins. People today are called to account for the immediate past and the present thrust of their own deeds. White Christian churches in America have a mixed record in acting for the civil rights of blacks. Church leaders have often ignored the racial needs in their own communities. They find it much easier to raise money to send missionaries to Africa, than to offer helping hands of Christian brotherhood to African-Americans.

As *Time* magazine declared in 1956, the Church may still be the most segregated institution in American society. Also in a recent *Time* article (Nov. 12, 1990),"Taking the Measure of American Racism," South African-born Mark Matha Bane states that one of the most segregated hours in America occurs at 11:00 a.m. on Sunday. That's the usual time of Christian worship and fellowship.

The reluctance of the Church to face up to racial problems presents a troublesome repetition of history. Even so, churches remain accountable for their role in allowing such problems to go unchecked, for giving silent support to racism. As the Scripture declares, "It is time for judgment to begin with the family of God" (1 Peter 4:17, NIV). That judgment centers on their selfishness.

Any survey of racism in American Christianity is like wading through a treacherous swamp. It proves distressing to both groups and to individuals. Frankly, all peoples have some prejudice about others. This treatise condemns deeds of white supremacy and declares the impact of Negro slavery on race relations. It reproves views that dehumanize any people. Many Christians don't want to be prejudiced, and they avoid admitting to any bias.

Yet, ethnic minorities often become as a rung of the social ladder, on which whites stand to elevate themselves and to increase their wealth. Church people in every area of life should admit their racial prejudices and forsake them. But knowing the need does not guarantee the deed. This urgent task faced Christians from the Early Church on. It first concerned Jewish apostles taking the gospel of Jesus Christ to the hated Gentiles.

Many assume that simple faith in Christ routinely expelled "racial prejudice." Yet the apostle Peter needed a special vision (Acts 10:7-22). A similar experience is essential to bring about right relations between whites and blacks. For generations, in both the North and the South, professed Christians have allowed old biased concepts to thwart the Civil War peace. That conflict and aftermath still infect the attitudes of church people, blunt the gospel, and disrupt race relations. Facing that trauma, Christians must truly worship the Lord God Almighty as the God of all peoples.

Recall the prophet-concepts of "burden" and "vision." The silence of organized Christianity during this prolonged struggle now requires strong prophetic words. Like a burdened prophet, Christians should speak out against racism. God gives the vision. Jesus taught that His followers should love their neighbors as themselves. Church people must not depend on the failed *status quo* to inspire necessary changes. Only a self-denying response to erase racism will help bring reconciliation. The times call for building bridges of friendship—not walls of distrust.

This probing review is like a "burden" received in mind and heart, one addressed particularly to Christians and to all fair-minded people. The timeless "vision" of God's kingdom must be renewed. Without that revelation, as the Scripture says, "the people cast off restraint" (Proverbs 29:18). Instead of simply doing the expedient thing, the Church must ask: What would Jesus do about racism in our land today? His compassionate dealing with a despised Samaritan woman offers a clear clue.

Really, any social attitudes of selfishness that support racial conflict stem from mankind's subtle, inner conflict over worshiping himself. Self-worship occurs on the same path that one takes when he thinks that he is better than other people. It may be that a Christian believes he has kept God's commandments, and by careful watch of conscience has avoided the common snares of Satan. Yet, in the very act of doing so, one may fall into secret pride before God, like a Pharisee in the temple. He prayed about himself: "God, I thank you that I am not like all other men . . ." (Luke 18:11).

Right racial relationships, whether casual or close, is when Christians truly accept others. A Christian person's spiritual relationship with others cannot be divorced from social justice. Indeed, Christian moral attitudes are grounded on respect for other humans as equal persons despite "racial" or cultural differences. Suspicion and fear of people with other skin colors are allayed as insights are gained to each person's worth. When the dignity and worth of persons are diminished, we are all degraded.

The purpose of this treatise is to trace the role of the Church and well-meaning Christians in the slave trade. It is to arraign the Church in condoning African slavery as an accepted Christian practice, as well as a desirable economic and social system. This shocking body of gathered facts shout for repentance and reconciliation. The study is not to arbitrarily assign long-time guilt, but to call for the Christian Church to respond unselfishly in love and justice to deal with racism now.

Infected by black slavery, this complex issue involves historical, religious, philosophical, social, political, economic, legal, and scientific aspects. Even the conflict is twofold— a personal spiritual struggle and a conflict in human relationships. An overview of the tangle is shown through events noted in the following 12 chapters. The account begins in history and proceeds to current events.

Political efforts, legislative and judicial, economic and educational efforts, all lack the moral thrust that resolving the conflict and building peace demands. The Civil War peace was lost on a devious trail of moral wrongs. Only the Church has the true message and the Divine commission to lead in righting moral wrongs with the gospel of Christ. Only if the Church lives out its Christian message, whatever the cost, can it rightly augment the ultimate solution of the age-old "Negro question."

God's Word draws each of us from racial bias to brotherhood: "He made from one, every nation of mankind to live on all the face of the earth, having determined their appointed times, and the boundaries of their habitation" (Acts 17:26, NASB). Bridges of friendship can be built with patience and respect for others, by God's uniting love. As individuals and peoples are reconciled to God, they become reconciled to one another. God calls the Church as a whole, and every person to turn from selfishness, to renounce the racist legacy, resolve the conflict, and build the peace.

Chapter I

Slavery and the Watersheds of Religion in America

Like Abraham, the Old Testament patriarch, Englishmen bound for the New World sustained themselves with the assurance that God led. God would raise up a new realm and a new people. As the English people planned their pilgrimage to Virginia, John Rolfe observed, they were "a peculiar people, marked and chosen by the finger of God, to possess it, for undoubtedly He is with us."[1]

King James I, on April 10, 1606, chartered two companies to support settlements in the New World. The London Company received dominion over land between the 34th and 41st degrees of latitude, with control 100 miles out to sea and 100 miles inland. The other, the Plymouth Company, received a similar grant farther north. Eight months later, January 1, 1607, the London Company expedition sailed, and sighted the Virginia coast April 26. The Royal Charter of Virginia clearly shows the religious motivation.

> We greatly commending, and graciously accepting of, their desires for the furtherance of so noble a work, which may, by the providence of Almighty God, hereafter tend to the glory of his divine Majesty, in propagating of Christian religion to such people, as yet live in darkness and miserable ignorance of the true knowledge and worship of God, and may in time bring the infidels and savages, living in those parts, to human civility, and to a settled and quiet government: do by these our letters patents, graciously accept of and agree to, their humble and well intended desires.[2]

The Jamestown, Virginia colony did not become known for its religious fervor like the later Plymouth, Massachusetts Puritan colony. However, the Jamestown settlers showed some Christian purpose. Soon after landing on Virginia soil in May 1607, they joined Rev. Robert Hunt ("an honest, religious, and courageous Divine," according to Capt. John Smith) in the first Protestant Holy Communion. Rev. Hunt, a vicar from Kent, England, was chosen by the colony's president, Edward-Marie Wingfield, and approved by Anglican Archbishop Bancroft as a man "not any way to be touched with the rebellious humors of a popish spirit, nor blemished with the least suspicion of a factious scismatick."[3]

From the beginning, the Church of England became by law the official church of Virginia. The second church, built in 1611 at the newly organized town of Henrico, was pastored by Alexander Whitaker. He preached a sermon, "Good Newes from Virginia," which found its way back to England, was published, and won wide notice. Among his achievements was his role in the conversion and baptism of Pocahontas. Whitaker also performed the wedding ceremony of John Rolfe and Indian maiden Pocahontas.

In 1619 a representative House of Burgesses was formed. They met in the Jamestown church choir loft as America's first elective assembly. Their decrees cited idleness and gaming as punishable offenses. They forbade immodest dress; and ministers were to reprove the intemperate, publicly if need be. They legislated fines for swearing, and even excommunication and arrest for chronic sinning. Morning and afternoon church services were required on Sunday, with those who neglected them subject to censure. The governor set apart "glebes," or lands to support the church and ministers in each of the four parishes of the colony. To promote evangelism among the Indians, each town must educate "a certain number" of natives and prepare them for college.[4]

In time, the colony's economy and social structure took precedence. They deferred an earlier passion to evangelize the Indians, and made efforts to Christianize the Negroes. Every feature of the colony's life became conditioned by a rapid-growing slave population. By 1667 Virginia lawmakers acted to distinguish between spiritual freedom from the bondage of slavery. The law-makers declared that although a slave converted to Christianity and received baptism, he remained bound to his master.[5]

This action fixed the excuse for enslaving blacks, considering them neither white nor truly Christian. An English lady of the West Indies wrote Rev. Morgan Godwyn, in Virginia, that one "might as well baptize puppies as Negroes."[6] By 1723 Virginia law banned manumissions of slaves except those approved by the governor and council for meritorious service. As freedom and opportunity increased for whites, the rights and freedom of blacks waned.

By 1743 Commissary James Blair told how fully slavery had merged the social structure of Virginia: "From an instrument of wealth, (slavery) had become a molding power, leaving it a vexed question which controlled society most, the African slave or his master." For over a century some expressed concern that slaves receive religious nurture as a feature of the social order. This was beside the aims of the Society for the

Propagation of the Gospel in Foreign Parts. Yet in 1731 George Berkeley accused American slaveholders for binding the blacks with "an irrational contempt . . . as creatures of another species who had no right to be instructed or admitted to the sacraments."[7]

A mix of political, economic, and ecclesiastical policy urged by immigration, soil, sun, and slavery, combined to create the "first South." In 1765, a Quaker missionary protested that "it is too manifest to be denied, that the life of religion is almost lost where slaves are very numerous."[8] Whatever godly purpose was at first pursued, became secondary to material goals. The drive for political power and economic gain soon confirmed the uprightness of slavery to reach those desired ends.

New England, however, is known as the place where Puritanism achieved its fullest flower. The four chief New England colonies were instilled with a peculiar corporate spirit. The concept of a "national covenant" bound the people of each commonwealth together in a public task. From the beginning, this sense of a common calling was strengthened by the conviction that the Reformation enacted was truly a decisive phase in the final chapter of God's plan for His Church in this world.

In 1620 the English Separatists sailed from Holland for England, and thence to the New World, launching as true religious pilgrims. Pastor John Robinson assured them: "The Lord hath more truth and light yet to break forth out of his holy Word." They viewed God's plan for this world as incomplete, not fully disclosed. They felt God was sending them on an errand into the wilderness. In His continuing revelation, they would be used by Him in forming a pure church amid vain and fleeting life.[9]

Like other Puritans, Robinson's congregation contended that the Church of England was not completely reformed, not really pure, in membership, worship, or in its government. The pilgrims in Holland ceased trying to reform the Church of England from within. Becoming Separatist, they fled England to escape the severe penalties of the law. They left friends and fortune behind, going first to Amsterdam, and then to Leyden in 1608.

The ship "Speedwell," sailing from Leyden, joined the "Mayflower," another vessel, in Plymouth harbor in southern England. The whole company finally took passage for the New World, sailing west on the "Mayflower," September 16, 1620. The overcrowded and under-provisioned ship had in addition to its crew of 48, 101 passengers: 56 adults, 14 servants and hired artisans (not Separatists), and 31 children, of whom at least 7 were waifs. During the 65-day voyage, one passenger died, and two were born. The first winter curtailed their good fortune; by spring half of the company had died of scurvy or general debility.[10]

Plymouth colony remains a classic instance of congregational Separatism in America. The so-called "Pilgrim Fathers" came from lower middle class backgrounds, with few academic pretensions or desires. Less than 20 university men came to the colony during its first three decades—only 3 of them, all ministers, remained. Because the colony attracted few immigrants, its churches were often without ministers. A Dutch visitor in 1627 saw the Plymouth Pilgrims marching in solemn procession to Sabbath meeting by drumbeat. Elder William Brewster, a layman, "taught twise every Saboth, and yt both powerfully and profitably, to ye great contemment of ye hearers, and their comfortable edification; yea, many were brought to God by his ministrie."[11]

Soon, New England's Puritans, including the Massachusetts Bay Company, Separatist and Nonseparatist alike, all gathered under the banner of Congregationalism. Rev. John Cotton, the leading Boston divine, listed the real distinctions: (1) rule practiced by the bishops and conformity demanded by law are burdens too heavy to bear; (2) use of the Book of Common Prayer violates the Second Commandment's prohibition against manmade images; (3) the highest earthly ecclesiastical authority is the local congregation; (4) only those who give evidence of conversion in their lives and conversation are eligible for church membership; (5) the church is formed by a voluntary covenant among believers.[12]

This church covenant presumed a prior contract: the covenant of divine grace. All communion between God and mankind found its basis in this covenant, in which God accepted those foreordained to receive His grace. The covenant bound God to man and man to God in union that was eternally secure. People so bound should stand before their peers, showing "their knowledge in the principles of religion, and of their experience in the ways of grace, and of their godly conversations among men."[13]

Christian life soon become soiled by slavery, undaunted by the strict dogma of Puritanism or by liberal Anglicans. Clergy and laypeople of all the colonial churches—Anglicans, Catholics, Congregationalists, Presbyterians, Baptists, Quakers, Methodists, Lutherans, and various Reformed bodies—were among the slave traders or slaveholders. Only the "communitarian" sects such as the Mennonites, Amish, and others withheld from the besetting evil.

At a General Court held in Warwick, Rhode Island, the Quakers passed a resolution against slavery, May 18, 1652:

> Whereas there is a common course practiced among Englishmen, to buy negroes to that end that they may have them for service or as slaves forever; for the preventing of such practices among us, let it be ordered, that no black mankind or white being shall be forced, by covenant, bond, or otherwise, to serve any man or his assignees longer than ten years, . . . at the end or term of ten years, to set them free as the manner is with the English servants. And that man that will not let them go free, or shall sell them away elsewhere, to that end they may be enslaved to others for a longer time, he or they shall forfeit to the colony forty pounds.[14]

There were both Indian and Negro slaves in the Old Colony as early as 1646. The authorities then announced their intentions of selling Indians or exchanging them for Negroes as punishment for offenses. The Bay Colony formally recognized the institution of slavery in its Code of Fundamentals, or Body of Liberties, adopted in 1641. It was the first of the colonies to do so. Three years later, this "peculiar institution" was implicitly recognized in the Articles of Confederation drawn up by the United Colonies.

The treatment of slaves was left to the individual colony. Each could decide who was a slave and the rules on how slaves should be treated. The slave code gauged the fears and perceptions of a colony, as to what laws the white settlers felt necessary to hold the slaves in check. In New England, as elsewhere, religion proved the moving force to expose blacks to book learning. Concern for the spiritual welfare of slaves led prominent Puritans, such as Cotton Mather, to found charity schools with Bible study as the chief subject.

In the late 17th century, Boston Puritan minister Cotton Mather insisted that masters treat their slaves "according to the rules of humanity" as persons with "immortal souls in them and not mere beasts of burden." Puritan masters were convinced it was wrong to work their slaves on the Sabbath. They also gave the Negroes medical attention when they were ill.[15]

Mather eventually formed a society to instruct Negroes in Christianity and performed slave marriages with Christian dignity. He told other ministers to preach "Thy Negro is thy neighbor" to their congregations. He supported what he preached saying: "I would remember, that my servants are in some sense my children . . . Nor will I leave them ignorant of anything, wherein I may instruct them to be useful to their generation." He added that "I will put Bibles and other good and proper books in their hands."[16]

Judge Samuel Sewall of Massachusetts wrote a pamphlet, "The Selling of Joseph," which appeared in 1701, as the first direct attack on slavery in New England. He urged masters to give religious instruction to their bondsmen. Yet Anglican clergy, working in the Southern colonies, often found it difficult to persuade planters to even offer book learning to slaves. The church there found itself hindered in an environment dominated more by "rice than by righteousness." Pointing up the problem, Judge Sewall wrote in 1705:

> Talk to a Planter of the Soul of a Negro, and He'll apt to tell ye (or at least his Actions speak it loudly) that the Body of one of them may be worth twenty Pounds; but the Souls of an hundred of them would not yield him one Farthing . . .[17]

In some respects the Anglicans had greater success in providing schooling for slaves. In 1695, Oxford graduate Thomas Bray was appointed commissary to Maryland. A gifted pastor and teacher, he eagerly helped those that "shall most hazard their persons in attempting the conversion of the Negroes or native Indians." Bray with several influential backers founded the Society for Promoting Christian Knowledge (SPCK) in 1699 in London. The society thus early entered the book business—buying, printing, distributing, and educating. In 1705 the society founded a Negro school in New York City. Forty years later, the Charleston Negro School began, in which two former slaves, Harry and Andrew, became teachers, trained and freed for that purpose.[18]

After Commissary Bray's first visit to Maryland in 1700, he returned to found a second society, the Society for the Propagation of the Gospel in Foreign Parts (SPG). In America less than six months, Bray realized the church was in difficult straits. To gain support for a suitable ministry, he proposed this society to insure the Church of England's place in "foreign parts," and to work for the conversion of Negroes and Indians. From the start, the society ordered its missionaries to "use their best endeavors, at proper times to instruct the Negroes." The society worked with another Anglican band, "the Associates of Doctor Bray," in founding a school in Philadelphia. This group opened schools in Williamsburg and Newport, with some support from Benjamin Franklin.[19]

Most colonial Christians did not oppose slavery because no part of the Christian Church ever took a firm stand. Even in New Testament times, the Church embraced both slaves and slaveholders. The Early Church Fathers and medieval authorities enlarged the scriptural advice to both parties. Catholics and Protestants alike shared the traditional acceptance of slavery, particularly of pagans. North American colonists pointed to an ancient and strong tradition to support slavery.

The rationale to promote slavery claimed substance in five points: (1) Africans could be enslaved because they were under Noah's curse upon his son Ham. (2) Israel, God's chosen people, had slaves. (3) Jesus Christ did not forbid slavery. (4) Slavery was merely the lowest level in a divinely approved social order. (5) The enslavement of Africans actually improved their lives, by giving them access to the gospel.[20]

Like some other church denominations, the Quakers made early efforts to give religious instruction to the Negro. Themselves persecuted, the Quakers of the Middle Colonies, who rejected war and violence, became the first white group that moved to aid the slave. Viewing slavery as a form of violence, they eventually freed their own slaves, and urged others to do the same.

Only Quakers, of the various church groups, believed religious instruction to be a step toward physical freedom as well as a means of spiritual salvation from the bondage of sin. From the time of the Germantown protest, the Quaker conscience was disturbed against slavery. By 1700 three Friends leaders urged plans for the mental improvement of slaves: George Fox, founder; William Penn, colonial proprietor; and George Keith of Philadelphia. Their followers in 1693 published the first antislavery tract in British America.

Prosperous Quaker communities in Rhode Island, the Jerseys, and Pennsylvania depended greatly on slave labor in the Caribbean. Yet George Fox knew the problems raised by American slavery. His famous letter of 1657, "To Friends Beyond Sea That Have Blacks and Indian Slaves," stressed Christian mercy and brotherhood. Preaching to slaves in Barbados 14 years later, he proposed that Christian servitude be limited to 30 years of bondage. Fox viewed Negro slavery as an institution, based on the ancient dualism of body and soul, matter and spirit. He believed that the relations of master and slave could be imbued with a divine spirit of love. This belief resembled that of many Catholics and Protestants.

William Penn bought and owned Negro slaves, however, and the Quaker dominated government in Pennsylvania passed a harsh slave code. As late as 1730 Quaker merchants in Philadelphia imported and sold West Indian Negroes. Also, the Rhode Island slave trade in the 1760s involved leading Quaker families. Though Quaker masters were perhaps more humane than most, they did not really Christianize the institution of slavery. But in 1756 the Society of Friends acted to induce owners to provide religious instruction for their slaves. Yet congregations did not receive Negroes as brethren entitled to equal membership or to Quaker burial.

Slave holding certainly provoked far more tension among the Quakers than among Anglicans, Congregationalists, or Catholics. The Quaker frame of mind enabled men to ignore human law and precedent, and to judge slavery by the divine Inner Light. The Quaker genius achieved a dynamic tension between an impulse to Christian perfection and a way of life seeking to crystallize the impulse in forms within the demands of reality.

In 1676 William Edmundson, an associate of Fox, sent out a general letter from Newport, Rhode Island, to Quakers in slave-holding colonies. He reviewed the ancient linkage between sin and bondage. He said that barbarian masters had allowed slaves the sinful liberty to follow the desires of their own corrupt natures, but denied them freedom to be servants of Christ. To obey the command to "make their condition your own," Quakers must enable their Negroes to fulfill the law of Christ. Edmundson inverted the traditional dualism when he reasoned that physical slavery and Christian liberty were incompatible. Negroes were slaves to sin because they were made slaves of men. This point was only a short step to the conclusion that slavery itself was sin.[21]

During the first half of the following century (18th), a half-dozen Quaker reformers condemned slavery. The greatest of these was John Woolman, a New Jersey Quaker, "perhaps the most Christlike individual that Quakerism has produced." He gave powerful stimulus to antislavery feelings. Slavery was entrenched in New Jersey by the middle of the 18th century, and it flourished among all religious groups, including the Quakers. From the time Woolman was obliged to make out a bill of sale for a slave (on behalf of his employer) in 1742, Woolman found himself fired with the urgent task of abolishing slavery. In his *Journal* for 1749, he shows his growing concern over slavery:

> Two things were remarkable to me in this journey [to the south]. First, in regard to my entertainment, when I ate, drank and lodged at free cost with people who lived in ease on the hard labor of their slaves, I felt uneasy . . . Where the Masters bore a good share of the burden and lived frugally, so that their servants were well-provided for and their labor moderate, I felt more easy. . . .

> Secondly, this trade of importing slaves from their native country being much encouraged amongst them and the white people and their children so generally living without much labor was

frequently the subject of my serious thoughts. And I saw in these Southern Provinces so many vices and corruptions, increased by this trade and this way of life, that it appeared to me as a gloom over the land. . . .[22]

Anthony Benezet, Woolman's coworker, was a leading antislavery propagandist in pre-Revolutionary War America. Quaker Benezet compiled, reprinted, and sold abolitionist books and pamphlets. Founding a school in 1770 for Negro children in Philadelphia, he declared: "I have found amongst the Negroes as great variety of talent as amongst a like number of whites." He also said the belief "that the blacks are inferior in their capacities, is a vulgar prejudice, founded on . . . pride or ignorance." For two years the class sessions were held in his home. The school had a few white students, 6 out of 46, in 1775. The basic reason for its existence lay in meeting a duty "to those oppressed people"—Negro slaves.[23]

Also in 1775, Benezet and a group of Philadelphia Quakers formed the country's first antislavery society. During the next two decades similar organizations began in several states, including Maryland (1790), Virginia (1791), and Delaware (1794). Anthony Benezet, in 1776, led the Society of Friends to expel its slaveholding members. John Wesley sided with Benezet's view. At the Christmas Conference of 1784, from which American Methodism dates its formal origins, measures were instituted to exclude slave owners or dealers from membership. Later, where slavery took deep institutional root, that discipline became progressively relaxed.[24]

However, when the Irish Methodist leader Robert Strawbridge founded the first colonial Methodist society in Maryland in 1764, a slave woman named Anne Sweitzer was among the charter members. Strawbridge became the first circuit rider of American Methodism. Building the meeting house at Sams Creek, Maryland, in 1764, he served new areas throughout parts of Maryland and Virginia.[25]

Black acceptance also faced a test in 1766 when Philip Embury organized the John Street Society in New York City. John Wesley had licensed Embury, a native of Ireland, to preach. Barbara Heck, Embury's cousin, became outraged when she found a card game in progress at a friend's home. She went to Embury and asked him to come at once and preach "to the sinners." He went and found five persons, one of whom was Betty, a slave of Barbara Heck. The group sang, prayed, and listened to a sermon on salvation.[26]

From that offhand gathering, these persons formed the John Street Society with Embury as their leader. The society met in Embury's house until their numbers overflowed. Much of the growth included slave and free blacks. Building a chapel in 1768, the membership planned to segregate the congregation. They built a ladder stairway to a gallery for the slaves. In time white males also used part of the gallery, duly crowding out the slave members. Within four years the congregation outgrew the chapel.

Joseph Pilmore, the second pastor of the church, wrote Wesley April 24, 1770, of the congestion: "Our house contains about 1,700 hearers; only about a third part of those who attend get in; the rest are glad to hear without. There appears such a willingness in the Americans to hear the word, as I never saw before. The number of blacks that attend the preaching affects me much."[27]

Others also tried to evangelize the slaves. Presbyterian Samuel Davies affected Virginia history, coming to the colony from Pennsylvania in 1747. He resolved that the gospel should reach all classes and conditions, with a special concern for the Negro in Virginia. In a letter to Philip Doddridge, dated October 2, 1750, he describes the vigor of his mission effort among Negro slaves:

I have also comfortable hope that Ethiopia will soon stretch out her hands unto God for a considerable number of Negroes have not only been proselyted to Christianity and baptized but seem to be genuine seed of Abraham by faith . . . I have baptized about 40 of them in a year and a half, 7 or 8 of whom are admitted into full communion and partake of the Lord's Supper. I have also sundry catechumens who, I hope, will be added to the church after further instructions.[28]

Jacob Green, a New Jersey Presbyterian, issued a perceptive prophecy with his denunciation of slavery in 1776:

What a dreadful absurdity! . . . that people who are so strenuously contending for liberty, should at the same time encourage and promote slavery! . . . However we may be free from British oppression.... our liberty will be uncomfortable, till we wash our hands from the guilt of negro slavery.[29]

Samuel Hopkins, a Congregational minister of Newport, Rhode Island, also criticized slavery. He, with Ezra Stiles, a Congregationalist colleague, planned to raise money to free slaves and return them as missionaries to Africa. In 1776 Hopkins dedicated his "Dialogue Concerning the Slavery of Africans" to the Continental Congress. This sharp attack assailed slavery as "very inconsistent . . . with worshiping God thro' Christ." Hopkins knew people commonly treated blacks as if they were "not . . . our brethren, or in any degree on a level with us, but as quite another species of animals, made only to serve us and our children." Yet this attitude violated "that benevolence, which loves our neighbors as ourselves, and is agreeable to truth and righteousness."[30]

Hopkins deplored "the inconsistence of promoting the slavery of the Africans, at the same time we are asserting our own civil liberty, at the risque of our fortunes and lives." He wondered what slaves thought about the patriotic arguments against Britain, when "they see the slavery the Americans dread as worse than death, is lighter than a feather, compared to their heavy doom; and may be called liberty and happiness, when contrasted with the most abject slavery and . . . wretchedness to which they are subjected." He concluded: "Oh, the shocking, the intolerable inconsistence! And this . . . is an open, practical condemnation of holding these our brethren in slavery; . . . the crime of persisting in it becomes unspeakably greater and more provoking in God's sight."[31]

The so-called Great Awakening of the mid and late 18th century inspired a belief in spiritual equality and increased the number of Negro slaves in Christian fellowship. Yet revivalism did not prompt pleas for their emancipation as a matter of course. Fervent religious convictions did not hinder George Whitefield, Anglican firebrand, or Jonathan Edwards, Congregational divine, from owning slaves. What the Great Awakening did do was re-emphasize the spiritual equality of whites and Negroes, providing a new ground for acculturation and a sharing of religious experience. This aroused a self-scrutiny which caused many white Americans to perceive the racial problem for the first time.

Whitefield owned some 75 slaves to run his Georgia Orphanage. He firmly believed that neither the colony nor his Orphan House could succeed without slave labor. As early as 1739 he attacked certain inhumanities of the slave trade, became a bitter foe of any harsh treatment of slaves, and urged their religious instruction. He conceded that the slave trade was advanced "in a wrong way." Since he could not change that, he said it would be fortunate if he could buy a number of Negroes and make their lives genial.[32]

By the time of the Revolution a master might have various motives for freeing his slaves. A few Methodists responded to John Wesley's severe stand against slavery. Yet, Thomas Coke, Wesley's emissary, found his life in peril during his American missions unless he restrained Wesley's anti-slavery precepts. Francis Asbury and other American Methodist Church leaders soon found this issue too touchy for a young church mainly concerned with conversion and expansion. Thus, the major thrust of 18th century revivalism ended with the missionary, not the abolitionist.

Finally, at the close of the 18th century, some of the British churches began Christian missions. The first American missionaries did not enter fields in Asia until 1812. British and American Christians, with religious freedom, using a common language, became the most zealous in promoting mission work. What was God doing while mankind was belatedly moving to evangelize the world? The slave traders brought to the doors of British and American Christians hundreds of thousands of heathen Africans, who, under slavery, learned the English language. They could not be taught by the Christian teacher who only knew his mother tongue.[33]

Since God rules over all mankind, He knows how to perform His purpose. He seemed to decree the redemption of Africa. Africans themselves must be trained for the task. The slave trader carried away the black Africans, bringing them into British and American civilization. The restraints of slavery forced them to acquire a knowledge of agriculture, mechanical arts, literature, science, and religion. Many Christians believed they could see God's hand in this. His providence towards the African race paralleled sending Jacob and his sons into Egypt, allowing the bondage of their progeny, so they might rise above their former pastoral state.

White Christians reasoned that such was the state of the black race in Africa. They slumbered for thousands of years in sloth and pollution. The slave trade carried the people away from a life of indolence to one of industry. Their minds were awakened by the very chains that bound them. The Providence which deigned that the slave trader ship the Negroes away from Africa also prompted the hearts of masters to teach them the gospel year after year.

The usual master, however, is unlike the ideal portrait painted as one who keeps slaves mainly to make them Christians. A further analogy of the value and divine purpose in the Egyptian bondage of the children of Israel, shows that Egyptians suffered 10 terrible plagues for their role. As the American slaves learned of Scripture, they related their lot with the bondage of Israel in Egypt. Also, the Negroes formed a faith that the God of Israel would one day deliver them. Should such inhumane means of slavery then be justified by the proposed end of the "salvation of souls"?

The Revolutionary generation made antislavery and Negro salvation questions subject to other concerns. When the federal Constitution was forged it dealt with slavery as an institution. Moral vexation spread in the

Constitution's provisions to end the slave trade, and in the prohibition of slavery in the Northwest Ordinance of 1787. By this time nearly every northern state had abolished or provided for the gradual abolition of slavery. Yet another century would pass, with rending strife throughout society, and pitched battle in civil war, before slavery was abolished.

The movement of Christian religion in America headed a flow of history which allowed the erosion of a treacherous chasm of slavery. The "American dream" of freedom, opportunity, and prosperity would become nightmares of selfish greed and conflict. Churches could not convert the many self-servers, or redirect professing Christians to truly obey God's Word about slavery. In fact, they twisted Scripture to pronounce divine approval of slavery as well as to denounce it.

The inner conflict against slavery that arose in the minds of individual Christians stems from the struggle that every person has in wanting to be more than everybody else. Ultimately, one desires to be God himself. With this early American attitude toward Providence, a law of history begins operation. The great assurance a person obtains from thinking that he is the agent of Providence causes him to believe that his life has been given a metaphysical orbit. Yet, without submission to God's control, this leads him, in accord with the primal law of all tragedies, to that *hubris*, selfish pride, which "goes before destruction" (Prov. 16:18).[34]

From the earliest colonial beginnings, American church people viewed white supremacy as fact. That guarded presumption remains key to the troubling *status quo* held by many individuals and churches. The inner conflict of personal selfishness and the outer struggle over the practice of slavery became eased amid the growing revolt for national freedom. The Revolutionary War against England would take precedence over all other conflicts.

Chapter 2

Scriptural Perspectives of Slavery and Racism

"With us," wrote William Gregg, South Carolina textile leader, "slaves are property, and it amounts to many millions, the protection and use of which is guaranteed to us by the Constitution; without that protection the Union is of no use to us."[1] As war clouds gathered a decade later, Gregg defined slavery as "rooted in nature and sanctioned by the Bible."[2]

Apologists claimed slavery needed no apology—the Bible spoke in its favor. Many Old Testament passages implied God's approval of slavery. Some of the persons He called out for special service, notably Abraham, owned slaves. In the New Testament, Christ came to fulfill the law, not destroy it. So everything in the old law that He did not change remained lawful. The apostles taught slaves to obey their masters. Proslavery men even said Paul's warning to servants to obey their masters was prompted by the actions of godless abolitionists of that day.

Those who argued from the Scripture against abolitionists declared slavery an appointment of divine mercy. Without it, millions of "Ham's offspring" in the South faced eternal damnation, blind to the gospel and away from God. The Creator blessed those savages by prompting Southern Christians to become their masters. Northerners were accused of serving Money rather than God, making huge profits in the slave trade and shirking the proper training of Negroes. The slaves faced poverty, crime, and death.

Yet, Southern whites were pressed to reconcile the natural rights doctrine of the American Revolution with slavery. Most owners simply declared the Caucasian enjoyed privileges by virtue of his superior race. They judged inferior Africans to be in the world with few, if any rights. Many proslavery men denied any order of natural rights, saying white men were made for freedom, and blacks for slavery. Instead of slavery being a matter of human rights, it was merely a matter of property rights.

Howell Cobb warned in his "scriptural" examination of slavery:

> . . . it must be remembered that we have to control a race of human beings who are under the influence of the most depraved and vicious propensities that ever marked the character of the

debased: individuals of which race seem to be incapable of redemption, either by kindness or severity.[3]

Some viewed the Bible as a system of government, not to be disputed. It commands all people to conform their choices to its requirements, as to that which in itself is good. The Bible cautions civil government: "Let every soul be subject unto the higher powers. For there is no power but of God: the powers that be are ordained of God. Whosoever, therefore, resisteth the power [government authority], resisteth the ordinance of God: and they that resist shall receive . . ." damnation . . ."" (cf. Rom. 13:1-7). Citing Adam Clarke's notes, these words charged Roman Christians to obey Caesar's government—a system sustained by slavery. Free choice barely survived; political authority was denied the common person. Declaring government in this extreme form of controlling human wills, God confirms the *principle, as in itself right*.[4]

The Jews brought slaves with them from Egypt. The Decalogue Jehovah gave to the Jews accepts and allows for the practice. The tenth article of this "constitution" secured the right of property in slaves: "You shall not covet your neighbor's . . . manservant, or his maidservant . . ." (Exod. 20:17, RSV). Stemming from this basic law of the chosen nation, God granted in their civil customs usage of a system of domestic slavery.[5]

A Hebrew might lose his liberty and become a domestic slave in six different ways (see A. Clarke's comments on Exod. 21):

1. He might sell his liberty because of poverty (Lev. 25:39).

2. A father might sell his child (Exod. 21:7).

3. Debtors could become slaves of their creditors (2 Kings 4:1; Matt. 18:25).

4. A thief could be sold to profit the one he had robbed (Exod. 22:3).

5. A Hebrew taken prisoner in war could be sold as a slave (2 Chron. 12:8).

6. A Hebrew slave who had been ransomed from a Gentile by a Hebrew could be then sold to one of his own nation. All who thus became slaves were emancipated in the seventh year, except those who refused liberty (Exod. 21:2-6).

The law further provided for domestic slaves in perpetuity. Leviticus 25:44-46 (RSV) declares:

As for your male and female slaves whom you may have: you may buy male and female slaves from among the [heathen] nations that are round about you . . . You may bequeath them to your sons after you, to inherit as a possession for ever . . .

Southerners thus argued that Christ himself recognized this law, as "it was originally designed to be, of universal obligation and force."[6] Had not Jesus said: "Do not think that I have come to abolish the Law or the Prophets; I have not come to abolish them but to fulfill them" (Matt. 5:17).

Advocates declared that no state in this Union was any more a slaveholding community than the Jewish people in Jesus' time. "In every congregation which he addressed, bond slaves may have mingled . . . not a word is known . . . declaring the relation of master and slave to be sinful." Paul's censure of "the teachers of abolition doctrines" was that they do "not agree to the sound instruction of our Lord Jesus Christ and to godly teaching" (1 Tim. 6:3). This reason confirmed that Christ approved slavery, and condemned all attempts to abolish it as a duty of the religion which He taught.[7]

The master-slave relation appears in some of Christ's most eloquent allusions, supporting some of His training parables: "Good teacher, what must I do?" (Mark 10:17). "No one can serve two masters" (Matt. 6:24). Among the parables are: "The servants asked him, 'Do you want us to go and pull them up?'" (Matt. 13:24-28); the one of the vineyard (Matt. 21), and of the talents (Matt. 25).[8]

Persons with a biased mind-set explain the Scriptures so they seem to condone forced slavery. Yet scriptural truths point out that God hates slavery, though He has permitted it along with other sins of men's hardened hearts. God through Moses also commanded: "You shall not give up to his master a slave who has escaped from his master to you; he shall dwell with you . . . you shall not oppress him" (Deut. 23:15-16, RSV).

Again, in one of the most complete passages on social justice in the entire Bible, God speaks through a prophet against all kinds of oppression. Ezekiel writes:

If a man is righteous and does what is lawful and right—if he . . . does not oppress any one, but restores to the debtor his pledge, commits no robbery, gives his bread to the hungry and covers the naked with a garment, does not lend at interest or take any increase, withholds his hand from iniquity, executes true justice between man and man . . . he is righteous, he shall surely live, says the Lord God (Ezek. 18:5-9, RSV).

Among other things, these words reveal that God opposes economic slavery as well as social slavery.

A number of other references against tyranny appear in the Old Testament (e.g. Exod. 22:21; Jer. 30:20; and Mal. 3:5). One of the mighty signs that God opposes political and social slavery concerns the rescue of Israel from Egypt. The Lord declared:

> "I have seen the affliction of my people who are in Egypt, and have heard their cry because of their taskmasters; I know their sufferings, and I have come down to deliver them out of the hand of the Egyptians . . . I have seen the oppression with which the Egyptians oppress them" (Exod. 3:7-9, RSV).

God called Moses to deliver them. When Pharaoh of Egypt refused to let the children of Israel go, God sent 10 plagues upon the Egyptians (Exod. 5-12). So, God opposes institutions of human slavery. Whether the slavery be political or economic, God says, "Let my people go." Among the Bible stories the Negro slaves learned in "Christian" America, the Divine rescue of Israel became their ground and dream of faith. Black Christian converts sang the gripping spiritual, "Let My People GO!"

In the New Testament, the apostle Paul declared that "there is neither Jew nor Greek, there is neither slave nor free . . . for you are all one in Christ Jesus" (Gal. 3:28, RSV). "Masters," he warned, "treat your slaves justly and fairly, knowing that you also have a Master in heaven" (Col. 4:1, RSV). When Onesimus, a converted runaway slave returned to Philemon, his master, he came "no longer as a slave but more than a slave, as a beloved brother . . . both in the flesh and in the Lord" (Philemon 16, RSV). By showing both master and slave were brothers under one Master—Jesus Christ—the New Testament blasts the foundation of slavery built on any alleged essential inequality of people.

Multiplied millions of persons of various conquered tribes and nations throughout history have endured slavery. Great empires of the world all used such captives in their social structures. The slavery which Scripture mentions refers only to that of captured peoples. Neither the Old or New Testaments attaches racial stigma to slaves. The Egyptian bondage of the children of Israel resulted from their number, not because of skin color. The institution of slavery as related in the Bible, of many peoples, is unlike African slavery so condoned in America.

Slaveholders argued that the principle of slavery was justified for three basic reasons:[9]

1. Because the Africans are a distinct race of people, who cannot amalgamate with the whites, and who, therefore, must exist as a separate class.

2. Because the Africans are, as a class, inferior to the whites in intellectual and moral development, making them incompetent to self-government.

3. Because the Divine procedure in the case of the heathen subdued by the ancient Israelites, domestic slavery is fully exemplified as the appropriate form of government for such inferior people.

Contrary to common belief, the Bible never uses either the word or the concept of "race." God's human creation has no such thing as a "race," only tribes and nations. Scripture writers do not mention any distinct or inferior people, in terms of Caucasian, Mongol, Negroid, or other divisions. Biblical differences among peoples are based on languages, families, nations, and lands (Gen. 10:5, 20, 31), not as races. The original divisions after the Flood are based on distinct languages (Gen. 11:6, 9) divinely imposed. Physical differences are not noted.

Some have explained Noah's prophecy concerning his three sons (Gen. 9:25-27) to refer to three races—Hamitic, Semitic, and Japhetic. The prophecy does apply to the offspring of Noah's sons, and the various nations to be formed from them. But we read of no mention about three separate races. The Bible speaks only of one race—the human race. "(God) has made from one blood every nation of men" (Acts 17:26, NKJV). The vision of the redeemed saints in heaven is one of "every nation, tribe, people and language" (Rev. 7:9, NIV). All ethnic differences have vanished.

Certain religious writers have interpreted the Bible from a "racist" framework. Such attempts wrest the Scripture. The origin of the concept of race occurred elsewhere than in the Bible. Later we shall see, rather than being a biblical category, "race" became a recognized category of evolutionary biology. Some thought the Negro provided the species link between apes and mankind.

Some viewed slavery as a "God-send" for the African, for the American colonies, and common civilization. An assumed proper rationale is stated from the pinnacle of "principled Christianity":

No one dreamed of robbery, injustice, or wrong to any one! All considered it a wide door which a kind Providence had opened

. . . the men who were worthy . . . did authorize, by a common public opinion, the practice of going to Africa, and negotiating a purchase with those who by the usages of barbarous war were condemned to death. They considered that thus to arrest the practice of putting prisoners to death was humane, and worthy of a Christian people; that to introduce them into civilized society, teach them the habits of civilized life, the principles and experience of Christianity, and . . . to send them back to regenerate their fatherland was an achievement worthy of the highest attainments of piety![10]

By the 1760s changes in cultural values thwarted traditional justifications for slavery. Insofar as the Enlightenment divorced anthropology and comparative anatomy from theological beliefs, it allowed theories of racial inferiority to flourish. Such theories were ignored by 18th century scientists, who generally shared the Christian belief in the common nature and origin of mankind.

For reasons unknown, the African's skin color became his defining trait. It aroused the deepest scurrile response in Europeans and Americans. Often called a "Moor" or "Ethiopian," he also was a "negro" to the Spanish and Portuguese, a "noir" to the French, and a "black" to the English. In all four languages the word implies gloom, evil, baseness, wretchedness, and misfortune.

Early in the 17th century, Samuel Purchas tested "the varietie of answeres" he had heard about the black race with reason and religion. In a marginal note he mentioned the theory that Negroes bore the curse of Ham, who was punished for knowing his wife in the ark. Purchas seemed to think it plausible. Yet it was absurd to attribute blackness to the sun's heat, since no black natives lived in the American tropics. Besides, the offspring of the early Portuguese remained white in Africa.[11]

If the color of Negroes resulted from the blackness of their parents' seed, as some affirmed, why were they reddish at birth and yellowish at age? It must be one of God's supreme mysteries, and simply showed the divine pattern of substance and accident, of unity and diversity. Purchas eloquently expresses his Christian faith, concluding that God had infinitely multiplied mankind,

. . . that we might serve that One-most God: that the tawnie Moore, blacke Negro, duskie Libyan, ash-coloured Indian, oliue-coloured American, should, with the whiter European become one sheepefold, under one Great Shepherd, till this mortalitie being swallowed up of life, we may all be one, as He and the

Father are one . . . filing Heauen and earth with their euerlasting
Halleluiahs, without any more distinction of Colour, Nation,
Language, Sexe, Condition, all may bee One in him that is ONE,
and only blessed for euer. Amen.[12]

This pronounced the very heart of Christian belief and the basis for all
attempts at converting blacks. Scholars continued to ponder the origins of
the African's color. Yet good Christians knew all men were created in God's
image. As Samuel Bowden wrote, all were black in the darkness of the tomb.
These concepts denied the theory that Negroes had descended from apes or
had a separate origin from the rest of mankind. Freethinkers and innovators
like the German physician, Paracelsus, and the Italian philosophers, Lucilio
Vanini and Giordano Bruno first advanced these ideas.

Theories of Negro inferiority gained in popularity with the growth of
the slave trade in the last quarter of the 17th century. In 1680 Morgan
Godwyn observed that traders and planters acted in their interest to
spread the belief that Africans were not really men. He said even if a
black skin did reflect the mark of Ham's curse, this failed to prove
Negroes were not human. Planters would hardly use brutes to oversee
the work of other brutes. Like Sir Thomas Browne, Godwyn stressed the
relativity of color, which suggests a common prejudice toward
blackness. He also countered the claim that Negroes were monsters
whose unions with human beings produced only sterile offspring.
Godwyn seemed to believe reports that Africans had "unnatural
conjunctions" with apres and drills.[13]

John Wesley in general thought of primitive people as bestial
idolaters. Yet he viewed the Africans in a different light. Most orthodox
Christians saw the barbarity of primitive people as proof of mankind's
degeneration from a holy state. Early antislavery writers like James
Ramsay and Granville Sharp warrant human nature with the fervor and
caustic wit of the first anti-Darwinists. Ramsay said if David Hume were
a West Indian slave, he would be a conjurer, and be rightfully flogged for
imposing on the credulity of his fellows. By linking the theory of racial
inferiority with Hume, Voltaire, and materialistic philosophy, antislavery
writers made the idea less pleasing.[14]

James Beattie, a Scottish philosopher, supported the truth and moral
feeling against the "sophistry and skepticism" of Hume and Voltaire. He
warned the inferiority of Negroes was used by writers whose real target
was the authority of Scripture. His *Elements of Moral Science*, a text used
in America, declared the issue of Negro slavery posed a decisive test for
religion and moral philosophy:

It is impossible for the considerate and unprejudiced mind to think of slavery without horror . . . If this be equitable, or excusable, or pardonable, it is vain to talk any longer of the eternal distinctions of right and wrong, truth and falsehood, good and evil.[15]

Beattie's attack formed part of a wider debate on the Negro's capacity for progress. The dispute involved the anthropological and physiological differences and induced arguments from such diverse figures as Buffon, Hume, Jefferson, Immanuel Kant, Samuel Stanhope Smith, and Charles White. Yet the complexities of racial theory should not obscure the ideological importance of the biblical account of a single human race descended from common parents. Even when qualified by racist stereotypes or by strained views of Canaan's curse, belief in a common origin implied all peoples share a common nature and destiny.

Genuine abolitionism against human bondage in America began in the great Quaker revival. It moved from an ideal of quietistic spirituality and self-denial in the mid-18th century toward renewed avowals of both mankind's sinfulness and the mercies of Christ the Redeemer. In Maryland, Virginia, and North Carolina the Quaker example aroused Methodists, Baptists, and Presbyterians who sought to recover the Christian zeal of the Great Awakening of the 1740s.

By the 1780s, views of sin and religious duty had gained wide acceptance. Revivalists had often urged that black slaves be Christianized and treated according to New Testament ideals. Yet none of the Great Awakening leaders denounced slaveholding as a sin or even as an evil. However, for both Quakers and Southern evangelicals like Freeborn Garrettson, David Rice, Carter Tarrant, and James Meacham, slaveholding should no more be sanctified than the vices of gambling, drinking, horse racing, and Sabbath-breaking that infected the planter class.

All evangelicals by no means demanded slave emancipation as a sign of individual and national repentance in the midst of the Revolutionary crisis. For men like Garrettson, who owned black slaves, the decision to sacrifice immoral wealth became a double emancipation, signifying new identities for both master and slave. That choice culminated Garrettson's conversion experience in 1775, freeing him from Satan's temptations. "All my dejection and that melancholy gloom, which preyed on me, vanished in a moment: a divine sweetness ran through my whole frame . . ."[16]

The abolition movement was mainly inspired by Christian teachers, not by secular men. God showed an ecumenical spirit by selecting as agents Morgan Godwyn, an Anglican; Richard Baxter, a Nonconformist;

and George Fox, a Quaker. The Quaker ethic of self-denial and
nonviolence helped expose the guile of the established churches on the
issue of slavery. The simultaneous development of antislavery in Britain
and America also proved Christianity was "capable of producing the
same good fruit in all lands."[17]

Among Quakers and early Methodists, public outcries against slavery
disclosed the self-serving expediency of the established churches. Under
the banner of "practical benevolence," the evangelical party led by
William Wilberforce and the Clapham Sect challenged the complacency
and worldly system of patronage within their own Church of England. By
the 1820s abolitionism was serving similar goals for evangelicals like
Thomas Chalmers and Andrew Thompson in the Church of Scotland. In
the northern United States followers of Charles G. Finney believed
silence or undue "prudence" regarding slavery epitomized the "satanic
doctrine of expediency" that morally weakened the Presbyterian and
Congregational churches.

In 1835 Henry Clarke Wright became an abolitionist champion of
nonresistance. Wright affirmed that "Christ is the Prince of moral
reformers—the great Captain of agitators in aggressive warfare, as well
as the Prince of Peace." Wright not only battled Unitarians and other
theological liberals, but also errant Puritans who ignored the claims of
divine sovereignty and were corrupted by "subserviency to the will of
man." He abhorred disorder, violence, and immorality, seeking the
restoration of "the Order of God's creation." Human presumptions of
authority must yield to the Divine will. Wright believed Negro slavery
was the most flagrant example of man's usurpation of divine dominion.[18]

A conflict flared between abolitionists and their Protestant opponents
who acknowledged slaveholding might become sinful and adverse to the
public welfare. Yet, they denied the concept that an institution approved
in the Bible could be really sinful. Henry Wright noted in his journal that
the New England clergy also feared that if reformers attacked a specific
embodiment of sin, then "that sin will assume such an importance that
everybody will think nothing is necessary to make them christians but
abstinence from that particular sin." Calvinists were wary of attempts to
impute unconditional evil to abstract "essences" or categories, such as
slaveholding and corporal punishment. All human relationships contained
a mixture of good and evil.[19]

Convinced that sin pervades every human work, Calvinists were
dubious of people who looked for salvation in holy causes or who
shunned the painful duties of life. It seemed like the papist fallacy that

salvation could be won by celibacy, monasticism, or noble works. Radical sectarians were also deceived who thought evil could be incarnate in institutions. Though imperfect, God meant them to be improved and made useful by pious human authority.

Even so, some abolitionists in Britain and America professed at least a modified Calvinist faith. Yet such reformers rejected the myth which always excused black slavery—that such servitude could be ennobled by Christian love and reciprocal duty. To the abolitionist, this exemplified the total rule of one human being over another. Theodore Weld defined this as a sacrilegious theory of "the prerogative of God, an invasion of the whole man—on his powers, rights, enjoyments, and hopes, [which] annihilates his being as a MAN, to make room for the being of a THING."[20]

For Weld, and most abolitionists, the slave's immortal soul made him a "God-like being" sheltered by God's authority. When the soul was inseparably joined to human "powers, rights, enjoyments, and hopes," external control over the body became spiritual destruction. Battling this evil as a scheming disguise of sin was virtuous action. The glaring existence of that baseness prompted even Calvinists to view some goodness in the human heart—in the disposition to "practical benevolence."

Meanwhile, the Church of Jesus Christ of Latter-Day Saints, known as Mormonism, was founded by Joseph Smith, Jr., in 1830, at Fayette, New York. Smith alleged a visit by an angel named Moroni. He revealed to Smith that a set of gold plates lay buried in a hillside near his home. Smith claimed that he found them in 1827. He believed these plates held the sacred writings of an ancient American civilization. Then, with the aid of a set of seer stones, known as "the Urim and Thummin," Smith allegedly "translated" these ancient writings into the *Book of Mormon*. He completed the task in 1830, and that same year founded the Mormon church. He published the book and his followers canonized it as holy scripture.[21]

Smith's book detailed the rise and fall of an ancient American civilization, supposedly stemming from a group of Israelites who had migrated from the Holy Land to the New World about 600 B.C. Led by a man named Nephi, these "Nephites," built a civilization on the North and South American continents, lasting until A.D. 400.

Smith's tale of these ancient Americans used racist concepts contrasting nonwhite racial inferiority with white superiority. Racism is seen in the *Book of Mormon* passages describing the conflicts and divisions plaguing the Nephite nation. Under the wise leadership of Nephi, these people built a complex, urban society as God's chosen people. Yet Nephi's two brothers, Laman and Lemuel challenged his authority.[22]

Laman and Lemuel, and their followers, were cursed with "skin of blackness" by "the Lord God." They were called the Lamanites, "a dark, and loathsome, and filthy people full of idleness and all manner of abomination." Smith also described another group who opposed the Nephites, the Amlicites. They painted red marks on their foreheads to show their rebellion. The Amlicites also became a dark-skinned people.[23]

Joseph Smith's *Book of Mormon* only alludes to the role and place of blacks generally. Yet his use of the term "black" synonymously with "red" to describe various dark-skinned peoples infers a dislike of contemporary blacks. At one point Smith discussed the wicked acts of Cain, a biblical counter-figure, labeled both by certain Latter-day Saints and by some non-Mormon Americans as the direct ancestor of black people.[24]

This young religious sect with Northern roots further spawned racist concepts, complementing Southern thinking. Brigham Young, Smith's successor, in his *Journal of Discourses*, wrote some degrading racial statements:

> You see some classes of the human family that are black, uncouth, uncomely, disagreeable and low in their habits, wild, and unseemingly deprived of nearly all the blessings of the intelligence that is generally bestowed upon mankind.[25]

> Shall I tell you the law of God in regard to the African race? If the white man who belongs to the chosen seed mixes his blood with the seed of Cain, the penalty, under the law of God, is death on the spot. This will always be so.[26]

In the 20th century, Joseph Fielding Smith, (grand-nephew of Joseph Smith), still said the Negro's curse was derived from Cain:

> Not only was Cain called upon to suffer, but because of his wickedness, he became the father of an inferior race. A curse was placed upon him and that curse has been continued through his lineage and must do so while time endures. Millions of souls have come into this world cursed with a black skin and have been denied the privilege of Priesthood and the fullness of the blessings of the Gospel.[27]

By 1852, William Goodell, an abolitionist historian, wrote of the "general decline of pure religion and sound morality" following the Revolution. This advanced a growing disregard for liberty and human rights, exemplified by such "flagrant iniquities" as the slave trade and Negro slavery. Goodell believed the decline of early antislavery commitment came chiefly from the American's quest for wealth.

Goodell documented the effects of such materialism on American Protestant churches. They moved from frank opposition to slavery into the Revolutionary period, and through stages of embarrassment, apathy, and apology. Religious revivals had "done little towards restoring the ancient standard of morals." The churches became an influence to relax moral judgement—adjusting itself to "the unexpected profitableness of the cotton manufacturer at the North." Churches served as agents to the "mean," "infidel," "blasphemous," "murderous" prejudice that "virtually predicates humanity upon the hue of the skin, that disbelieves that 'God had made of one blood all nations of men,' that arrogates to less than one-sixth part of the human race the exclusive monopoly of our common humanity ..."[28]

As Winthrop Jordan has perceived:

The concept of Negro slavery . . . was neither borrowed from foreigners nor extracted from books, nor invented out of whole cloth, nor extrapolated from servitude nor generated by English reaction to Negroes as such nor necessitated by the exigencies of the New World. Not any one of these made the Negro a slave, but all.[29]

Overarching these factors that produced Negro slavery is the manner in which a black person is perceived. Was he "created in the image of God"—or not? White Southerners, trying to prove Negroes were inferior, often consigned them to a lower creation, other than human. Some extremists pushed Negroes to the brink of the abyss separating man from monkey. In 1854, J.C. Nott published *Types of Mankind* to prove the separate origin of Negroes. He said domesticated blacks reverted to wildness when left to themselves.

In 1856 George M. Stroud wrote *Sketch of the Laws Relating to Slavery*. He captioned his major chapter, "Slaves Are Things," citing the Louisiana Code that declares

. . . a slave is one who is in the power of a master to whom he belongs. The master may sell him, dispose of his person, his industry and his labor: he could do nothing, possess nothing, nor acquire anything but what must belong to his master.[30]

Charles Darwin, in 1859, wrote a benchmark volume. *Origin of the Species*, sub-titled, "The Preservation of Favoured Races in the Struggle for Life." Although he had species of animals in mind, he clearly thought of races of men in the same fashion. Darwin strongly opposed slavery on moral grounds, but he was convinced of white superiority. He once wrote:

> I could show fight on natural selection having done and doing more for the progress of civilization than you seem inclined to admit . . . The more civilized so-called Caucasian races have beaten the Turkish hollow in the struggle for existence. Looking to the world at no very distant date, what an endless number of the lower races will have been eliminated by the higher civilized races throughout the world.[31]

As 19th century scientists converted to evolution, they also were convinced of racism. They believed the white race superior to other races, as based on Darwinian theory. The white race had advanced farther up the evolutionary ladder, and would either eliminate the other races in the struggle for existence, or assume the "white man's burden" and care for those inferior races that could not survive otherwise.[32]

Such racist views were held by most, if not all, 19th century evolutionists. A reviewer in a modern scientific journal says:

> After 1859, the evolutionary scheme raised . . . questions, particularly whether or not Afro-Americans could survive competition with their white near-relations. The momentous answer was a resounding no . . . The African was inferior—he represented the missing link between ape and Teuton.[33]

One writer in 1875 claimed that Mosaic history in Scripture was only the history of the Caucasian race. How other races came into being was unknown, and need not be known. If Negro muscles or brains were made to promote the comfort of Adam's descendants, they might be preserved. Otherwise, they would be exterminated.[34]

Joining the Southerners who argued the races were created separately, and those who supposed Negroes to be less than human, was the commotion caused by the nonhuman theory. John W. DeForest, novelist and Freedman's Bureau official in North Carolina said:

> There was a prodigious movement in the Southern mind in consequence of Dr. Cartwright's discovery that God created three kinds of beings, to wit, man, "living creatures," and beasts; and that the Negroes, being . . . "living creatures," are lower than humans, though not as low as animals. This remarkable "reading," having been popularized by a writer signing as "Ariel," was used with great effect by Governor Perry [of South Carolina] against universal suffrage . . .[35]

"Ariel" published an array of "biblical facts" to show the Negro was created as a beast, the slave of Adam. This beast was denied immortality; it was the tempter in the Garden of Eden. God destroys all nations that mix with the beast or allow it equality. These "facts" also declared mulattoes crucified Christ.[36]

"Prospero" conceded humanity of a low order to Negroes by a "preadamic" creation. Negroes, as progeny of the preadamic men, came closer to the chimpanzee than to the Anglo-Saxon. The Caucasian, head of all races, found himself tempted in the Garden of Eden by one of the "preadamites," called a serpent. Later, Cain went among these creatures, who welcomed the felon and gave him a wife. The heinous crime of mixing preadamite blood with the blood of Adam was punished by the Creator sending a flood over the area occupied by these vile creatures. However, the unmixed preadamites were spared with the pure Caucasians. After the flood, the Caucasians drove the Negroes into Africa. In the South, whites repeated Cain's sin—not by owning preadamites, but by mixing with them. Because they polluted their blood with that of the lowest humans, they were chastised by serving their partners in crime.[37]

Wresting the Scripture and science, "Ariel" and "Prospero" produced the imagined gruesome mulatto offspring. Charles Carroll, following "Ariel," viewed Negroes as lower animals in 1900. Albert Stowe Lee-craft in 1923 ranked Southerners as superior Caucasians, inferior Negroes and mulattoes as "mule niggers." He believed Negroes could attain immortality if they obeyed the white man. Yet "mule niggers," being neither white nor black and conceived in breach of divine law, were denied everlasting life.[38]

Southerners viewed both history and science for evidence to use against the Negro. Whites believed the character of each race was grounded on history. The Creator made Negroes to be servants of white men, and this surmise was basic in the history of black-white relations. Some more modern white supremacists, swayed by the concept of social evolution, believed racial distinction stemmed from natural forces.

However, the Southerner mostly based his use of slavery on religious, not scientific arguments. He was disturbed unless, by fundamentalist belief, divine support backed his racist views. He even looked for "the will of God" behind the "voice of Nature." Thus, Senator Garrett Davis of Kentucky declared "the great God who created all races never intended the negro, the lowest, to have equal power with the highest, the white race."[39]

If the races were made unequal, rancor toward any Negro was an "instinct of manhood, the elevation of the soul, the pride, and dignity of race which God Almighty implanted in the breast of every reasonable creature."[40] The white had no shame to hide. He could proclaim his virtue "from the housetop." Because of the law of nature, which God's law set, coloreds must work as bootblacks, cooks, farmhands—only as menials of whatever sort.

From the mid-19th century and beyond the middle of the 20th century, prevailing worldwide scientific racism spoiled the social, political, and even religious realms. The seeds of evolutionary racism came to fullest and most frightful fruition in the National Socialism in Germany. Philosopher Friedrich Nietsche, a peer of Charles Darwin and an ardent evolutionist, popularized in Germany his concept of the master race. During the early to mid-20th century, Adolph Hitler gained power and made this philosophy national policy. The horrific result was the slaughter of over 6 million Jews. But the color of skin was not the issue.

In recent decades, only a few evolutionary scientists openly espouse the idea of a long-term development of the various races from more than one ancestral line. In modern terminology, a race of people may involve a number of individual national and language groups. This reflects a much broader generic concept than any of the biblical divisions. In biological taxonomy terminology, it is like a "variety," or a "sub-species." Yet biologists use the term to apply to mankind as well as to sub-species of animals.

A modern evolutionist, George Gaylord Simpson, has written: "Races of men have, or . . . had, exactly the same biological significance as the sub-species of other species of animals."[41] The influence of such basic evolutionistic concepts breed racism. The bias is to accept struggle between "natural" races, and allow the strongest to survive, thereby advancing evolution.

Blacks presently struggle to be accepted as equals in American society. Scripture declares all people, of any skin color, were created in the image of God. This basic Christian belief either eludes the minds of many church people, or is denied as fact. The plea for human rights with outcries of race discrimination is not simply a protest of secular humanism. Since God created all people, all—no matter their skin color—stand equal before Him. But the Revolutionary War would not bring freedom and equality to the black slaves in American society.

Chapter 3

Revolution, Religion, and Slavery in a Free Country

Nearly a century before the end of the Revolutionary War, a group of Pennsylvania Quakers issued a stirring protest against slavery February 18, 1688. They invoked the Golden Rule, making its truth a benchmark to generations that followed:

> There is a saying that we should do to all men like as we will be done ourselves, . . . Here [in America] is liberty of conscience, which is right and reasonable; here ought to be likewise liberty of the body . . . But to bring men hither, or to rob and sell them against their will, we stand against . . . Pray, what thing in the world can be done worse towards us, that if men should rob or steal us away, and sell us to strange countries; separating husbands from their wives and children . . . have these poor Negroes not as much right to fight for their freedom, as you have to keep them slaves."[1]

The 1763-1800 period is known as the "revolutionary era." The year 1763 helped England and her American colonies, when the Treaty of Paris ended 50 years of conflict. France's power in North America ended, and Spain was pushed to remote areas west of the Mississippi River. England took Quebec and Florida, improving Anglo-American relations in the New World. Yet in 12 years, good feelings turned bitter, causing 8 years of declared war.

The Protestant mind-set of the American people, despite the secularized Puritanism, viewed the English king's rule with great suspicion. Memories of earlier religious persecution strengthened this hostility, and rumors of sending a bishop to America bolstered it. Most people stood biased against such a prelate, along with "dissenters" who suffered discrimination in some colonies.

In the decade of the 1760s, fear of English Anglican intrusion reached its peak. By the 1770s that dam of bias burst, and in New England, Jonathan Mayhew, of Boston's West Church (Congregational), led the fight against "all imperious bishops." Any attempt by England to send a bishop to America meant an attack on American liberties, both civil and religious.

This spurred the revolution in men's hearts, to which John Adams believed the Declaration of Independence in 1776 gave only delayed expression. Its source of strength lay in the religious foundation, which was Nonconformist, Dissenting, and Puritan in nature. New concepts of freedom and equality took shape. Ideas of God, man, human rights, the state, and history developed. These stemmed from the Enlightenment's outlook on reality. The July 4, 1776, Declaration made such ideas a cornerstone of the American political tradition. They gained further substance later in state constitutions, and in the federal Constitution.

Church history during this turbulent epoch is important for several reasons. First, churches endured much confusion and decline by the intense political and military action. Second, a lengthy political crisis flared from the Stamp Act. It extended to Jefferson's election as president amid advanced Enlightenment philosophy, natural theology, and secular thought. Political issues received priority, and traditional theological questions were viewed in legalistic ways. Third, the churches had to respond to the new political events created by the War for Independence and the Treaty of Paris (1783). Most churches encountered major changes. Fourth, all religious groups received new opportunities for increased activity and growth by adjustments of church and state relationships. They helped bring about these changes.

A "Great Awakening" swept through the North American colonies between 1740 and 1790, with mixed results among the blacks, both slave and free. They gladly heard and accepted the gospel that Christ's suffering, death, and resurrection made persons one with God. Some evangelical preachers recorded conversions among the slaves. Yet these preachers had to balance the faith in the Christ they preached with the slavery and abuse endured by the blacks.

Many preachers of this period believed the predestination doctrine explained this conflict. They said God had predestined some persons for damnation, and some for salvation. Many whites thought God predestined all blacks for damnation. Some evangelists taught that slavery was a natural station in life for Negroes. Even those who held a modified view believed slavery benefited the slave. These whites maintained that Africans lived better as slaves in America than as "savages" in their homeland. This became known as "the noble good theory" of slavery.

Between 1766, when the first American Methodist society began in New York, and the onset of war with England a decade later, the movement gained only 3,148 members. Of these, 2,500 lived around Baltimore and in Brunswick County, Virginia. Non-conformity prevailed there from earliest colonial days. English-born Francis Asbury became an early Methodist leader in America, taking a forceful role, in 1771. But Methodism *per se* was neither strong enough nor convincing to exert much influence except with the Anglican church, its parent body, when the Revolution began.[2]

The revolutionary era brought decline for American Christianity. The churches receded to a lower level of vitality during the two decades after the end of hostilities than at any other time in the country's religious history. The war itself started the decline, prompting partisan ministers to flee when opposing armies approached. The general disruption and devastation of the war left the churches disorganized and their members preoccupied by pressing military or political questions.

By the end of the period, church membership so decreased that not more than 1 person in 20, had church connection. Membership became increasingly nominal in many churches. Tory ministers fled; Patriot ministers often found their labors hindered. Most of the college faculties became scattered and their facilities seized for military use. This greatly hampered the recruitment and training of the clergy. As religious "enthusiasm" met scorn, revivalism halted everywhere except in some remote areas of the South.

Thomas Jefferson became known as "the St. Paul of American democracy" because of his vital roll in the history of American religion (1743-1826).[3] Jefferson's philosophy of religion and his political theory form a unified whole. He served as the key architect of the United States' solution of the problem of church and state. The major Founding Fathers decided to put their trust in man, education, and reformed political institutions.

Jefferson believed each custom became a progressive function in its stage of moral evolution. Though a slave owner, his opposition to slavery agreed with this humanitarian view of government. His draft of the Declaration of Independence, prepared July 2, 1776, had a clause "reprobating the enslaving the inhabitants of Africa [which] was struck out in complaisance to South Carolina and Georgia, who had never attempted to restrain the importation of slaves, and who on the contrary wished to continue it."[4] In 1779, at the Virginia Legislature, Jefferson said, "Nothing is more certainly written in the book of fate than that these people [referring to the Negroes] are to be free."[5]

Benjamin Franklin wrote about slavery in his *Observations Concerning the Increase of Mankind*. He owned Negro servants as late as

1750; his desire to get rid of them seemed more from racial prejudice than humanitarianism. Franklin mentioned Negro slavery mostly in this essay, until his contact with Thomas Paine. Paine's first article printed in America (March 1775) attacked slavery and the African trade. A month later Paine and Franklin helped found the first antislavery society in America. Franklin became a leader of Pennsylvania's Society for Promoting the Abolition of Slavery.

Aside from Quakers, colonial Christians exerted little effort to improve the Negro's lot. Yet just before the Revolutionary War two developments forecast better times for the blacks. These were the growing hostility to the slave trade, and Negro efforts to better themselves. Opposition to the slave trade increased partly because of the fear of slave insurrections.

Shortly before the war, colony after colony showed displeasure over slave imports. The Massachusetts Legislature passed anti-slave trade laws in 1771 and 1774, but the royal governor vetoed them. In 1774, both Rhode Island and Connecticut voted to prohibit the trade. Rhode Island stipulated that any slave brought within her boundaries would be set free. Pennsylvania, in 1773, struck at the slave trade by levying a duty of 20 pounds on each imported slave. Three Southern colonies passed confining measures: Virginia and North Carolina in 1774, and Georgia in 1775.

These widely adopted measures against importing slaves ensued to prevent the uprising of a numerous black population. They also served as an attempt to rebuke Parliament for passing unsuitable laws. This is why the Continental Congress, April 6, 1776, voted that no slave be imported into any of the 13 united colonies. Such action against the slave trade ensued also because of an increasing impact of a philosophy of human freedom, as the crisis grew.

In 1774 a group of Negroes expressed wonder and dismay that the colonists sought independence from Britain without giving regard to the slaves' pleas for freedom. As Edmund S. Morgan observed, to a large degree, "Americans bought their independence with slave labor."[6] They focused on white, selfish pride.

The general policy in early America excluded Negroes from military service, and bearing arms. Yet manpower shortages eventually overruled the aversion to give the Negro a gun. Whites viewed the arming of slaves as risky in time of war for fear they might side with the enemy. Slaves and free Negroes had fought in Queen Anne's War (1702-1713), King George's War (1744-48), and the French and Indian War (1754-1763).

They fought and died along side General Braddock and George Washington in 1755, and took part in the capture of Fort Ticonderoga and Crown Point in 1758. They also served aboard most of the ships in the colonial navy, receiving the same food, pay, and treatment as white sailors.[7]

Using Negroes in the colonial militia set a practice for the early months of the revolt against England. Blacks fought in the first armed conflict of the Revolution, the Battle of Lexington and Concord, April 19, 1775. Among the Negroes fighting in this skirmish were Epheram Pomp Blackman, who later served in the Continental Army, and Prince Estabrook became a casualty. Also, a Lemuel Haynes later became a notable minister in white churches.

Two months later at Boston, in the Battle of Bunker Hill, Negroes and whites used ammunition of nails and scraps of iron, as well as musket balls. They cut down the advance of the British army twice and retreated only when the ammunition was gone.[8]

This early use of Negro soldiers became restricted by the end of 1775. The newly formed Continental Army was forced to adopt a no-Negroes policy. The military establishment which represented all of the states had to respond to their viewpoints. Continental commanders were informed that most Negroes were slaves, whose enlistment violated the property right of their masters. The high command, meeting at Cambridge October 8, 1775, decided the federal army would not be a refuge for runaways. They agreed on a policy to exclude both slaves and free Negroes. Both the civilian and military authorities of the central government decided that the army was off-limits for the Negro.

By the summer of 1777, entering the war's third year, this policy became reversed. Negro enlistments met decreasing opposition as the war dragged on and it became more difficult to raise volunteer forces. Recruiting officers received pay for each enlistee, with little selectivity. Black recruits were also enlisted by men who wanted an officer's commission, which could be obtained by bringing a specified number of volunteers into camp. Allowing Negroes to become soldiers gained support when Congress in 1777 fixed quotas for each state. To meet manpower requests for Washington's army, recruiters began to send any available blacks. This spared an equal number of white men for the state or county militias, who usually served short-term local enlistments.

Outside the South, by the summer of 1778, the Continental Army had a mixture of black men. An official return of Negroes, dated August 24,

1778, and signed by Adjutant General Alexander Scammell, totaled 755, scattered over 14 brigades. General Samuel Holden Parson's brigade, recruited mostly from Connecticut, was noted as the detachment with the highest percentage of Negroes. Despite its relatively small black population, New England supplied more Negro soldiers than any other region. Meanwhile, in middle Massachusetts an observer reported most regiments had "a lot of Negroes." There were 225 to 250 blacks enrolled in the Rhode Island First Regiment.

No matter where he served, in the Continental Army, the state or local militia, the typical Negro soldier was a private, placed in the rank and file. Even more than any other privates, he lacked identity—often listed in the rolls only by terms such as "A Negro Man." Yet, blacks fought alongside whites in every battle.

In 1779, when the warfare shifted from the North to the South, Virginians allowed slaves into the patriot army. These men became part of regular combat units where they ate and fought alongside white soldiers. Many served as sailors—some as ship pilots. Caesar, the slave of Carter Tarrant of Hampton, became a known pilot in the Virginia service. During his duty, the boats he piloted had a number of contests with the enemy. He served four years as pilot of the "Patriot." Once when he was at the wheel, the "Patriot" captured a brig carrying stores for British troops.[9]

As Americans, Negroes felt roused also by the high goals of the Revolution. Breaking with England, the leaders of the new nation invoked the spirit of liberty, claiming that war was waged to extend the limits of human freedom. Ideas of liberty and the rights of mankind, so vital to slaves and others of lowly status, were most clearly expressed in the Declaration of Independence.

The Continental Congress approved this ringing statement July 4, 1776. It stated that all men were created equal and were endowed with certain rights that must remain: life, liberty, and the pursuit of happiness. Such language caused Negroes to view the Declaration as a freedom manifesto for mankind rather than simply a verbal attack against a king across the ocean.

The desire for freedom led many slaves to join the British, who had a greater manpower shortage then the colonists. They received the blacks from the start, and freely released the slaves of American rebels who came to them. Lord Dunmore, Royal governor of Virginia, issued a proclamation in November, 1775, declaring all slaves free who would join His Majesty's troops.

After the war fought for liberty ended, many Americans became more aware of the wrongness of holding people in bondage. The conviction that slavery did not match the ideals of the war arose in many quarters. Such views caused the formation of abolition societies, showed concern for blacks displayed by religious groups, and in the antislavery moves by the state and federal governments. The Pennsylvania Society, first formed at Philadelphia in 1775, was revived in April, 1784. Less than a year later New York organized a society, with John Jay as president. New Jersey was next, and by 1790, Delaware, Connecticut, and Rhode Island followed, with divers local societies besides the state-wide organizations.

The abolitionist societies worked by quarterly meetings, and through special and standing committees. They tried to assist the bondmen by urging the abolition of the slave trade, foreign and domestic, and by the gradual abolition of keeping slaves. They sometimes paid a master to free a slave. Or, they guaranteed a master that if he freed a slave, they would be legally responsible if the slave failed to support himself. Pennsylvania abolitionists censured slavery by refusing to buy the products of slave labor.

Church groups moved to support the work of the abolitionist societies. Most, if not all, religious denominations had renewed interest in their black brothers. The Quakers opened an attack on human bondage, and their sway prompted Pennsylvania to abolish slavery in 1780. It was the first state in America to pass a law for the gradual abolishment of slavery. Yet in Pennsylvania, slaves were still reported in the 1840 census.[10]

The Baptists progressed by the licensing of preachers, slave and free. Among the blacks were George Liele and David George, who both left America with the British. Also licensed was Jesse Peter, who in 1783 took the church at Silver Bluff, South Carolina, the first Negro Baptist church in the United States. Another early Negro Baptist was South Carolina-born Joseph Willis, who, prior to 1798, became a licensed preacher and moved into the Mississippi Territory. He may have delivered the first Protestant sermon west of the Mississippi River. He became the first moderator of the first Baptist state-wide organization—the Louisiana Association.[11]

Antislavery opinion among Methodists was strengthened by John Wesley's castigation of human bondage. In 1780, six years after Wesley wrote his *Thoughts Upon Slavery*, the Methodist conference at Baltimore expressed disapproval of members who held slaves. The conference required traveling preachers to free their slaves. This stand was reaffirmed in 1784, but in the next year the conference suspended the rule against slaveholding.

In a sense, the American Revolution had been a civil war which pitted colonist against colonist. Loyalists holding allegiance to the king of England endured intense persecution at the hands of the Patriots for American liberty. Anglican churchmen were among those suspected of Tory sympathies. In 1775, this group also included some 3,148 members of Methodist societies.

John Wesley aggravated the touchy situation when he published an indiscreet attack against the Patriot cause. This political pamphlet, "A Calm Address," provoked intense anti-Methodist protest. Frequently insulted, threatened, and jailed, Methodist missionaries returned to England. Among Wesley's appointees, only Francis Asbury remained. He had to go into hiding during the war, living in virtual exile for over two years.

Asbury noted in his journal, Friday, March 13, 1778:

> I was under some heaviness of mind. But it was no wonder: three thousand miles from home—my friends have left me—I am considered by some as an enemy of the country—every day liable to be seized by violence and abused. However, all this is but a trifle to suffer for Christ, and the salvation of souls. Lord stand by me![12]

The war upset Methodist circuits, turning many meetinghouses into makeshift hospitals. Methodist preaching was silenced in some colonies, driving societies underground. Yet those troubled times did not halt their spread. By the war's end, Methodist membership had grown toward 15,000—an increase of over 450% in eight years! Despite adversities, revivals in Virginia offset other losses, so the over 3,000 members in 1775 trebled by 1780. For instance, at the annual conference of 1778, five old circuits were canceled in Pennsylvania, Maryland, and New York, but six new ones were opened in Virginia and two in North Carolina. By 1784, four-fifths of the country's 15,000 Methodists lived south of the Mason-Dixon line.

That year meant a time of decision for Methodism in England and America. In February John Wesley settled for England the "Deed of Declaration," vesting the 359 Methodist chapels in a self-perpetuating annual conference of 100 preachers. September 1, he recorded in his diary the fateful decision concerning Methodist ministry in America. He wrote: "Being now clear in my own mind, I took a step . . . and appointed Mr. [Richard] Whatcoat and Mr. [Thomas] Vasey to go and serve the desolate sheep in America."[13]

A few days later, Wesley, Thomas Coke, and James Creighton, all priests of the Church of England, ordained Whatcoat and Vasey. Then Wesley, "assisted by other ordained ministers," also ordained Coke to be a superintendent in the United States. The three were sent out with this authorization: "Know all men, that I, John Wesley, think myself to be providentially called at this time, to set apart some persons for the work of ministry in America."[14]

The three Methodist emissaries set sail in September, 1784, landing in America after stormy passage, in November. In December, at Baltimore, they convened a "Christmas Conference" to organize the American church. From Francis Asbury's effort to notify the distant circuits, 60 preachers attended. They formed an Episcopal Church, with superintendents, elders, and deacons. Asbury and Coke were elected unanimously as superintendents. Asbury was ordained successively as deacon, elder, and superintendent by the three English ministers. Philip William Otterbein of the German Reformed Church assisted them in the latter rite.

With Francis Asbury at its head, American Methodism surged forward, while the English movement began lapsing into formalism and stagnancy. During the next century Methodism was the driving force of evangelical Arminianism in this country. Spreading mainly by domestic evangelism, it grew faster than all other Protestant churches. The chief traits of the American Methodist message were its emphasis on personal religious experience, its prescribed views of Christian behavior, and its simple doctrine. An experience of regeneration (new life in Christ), by repentance (turning from a life of sin), were required for church membership.

The specific behavioral and moral demands placed upon the regenerate Christian were basically Puritan, including prohibitions on alcohol and slaveholding. The doctrinal message was grounded on three essential points: (1) God's grace is free to all; (2) man is ever free to accept or reject that grace; and (3) the justified sinner, with the aid of the Holy Spirit, must seek Christian perfection (i.e. freedom from willful sin).

As the colonial period ended (1775) three large ecclesiastical blocs, all of British background, made up 80 percent of Americans who were affiliated with any church. They were evenly dispersed among the Congregationalists of New England, the Anglicans of the South, and the Presbyterians who flourished in the Middle Colonies. Small but potent Quaker, Baptist, and Methodist groups added almost three percentage points to the British Protestant total. Also, Dutch Reformed churches, strongest in New York and New Jersey, became aligned with the English-speaking population. Roman Catholics and Jews composed only about 0.1 percent of the population. By the neglect of evangelism among the slaves, the largest non-British minority in the colonies was African.

The Congregational churches did not face upset by the revolutionary era's turmoil as did the Anglicans and Methodists. Outwardly the Congregational position was improved. The Anglican challenge became weakened by the taint of Toryism and by great physical losses. Congregationalism rode the crest of patriotism, inciting the revolutionary spirit and providing the institutional and theoretical groundwork for America's independence.

Yet the Puritan ideal, of which these churches were the wardens, was corroded by the Enlightenment's demand for simple "common sense." The "orthodox" churches became nearly as infused by rationalism and formalism as the Arminian churches which relied on human reason and ability. Church membership became nominal, and revivals were erratic and limited. Any "religious enthusiasm" flowed through the Baptist and Methodist churches. After earlier visits by itinerant evangelists, Jesse Lee started Methodism in New England, beginning a circuit at Norwalk, Connecticut, in June, 1789. He also preached at Fairfield, Danbury, and New Haven, and then founded a circuit in Rhode Island.[15]

The revolutionary era gradually broke the bonds between the Presbyterian church and Congregationalism that the Great Awakening had forged. Just prior to the war, they united in a general convention to resist any imposition of an Anglican episcopate on the colonies. Yet in theology, polity, and internal spirit they moved apart. By the end of the 18th century, revivalism and the western missionary challenge would again unite the two churches.

During the same period the Baptists advanced from the revival fervor infused into their ranks by the Separates. They joined forces with the Calvinistic Baptists in New England and nearly engulfed the older Arminian Baptists. In 1740, only 25 Baptist churches existed in all New England: 11 each in Rhode Island and Massachusetts, and 3 in Connecticut. By 1790, despite the times, these had increased to 38 in Rhode Island, 92 in Massachusetts, 55 in Connecticut, 15 in Maine, 32 in New Hampshire, and 34 in Vermont—a total of 266 churches.[16]

As revivalism increased faster in the South, Baptists made larger gains. In 1790 Virginia alone had almost as many churches (218) as all of New England. The union of the Separates and Regulars in 1787 poised them to advance with the westward movement into Kentucky and Tennessee. Thereby, the Separate Baptists made steady progress through personal and mass evangelism, opposing all forms of religious favoritism in Virginia. They were joined by the Presbyterians, and by many statesmen, such as Thomas Jefferson and James Madison—both nominal Anglicans.

Feelings against the established church prevailed at the outbreak of the war. The assembly passed a series of bills to remove all traces of religious inequality. In 1776 compulsory taxation for clergy support was set aside. The basic guarantee of religious freedom was enacted in 1785, and in 1799 the old glebe lands were returned to public domain. In the long struggle to enforce the First Amendment to the federal Constitution, John Leland and Reuben Ford ably led the Baptist cause.

With the ratification of the federal Constitution (1787) and its first 10 amendments (1791), Protestants as a whole possessed liberties found nowhere else in the world. Though Roman Catholics faced various legal measures, they had more freedom than in any other Protestant land. Meanwhile, humanists, deists, Unitarians, and persons with no professed religion could also freely voice their views and aspire to the highest office in the land.

One might think only a dissenter would construct the Constitutional safeguard with regard to religion. Rather, an Anglican, Charles Pinckney, of South Carolina, proposed that "no religious test shall ever be required as a qualification to any office or public trust under the United States." August 30, 1787, Pinckney's clause was added to Article VI, stating that elected officials could be bound to their duties either by "oath or affirmation." This allowed Quakers, whose religious convictions refused oath-taking, to participate fully in the Federal Government.

A patriotic spirit overarched all such circumstances of the various churches, pervading every aspect of the country's feeling and thought. When the Founding Fathers designed the new republic's Great Seal, they showed acceptance of the old Puritan concept that Providence had assigned a world mission to the American nation. In effect they reaffirmed the words Massachusetts Bay Governor John Winthrop proclaimed in 1630: "The God of Israel is among us. . . . We shall be as a city upon a hill." E PLURIBUS UNUM (One out of many)—ANNUIT COEPTIS (He [God] has smiled on our undertakings—MDCCLXXVI—NOVUS ORDO SECCLORUM (A new cycle of the ages).[17]

During the decades closing the 18th century and opening the 19th century, the Baptists and Methodists began active programs of evangelization. Their efforts were aided by more mobility, ardent experientialism, and candid preaching. Bishop Benjamin T. Tanner, of the African Methodist Episcopal Church, clearly describes the fervent methods which induced the changed religious spirit in the South—for whites and blacks alike:

> While the good Presbyterian parson was writing his discourses,
> . . . the Methodist itinerant had traveled forty miles with his horse
> and saddle bags; while the parson was adjusting his spectacles to
> read his manuscript, the itinerant had given hell and damnation to
> his unrepentant hearers; while the disciple of Calvin was waiting
> to have his church completed, the disciple of Wesley took to the
> woods and made them re-echo with the voice of free grace,
> believing with Bryant, "The groves were God's first temples."[18]

After the Revolution, religious activity increased in the free or partially free black communities of the North. Local churches accepted both white and black members, but special seating was assigned to the blacks, who often outnumbered the whites. By 1790 the Methodist church reported 11,682 "colored" members, almost a fifth of the total membership. Some credited the Baptists for converting even more Negroes. Reports from scattered parishes show that these two church groups were more successful than any others.

For the revolutionary generation, slavery and antislavery questions were of lesser concern than other issues. The federal Constitution made a compromise with slavery as an institution. The men who met at Philadelphia to write the document came to found a strong and united nation—not to solve the slavery question. To keep the loyalty of slaveholders and slave traders in both the North and the South, they sheltered slave property in three sections of the Constitution:

1. They gave the African slave trade 20 more years in which to cease operations.

2. They provided that all runaway slaves had to be returned to their owners.

3. Because slaveholders were to be taxed for their slaves, as property, they were allowed three votes for every five slaves owned.[19]

By 1787, several states had acted to outlaw the slave trade. Foes of this awful traffic in human beings hoped the Constitutional Convention would act to stop this evil. The Pennslyvania Abolition Society drafted a memorial imploring the convention to include the slave trade in their deliberations. The society gave it to Ben Franklin to present.[20]

Franklin's task included avoiding the suspicions of Southern convention members. The Constitutional Convention had already endured heated debates over representation in the Congress. It focused on the question as to how the slaves should be counted. Most Northern delegates viewed slaves only as property, which did not deserve representation. The so-called three-fifths compromise finally written into the Constitution shows the strength of the proslavery interests at the convention. The compromise stated:

Representatives and direct Taxes shall be apportioned among the several States which may be included within this Union, according to their respective Numbers, which shall be determined by adding the whole Number of free Persons, including those bound to Service for a Term of Years, and excluding Indians not taxed, three-fifths of all other persons. (Article I, Section 2).

When the slave problem came before the convention, a fiery argument ensued. Fear of rupture at this point led the states of the North and upper South to compromise with the states of the lower South by extending the slave trade for 20 years. The provision finally adopted for the Constitution reads:

The Migration or Importation of such Persons as any of the States now existing shall think proper to admit, shall not be prohibited by the Congress prior to the Year one thousand eight hundred and eight, but a Tax or duty may be imposed on such Importation, not exceeding ten dollars for each Person. (Article II, Section 9).

Little opposition met the proposal that states return fugitive slaves to their owners. The public duty to return runaways, as stated in several Indian treaties between 1781 and 1786, was set up in the Northwest Territory in 1787 along with the prohibition of slavery. This provision came before the convention late, on August 28. The slave owners had already won such acceptance of slavery that the question of fugitive slaves was anticlimactic. Roger Sherman of Connecticut declared he saw "no more propriety in the public seizing and surrendering a slave or servant, than a horse," but his New England colleagues gave no support.[21]

The inserted item declares:

No Person held to Service or Labour in one State, under the Laws thereof, escaping into another, shall, in Consequence of any Law or Regulation therein, be discharged from such Service or Labour, but shall be delivered up on Claim of the Party to whom such Service or Labour may be due. (Article IV, Section 2).

The founders of the Constitution staunchly proposed that "government should rest on the dominion of property." To the Southern fathers this meant slaves, and commerce and industry to the Northern fathers. The Constitution granted the institution of human slavery to protect this property, but 75 years was needed to undo the bondage allowed in the 1787 Philadelphia convention.

The adoption of the federal Constitution marks an era in the political history of the United States, and of Negro Americans. Freed from British rule, Americans could no longer lay the onus of slavery at the door of their mother country. Americans met the challenge and duty of their new political freedom by framing the methods and safeguards that ensured the continued enslavement of blacks. Ironically, the freed whites extended Negro slavery beyond its term in the British empire. The revolution that liberated American colonists did not include freeing black slaves.

Widespread moral dissent emerged, however, in the prohibition of slavery in the Northwest Ordinance of 1787. Nearly every Northern state had either abolished or provided for the gradual abolition of slavery. As the country matured, the questions, remorse, and protest continued, all nurtured by Christian conviction and patriotic idealism. Objections to slavery were clearly expressed even in the South, where the institution was firmly entrenched. In fact, between 1808 and 1831, Southerners were more vital to the antislavery movement than Northerners.

Yet, believers in the *status quo* held sway in the thoughts and plans of most people. Though slavery was recognized as a serious problem by political and religious leaders alike, they relied on the overrated cure of time. A religious reawakening must occur. Neither slavery nor the conflict of racism would heal themselves or fade away in time. Freedom would not prevail for African-Americans until the conflict was resolved in true reconciliation.

Chapter 4

Christians and Abolitionist Action

In the decade of the 1830s, "Sir, and Ma'am, may I help you," became a likely tactic as American society enjoyed the Jacksonian democracy. This time of increased popular knowledge and the enlargement of economic opportunity provided common ground for a new perception of brotherhood. Those who suffered received more sympathy, coupled with greater interest in the progress of the whole human race. Seemly words of encouragement were, "That will suit you just fine." This decade launched an antislavery impulse.

American church people had long been "sold" on a questionable "bill of goods" in their dealings with slavery. As concern for all mankind increased, the dogmas of Calvinism lost authority, uniquely in the Presbyterian and Congregational denominations. To the many Calvinists of New England and the West (beyond the Eastern high-lands), the democratic faith in the common man conflicted with the central Calvinistic doctrine of original sin.[1]

Basically, the original sin meant Adam's disobedience to God in the Garden of Eden. But Calvinists believed it included also our sin; we like branches in the root sinned in Adam. Totally depraved in all our faculties of soul and body, we cannot will or do any good. We do not really face blame for our sins until God's Holy Spirit endues us with the power of His elect.[2] Yet fiery evangelists holding revival meetings stirred both an inner personal struggle and a general conflict among professed Christians that holding slaves denotes sinfulness. People's aroused consciences wondered if slavery expressed a sin against God and a black-skinned people with a strange culture.

Since slavery's beginning in the first English settlement at Jamestown, Virginia, in 1619, people ignored any possibility that slavery stood as sinful. Many church people held the Calvinist definition of original sin, and avoided direct accountability to God. They also identified blacks as sub-humans, so the slaves could be claimed as property. For centuries, a large number of Christians continued their faulty thinking and actions in the shameful use of slavery. Only "Holy Ghost revival" could bring the change of mind and heart needed to halt that sinful practice.

Most abolitionists declared slavery to be a sinful crime. The abiding concept of racial bias stems from the longtime confusion as to whether the use of slaves is sinful. Then, at what point do racist attitudes become sinful, even after slavery is abolished? Ever since the Civil War churches have been as much perplexed about how to deal with racism as they were about slavery. The Church has mostly lacked the love and humility to use the power of Christ's cross that truly offers salvation for all mankind.

Unitarian and evangelical zealots joined to kindle the first flame of antislavery feeling which blazed across the nation. Yet, evangelists like Charles G. Finney shunned being a political agitator to be a "soul winner." Also among those revivalist radicals were Theodore Weld; Arthur Tappan, first president of the American Anti-slavery Society; and Joshua Leavitt, editor of *The Evangelist* and also *The Emancipator*. Revivalists like Edward Norris Kirk, Nathaniel S. Beman, and Jacob Knapp, with many Methodists and New School pastors, added impetus to the movement.[3]

Methodists, like other churches, switched their interest in freeing the Negroes to offering religious instruction. Methodist decrees favoring emancipation passed the 1796 General Conference. Traveling preachers should not hold slaves; slave sellers among the church membership faced expulsion. But such rules were never enforced. By 1808 every item about slave holding members was erased from the discipline. By 1824 the conference told preachers to prudently teach the Bible to slaves. Negro preachers and official members received full grants, and the annual conferences sent black preachers to travel as missionaries among the slaves.[4]

White abolitionist William Lloyd Garrison denied gradualist urging emancipation of slaves sometime "between now and never." He headed a little Baptist temperance journal when Benjamin Lundy, a New Jersey Quaker, turned him to the antislavery cause in 1829. In Boston, Garrison, at 26, began to publish his *Liberator* (January, 1831), supported by Negro abolitionists. He labeled slavery as a sinful violation of the rights of mankind. Garrison claimed the government was protecting evil, and publicly burned a copy of the Constitution—because it viewed humans as property.[5]

Garrison founded the American Antislavery Society in 1833, following the British evangelical example. His zealous evangelical faith chafed under ecclesiastical prudence and compromise. In 1832 he appealed:

I call upon . . . the just . . . all who have experienced the love of
God in their hearts . . . upon the Christian converts . . . to sustain

. . . power enough in the religion of Jesus Christ to melt down . . . stubborn prejudices, to overthrow the highest wall . . . to break the strongest caste, to improve and elevate the most degraded, and to equalize all its recipients.[6]

The *Liberator* reported that Rev. Robert B. Hall told the New England Anti-Slavery Society in 1832: "A prejudice is generated in our youth against the blacks, which grows with our growth and strengthens with our strength, until our eyes are opened to the folly by a more correct feeling. . . ."[7]

The abolitionist demand for immediate emancipation also called for sudden racial brotherhood. If people could be turned to the one, they would also be changed to the other.[8] Crusader Theodore Weld wrote to Garrison in 1833, that God gives every man the right to be "a free moral agent," and "he who robs his fellow man of this tramples upon right, subverts justice, unsettles . . . human safety, and . . . assumes the prerogative of God."[9]

Such abolitionist feelings faced the developing sectionalism and political differences stemming from economic issues. These prompted an explanation of the system of slavery to insure its place in society. One writer declared in *DeBow's Review*, "This alliance between Negroes and cotton, . . . is not the strongest power in the world," but Christendom's welfare absolutely depends on its strength and security.[10]

When "King Cotton" ruled the economy, many writings claimed the sub-humanity of Negroes and argued that slavery was their natural state. The right to enslave enjoined defense by laymen, scholars, and by the Church. Few really perceived black slaves on the same level as white people—before God or anyone else.

Southern ideas thrived in Richard Furman's *Exposition of the Views of the Baptists relative to the Coloured Population* (1823):

While men remain in the chains of ignorance and error, under the dominion of . . . lusts and passions, they cannot be free. And the more freedom of action they have . . . they are . . . more qualified by it to do injury, . . . to themselves and others. It is, . . . firmly believed the general emancipation to the Negroes in this country would not, . . . be for their own happiness . . . it would be extremely injurious to the community at large.[11]

By 1827 slavery had been abolished in all the Northern states. Societies to spread the antislavery movement were organized in every state of the Union, except in the extreme South. This early movement became mostly moral and religious. Its center of activity and support moved in the so-called border states, especially in Kentucky and Virginia, where they viewed slavery as a moral evil. Prior to 1830, Lundy, advocating emancipation, traveled freely through the South and gained a kindly reception.

But the antislavery spirit in the Methodist Church had ebbed before 1830. For 10 years, little agitation moved in the General Conference, partly because the abolition societies seemed so radical and violent that church people avoided associating with them. Many of the early organizations formed by white people to help the slaves saw the problem as best resolved by deporting Negroes to Africa. With slaveholder assent and the aid of the United States Congress, the American Colonization Society founded such a colony in Liberia in 1821. Some 12,000 blacks were sent, mostly slaves freed on the condition they would accept deportation.

While Christian moderates knew the evils within slavery, they condoned the institution itself. Abolitionists and "immediatists" became uncompromising, with the failure of colonization attempts, apologists and secessionists became extreme. Some defended slavery as morally neutral, being whatever master and slave made of it. Great effort arose to evangelize the slaves, to improve their morals, to teach them obedience, and urge masters to have mercy. Thus total condemnation of the institution seemed improper.

Methodist evangelist Peter Cartwright said preachers in the Methodist Episcopal Church "didn't feel it their duty to meddle with it politically," but they opposed slavery as a moral evil. Cartwright claimed early ministers worked the release of thousands of "this degraded race of human beings." "If Methodist preachers had kept clear of slavery themselves, . . . bearing honest testimony against it . . . thousands more would have been emancipated . . ."[12]

Though slavery produced many moral evils, Cartwright said:

I have never seen a rabid abolition or free-soil society that I could join, because . . . the means they employ are generally unchristian. They condemn . . . the innocent with the guilty; . . . if force is resorted to, this glorious Union will be dissolved, a civil war . . . death and carnage will ensue, and the only free nation on the earth will be destroyed."[13]

Many Northerners advised moderation. Abolition began crushing more than slavery—it threatened the "American dream." Poet James Russell Lowell wrote, ". . . the world must be healed by degrees." Brown University's Francis Wayland said slavery could be eradicated only by "changing the mind of both master and slave, by teaching the one party the love of justice and the fear of God"—elevating the other to the proper level of individual responsibility.[14]

With only half-hearted approval from most churches, the abolitionists advanced like a religious crusade. The growing humanitarian movement sweeping the Northern United States became a popular ally. Abolitionist action became enmeshed with peace movements, temperance, women's rights, and other reform programs to better all needy people in America. Yet such national reform movements during Andrew Jackson's presidency (1829-37), and that of Martin Van Buren (1837-41), did not help the Negro. Both Jackson and Van Buren opposed voting rights for free Negroes. As states extended this right to all adult white males without regard to property, several states repealed the right to vote from property-owning blacks who had voted before.

In 1839 President Van Buren asked for the law against the African slave trade to be amended to preserve the "integrity and honor of our flag." By June, 1841, President John Tyler (1841-45) knew that the slave traffic was on the increase. The blatant abuse of the slave trade law did not arouse public action against those who profited from the scandalous trade. It became more than sectional; New York merchants like those of New Orleans gained from the illicit traffic.[15]

Every time a new state joined the Union, or settlers moved to fresh land, the thorny question of slavery pricked the national conscience more deeply. Would slavery be extended indefinitely in space and continue infinitely in time? Should the new territory be slave or free? In the passion to preserve both liberty and union, if one must choose, which came first?

Even in 1822, Richard Furman, South Carolina's leading Baptist cleric, claimed, "the right of holding slaves is . . . established in the Holy Scriptures, both by precept and example." He admitted the golden rule was urged "as an unanswerable argument against holding slaves." Yet that rule, he advised, is not used in a vacuum. One must weigh the social context, with "a due regard to justice, propriety and the general good." Thus, neither the spirit nor the letter of the Scripture demands the abolition of slavery.[16]

In 1823, some with slave interests tried to foist their "Institution" on Illinois. "At one meeting of the Friends of Freedom in St. Clair County, more than 30 preachers of the gospel . . . opposed the introduction of slavery into the State." "The pulpit," said one, "thundered anathemas against . . . slavery. The religious community coupled freedom and Christianity, which was one of the most powerful levers used in the contest." "The clergy of Illinois," said the annals, "were . . . opposed to the Convention (which favored making it a Slave State)," and they "exerted great influence in securing the rejection at the polls."[17]

Slavery was not an economic issue in Michigan Territory, but mostly a matter of social classification. An April 13, 1827, law was titled: "An Act to regulate blacks and mulattoes and to punish the kidnapping of such persons." Although Negroes could not be lawfully held as slaves, this did not recognize their status either as residents or as respected persons with civil rights.[18]

Detroit had large numbers of dedicated anti-slavery Quakers. They moved from Niagara, New York, to Detroit in 1832-33. Both proslavery and antislavery feelings sharply rose to riot fever. It became known as the Blackburn riot of 1833. Though the number of slaves in Detroit had declined to a mere few, Mr. and Mrs. Thornton Blackburn were arrested on fugitive slave charges June 14, 1833. Other blacks rescued them and enabled their escape into Canada.

As the 1830s progressed, many whites joined Garrison in the anti-slavery movement. Levi Coffin, Indiana Quaker and banker, began using his Newport home to hide runaways. He was soon called the "President of the Underground Railroad." After Charles G. Finney's conversion under the preaching of Presbyterian George W. Gale, his revival preaching won much support for antislavery.[19] Though theologically distinct from radicals like Garrison and Wendell Phillips, Finney agreed with them in respect to slavery. Finney's broad impact built up strong antislavery feelings in the Midwest, mainly around Oberlin, a Congregational college in Ohio.

In 1834, Theodore Weld, with Finney's blessing, took the antislavery gospel to Lane Theological Seminary in Cincinnati. After sessions of debate the students denounced the Colonization Society. One group of dissidents moved to Oberlin to avoid disciplinary measures by the seminary, when Oberlin College was little more than a "bivoac in the wilderness." Led by Asa Mahan, and later Finney, with funding from the Tappans of New York, Oberlin became a center of abolitionism and revivalism.

During 1836-37, Charles Finney, then president of Oberlin, gave a series of "Lectures to Professing Christians" in New York City. He linked conversion and Christian commitment to social issues. His first address, titled "Self-Deceivers," declared the Church had long acted too much on "the Antinomial policy." It had

> laid greater stress on orthodoxy in those doctrines that are not
> practical, . . . A man may be the greatest heretic on points of

practice, provided he is not openly profane and vicious, and yet maintain a good standing in the church, . . . when it is attempted to purify the church in . . . practical errors, she cannot bear it. Why else is it that so much excitement is produced by attempting to clear the church from participating in sins of intemperance, and Sabbath-breaking and slavery?[20]

In Finney's third address, titled "Doubtful Actions Are Sinful," he further states:

Who, . . . can say, that he has no doubt of the lawfulness of slavery? . . . it is . . . proposed, both at the north and at the south, to pass laws forbidding . . . discussion on the subject. Now suppose these laws should be passed, . . . enabling the nation to shelter itself behind its doubts whether slavery is a sin, that it ought to be abolished immediately . . . If they . . . hold their fellow men as property, in slavery while they doubt its lawfulness, they are condemned before God . . .[21]

Finney's fourth lecture, "Reproof a Christian Duty," cites what a Christian should rebuke. Under the listing of "Slavery," he exclaims:

What! shall men be suffered to commit one of the most God-dishonoring . . . sins on earth, and not be reproved? It is a sin against which all men should . . . lift up their voice like a trumpet, till this giant iniquity is banished from the land and from the world.[22]

Theodore Weld also cited antislavery in his writings, *The Bible Against Slavery* (1837), and *Slavery As It Is* (1839). Mobs often pursued him, making him the target of bricks and eggs when he lectured. Like other abolitionists, he opposed the institution of slavery, and its perpetuation. When Southerners used Scripture to support slavery, abolitionists claimed it violated Christ's teachings. Jesus taught love of one's neighbor and universal brotherhood. Also, the apostle Paul declared, "Love does no harm to its neighbor" (Rom. 13:10). Abolitionists charged that slavery ruined the Christian way by denying the rights of black people.

Abolitionists further declared slavery would trigger failure. Slaves spurred the waste of natural and human resources throughout the South. That area's culture and industry suffered. The master-slave relationship nurtured the baser aspects in each of their natures. Weld declared, "Arbitrary power is to the mind what alcohol is to the body; it intoxicates."[23] Since Southern whites feared slave revolts, that fear spawned violence and bloodshed.

In Alton, Illinois, a kindred rage occurred. Rev. Elijah P. Lovejoy, a Presbyterian minister and newspaper editor, resisted a gang protesting his antislavery passions. While protecting his press, Lovejoy was killed November 7, 1837—America's first martyr to freedom of the press. Because Lovejoy died defending his fourth printing press (all destroyed since being driven from St. Louis), this showed the conflict of slavery and freedom in this country.

The tragedy moved Edward Beecher, then president of Illinois College, toward abolitionism. Beecher wrote a dramatic narrative of the Alton riots, and in 1845 issued a series of articles on "organic sin," giving evangelical abolitionism some major ethical and theological insights. This aroused William Ellery Channing in Boston to organize a meeting at the Faneuil Hall with Wendell Phillips as the abolitionist orator.

In an address to the Massachusetts Anti-Slavery Society in 1853, Wendell Phillips proclaimed the abolitionist position:

> They print the Bible in every tongue in which man utters his prayers; and get the money to do so by agreeing never to give the book, . . . to any negro, free or bond, south of Mason and Dixon's line. The press says, "It is all right"; and the pulpit cries, "Amen." The slave . . . sees in every face but ours the face of an enemy. Prove to me now that harsh rebuke, . . . and pitiless ridicule are . . . always unjustifiable; else we dare not,... throw away any weapon which ever broke up . . . an ignorant prejudice, roused a slumbering conscience, shamed a proud sinner, or changed, in any way, the conduct of human being. Our aim is to alter public opinion.[24]

Such men perhaps relied on Garrison's *Liberator* to aid their effectiveness. Methodist presiding elder Orange Scott, a convinced evangelistic churchman, turned most of the New England conference to abolitionism in 1835 by sending them a three-month subscription to the magazine. Scott said that Garrison destroyed the dream of recolonizing the Negroes in Africa. Without this stumbling block, even Unitarians spoke against slavery in evangelical pulpits.[25]

Opposing slavery *as a sin* fit Methodist perfectionism, New School revivalism, and the moral concerns of radical Quakers and Unitarians. Most people's political interests increased during Andrew Jackson's presidency. For those who felt the revivals of 1828-36, that interest required a moral platform. The abolition of slavery became basic, meeting their religious traditions. John Wesley had called the traffic in human beings the "sum of all villainies." Samuel Hopkins denounced those in his Newport, Rhode Island, congregation who gained from slavery. The 19th century revival preachers were spiritual heirs of Wesley, English Methodist, and Hopkins, American Congregationalist.

This reforming thrust amenable to the Wesleyan concepts of perfectionism (in love) permeated the abolitionist's crusade against slavery. It may be said definitely:

> Abolitionism was absolutist . . . in its moral perceptions; . . . perfectionism demanded complete consecration to the known will . . . of God. This . . . provided a ready springboard for . . . answers to moral . . . questions. The relationship between perfection and the anti-slavery crusade, . . . was not coincidental. Converts of revivalism saw that the law of love . . . was being vitiated by slavery. They had to act against it.[26]

John Noyes, the Oneida perfectionist, warned William Lloyd Garrison that the abolitionists could succeed in their stand only if such efforts matched perfectionism ideals. Garrison finally espoused perfectionism, but Benjamin B. Warfield said it resembled that of the more Wesleyan Asa Mahan, than that of the mystical Noyes.[27] Garrison's leaning toward revolution rather than reform, caused a rift between himself and evangelical abolitionists.[28]

Turmoil arose between evangelicals and the radical Unitarians in 1836 and 37. It occurred while the Quaker sisters Sarah and Angeline Grimke toured New England as agents of the antislavery society. Their example swayed the infant movement for women's rights, about which advocates of abolition were divided. Garrison wanted to force the society to accept women as equals with men. Yet his plan of "universal reform" made Christianity a target of attack rather than means for reform. He urged freedom for slaves and legal equality of the sexes. But he condemned the "sinful" government of church and state that allowed these evils to exist.[29]

Throughout 1838 Garrison's campaign against the Church and its clergy was as furious as that against the slave traffic. By controling the official publication, and the disunion of the abolitionist organization, he ejected his foes at the annual meeting in 1839. Using similar tactics the next year, he seized control of the national convention in New York. Weld, abolition convert James G. Birney, and Arthur Tappan—both New York state and national president from the start—led evangelicals into the American and Foreign Anti-slavery Society. Boston clerics had begun a separate Massachusetts group.

That day in 1839, when Garrison seized control of the American Antislavery Society, was crucial for the Church. Evangelicals, as one writer put it, stood "between the upper and the nether millstones of a pro-slavery Christianity, and an anti-Christian abolitionism."[30] The first party explained both Scripture and ancient creed to sanction slave oppression. The latter associated freedom with infidelity and championed revolution against church and state. True morality must grow in human hearts beyond the movements to support it, and liberty must be a braver Christian force than mere symbols of patriotism, to free the slaves.

By 1845, the unity of the abolition movement became shattered. Garrison had ousted the evangelicals from the American Antislavery Society. Methodist bishops removed the radical abolitionists from their fold, but that wedge split the church, North and South. Old School theologians sided with proslavery Southerners to drive the revivalist synods out of the Presbyterian church and to form a biblical, theological defense of the South's "peculiar institution."

Meanwhile, Congregationalists and New School Presbyterians endured the charges of fanaticism aimed at Finney's Oberlin College when the perfectionist revival broke out there. The former group also struggled in New England to repel Garrison's attacks against the Church, the Bible, and ancient Christian creeds. They saw that religious and social radicalism brought the faith reproach.

Such strife greatly damaged the antislavery cause, especially in New England. The advice of moderate men prevailed—of church leaders with mystic and other-worldly goals, and of editors and church officials more anxious for the peace and prosperity of their flocks. The Christian witness against the nation's most glaring evil ceased. Dismayed, Weld, Birney, and many evangelicals began to reprove the sins of the Church as much as those of secular society. Birney declared in 1850 that churches had been "in the rear of society" for a decade. He wrote, "With the exception of small denominations, . . . the church cannot disappoint me much in its anti-slavery measures, because I look for so little . . . from it."[31]

The Lutheran Synod in North Carolina noted in 1836 "the impropriety and injustice of the interference . . . of any religious or deliberative body with the subject of slavery or slaveholding, emancipation of abolitionism. . . ." Charging "affected patriots" and "more than rotten-hearted benefactors of this much commiserated race," the synod firmly resolved it would "not at any time enter into a discussion of slavery."[32]

A Christian antislavery crisis broke during the same year at the Methodist conferences in New England and upper New York, as bishops checked their churches' feelings. In 1835 Bishop Elijah Hedding moved

Orange Scott from the Springfield to the Providence District. The next year Scott was removed from any presiding, perhaps because he led the antislavery delegation at the General Conference in Cincinnati. He accepted a pastorate in Lowell, Massachusetts. There he joined colleague Joel Parker, "to secure the outpouring of the Holy Spirit among the people" and so "to bring all over to the cause of Christ and the bleeding slave." The city soon became a center for Methodist abolitionists.[33]

Despite voices such as Scott's, the Methodist church ignored the slavery issue. In 1836 the bishops warned against voicing that issue in the church. In an Episcopal letter, they said, "the only safe, scriptural, and prudent way for us . . . to take is wholly to refrain from the agitating subject . . ."[34] Bishop James O. Andrew was one of the signers of the letter, and a focal point in the conflict that split the church in 1844.

Bishop Andrew became an owner of slaves when his first wife died. His second wife was also a slaveholder. Knowing this angered foes of slavery, Andrew offered to resign. People against slavery felt that a bishop as a slaveholder made the church show support of slavery. Yet, others urged Bishop Andrew not to resign. Those for slavery believed that to yield on this point would oust the very principle of slavery. The issue was settled when the Southern delegates met in 1845 at Louisville, Kentucky, and formed the Methodist Episcopal Church, South.[35]

Orange Scott took inactive status in the conference to become an agent of the American Antislavery Society. Defying Bishop Hedding, Scott set lectures at the seat of Methodist conferences. Hedding asked Wilbur Fisk, Nathan Bangs, and other leading New York City clergy to speak against abolitionism, giving them use of the conference floor. When Hedding made charges against Scott in 1838, the conference voted "not guilty" by a large margin. Shortly, 300 pastors in Eastern districts joined the antislavery cause, with *Zion's Herald* (the Boston Methodist weekly) as its champion. And Scott successfully evangelized western New York.[36]

By 1843, doubting any future antislavery success within the church, Orange Scott, LaRoy Sunderland, and Luther Lee led several thousand New York laymen and pastors into the Wesleyan Methodist Church. They quit the Methodist Episcopal Church because of the conflict they sensed between the Wesleyan doctrine of sanctification (perfect love) and slavery. They renounced episcopacy as well as the compromise with the slaveholders. This action soon weakened abolition in the mother church by relating it with schism. But the New Englanders, threatening to join the Wesleyans, forced the North-South division at the General Conference the next year.

Similar crisis beset the antislavery party in the Presbyterian church. The General Assembly in 1837 expelled the New School as a covert "deal" between discreet Scotch-Irish churchmen who opposed the revivalists' doctrinal heresies and Southerners who feared their antislavery creed. The latter ignored the theological issues that Finney, Albert Barnes, Lyman Beecher, and George Duffield raised when they espoused free will and natural ability. During the 1837 General Assembly, delegates from the moderate New York, New Jersey, and Philadelphia presbyteries offered to abandon the church's stand against slavery. That is, if Southerners would help them oust the growing "Puritan" party.[37]

Princeton scholars and Southern preachers wrote a defense of slavery, printing it in *The New York Observer* to curb evangelical foes. They argued God chose some to be masters and some to be servants, just as certain men were elected to be saved and others to be damned. Scripture showed God's sanction of slavery—the Old Testament by law and example—the New Testament by silence. The apostles never set the Church as "a moral institute of universal good," but as a way of personal salvation, unto everlasting life.[38]

Pioneer Baptist missionary, John Mason Peck, who hated all enslaving forms, made a *Journal* entry on the first day of 1842:

> January 1, Nashville. A negro boy . . . about twelve years old . . . stood by the auctioneer . . . crying and sobbing,.... it was the first human being I ever saw . . . for sale, . . . Slavery in Tennessee is certainly not as oppressive, inhuman and depressing as the state of the poorer classes of society in England, Ireland, and many parts of Continental Europe; yet slavery in its best state is a violation of man's nature and of the Christian law of love.[39]

Although Garrisonian antislavery tumult offended Christian churches of the North, the belief grew that Christians ought not to hold slaves. Such feelings also caused strife among the Baptist churches of the Northern states, and threatened their union. The slavery dispute appeared in the Minutes of the General Convention for several years before the final break, climaxing in 1844. The slavery issue troubled Baptist churches represented in the convention meeting that year, so they adopted the following:

> Resolved, . . . as members in this Convention in the work of foreign missions, we disclaim all sanctions either expressed or implied, whether of slavery or anti-slavery; but as individuals we are free to express and to promote elsewhere our views . . . in a Christian manner and spirit.[40]

The convention gave the Executive Board a mandate to preserve this attitude of neutrality. Yet that December, in response to a question by a Southern body, the board replied with a new rule:

> If any one who should offer himself for a missionary, having slaves, should insist on retaining them as property, we could not appoint him. One thing is certain, we can never be party to an arrangement which would imply approbation of slavery.[41]

In April, 1845, the American Baptist Home Mission Society, having similar discord with most of its Northern attendants, adopted certain resolutions. They declared it to be "expedient that the members . . . should hereafter act in separate organizations at the South and at the North in promoting the objects . . . originally contemplated by the society." These actions by the Northern Baptists made denominational unity futile.[42]

Called by the Virginia Foreign Mission Society in May, 1845, 310 delegates from Southern churches met at Augusta, Georgia, to organize the Southern Baptist Convention. Its constitution copied that of the first General Baptist Convention: "For eliciting, combining, and directing, the energies of the whole denomination in one sacred effort for the propagation of the gospel." Two boards were founded, one for foreign missions located in Richmond, and one for domestic missions at Marion, Alabama.[43]

Roman Catholic Bishop John England of Charleston observed in 1840, that slavery is not "incompatible with natural law." When a slave is justly acquired by a master, the institution is "lawful not only in the sight of the human tribunal, but also in the eyes of heaven." Such a defense underlay the concepts of Southern theologian and laity alike. They held the common biblical texts on Negro baseness, patriarchal and Mosaic sanction of slavery, and the apostle Paul's advice of obedience to masters.

It seems a verse of Cecil Francis Alexander's poem, "All Things Bright and Beautiful," voiced the thoughts of many religious people who remained silent on social evils. They ignored the evils of snobbery, selfish pride, and slavery because they believed God had arranged that people would be born in distinct social strata.

> The rich man in his castle,
> The poor man at his gate,
> God made them, high or lowly,
> And ordered their estate.[44]

Peter Cartwright described the changing rationale of slavery within the Methodist Episcopal Church in his 1856 *Autobiography*:

Methodism increased and spread; and many . . . preachers, . . . not able to own a negro, and who preached loudly against it, improved and became popular among slaveholders; . . . married into those slaveholding families . . . began to apologize for the evil; . . . to justify it, on legal principles; then on Bible principles; till . . . it is not an evil but a good! it is not a curse, but a blessing! . . . you would go to the devil for not enjoying the labor, toil, and sweat of this degraded race . . . without rendering them any equivalent whatever![45]

Every major religious body in America knew the tension between slavery and abolition during the 1830-1860 period. Three groups split over the slavery issue. The Methodists divided first as the conflict peaked with the North urging abolition of slavery against Southern holders. Bishops tried to temper every resolution, but one could not fit "All slaveholding is a sin against God" with "We believe that the Holy Scriptures . . . authorize the relation of master and slave." In 1844 the Methodist Episcopal Church, South, seceded from its northern counterpart—lasting until 1939.[46]

Two reports typify the breach in Methodism. South Carolina's Bishop William Capers defended the slaveholders in 1836, saying:

We denounce the principles and opinions of the abolitionists in tot, and . . . declare our . . . belief that whether they were originated, as some business men have thought, as a money speculation; or, as some politicians think, for electioneering purposes; or, as we . . . believe, in a false philosophy, . . . setting aside the Scriptures, through a vain conceit of a higher refinement, they are . . . erroneous and . . . hurtful.[47]

The abolition convictions were framed by resolutions adopted by the Methodist Anti-slavery Convention meeting in Boston in 1843:

Resolved, . . . holding or treating human beings as property, or claiming the right to hold or treat them as property, is . . . violation of the law of God: it is . . . a sin under all circumstances, and in every person claiming such right, . . .

Resolved, that as the unanimity . . . which should ever characterize the people of God cannot exist so long as slavery continues in the church, we feel it our . . . duty to use all such means as become Christians in seeking its immediate and entire abolition from the Church of which we are members.[48]

A similar Baptist schism ensued in 1845. Though the current issue was the appointment of a slaveholding missionary, the basic conflict engaged slavery's friends and slavery's foes. Baptist missionaries and agents who once moved freely through the states, now faced either preference or hostility. After the 1845 break, Baptists in the South, like the Methodists, continued religious and moral teaching among the Negroes. They often shared the same building and the same services.

The Presbyterians, the last church body to divide, maintained a semblance of North-South structural unity until 1857. That year the General Assembly ("New School") expressed "deep grief" that Southern churchmen tried to defend slavery as "an ordinance of God." This "new doctrine" could not be tolerated, the ruling body declared, because "it is at war with the whole spirit . . . of the Gospel of love and goodwill, as well as abhorrent to the conscience of the Christian world." This sharp rebuke prodded 21 Southern presbyteries to withdraw and form the Presbyterian Church, U. S.[49]

The *New York Evangelist* newspaper published, in November 21, 1835, the stark contrast of North-South views of Presbyterians. South Carolina Presbyterians had written:

> Resolved, that in the opinion of this presbytery (Charleston Union), the holding of slaves, so far from being a sin . . . is nowhere condemned in his Holy word . . . it is in accordance with the example, . . . the precepts of patriarchs, prophets, and apostles; and that it is compatible with the . . . best good of those servants whom God may have committed to our charge, . . . therefore, they who assume the contrary position, . . . as a fundamental principle in morals and religion, that all slave-holding is wrong, proceed upon false principles.[50]

Michigan Presbyterians stated a drastic contrast:

> Resolved, that this synod . . . believe the buying, selling and owning of slaves in this country to be A Sin before God and man: that . . . slavery is a great moral, political, physical and social evil, and ought to be immediately and universally abandoned . . . it is our duty, by the use of all . . . means, and . . . by cultivating a spirit of . . . prayer for the enslaved, and their masters, as well as . . . the dissemination of truth . . . to hasten . . . universal emancipation.[51]

The charade of the household of faith dividing America brought lasting shame to the Christian religion. Some upraised the Bible to extoll liberty for all peoples, but others used Scripture to justify and endorse slavery. Most Northern churches declared that slavery was a sin; those in the South deemed it a blessing. Some ministers freed their slaves, while others kept theirs. To whom does one turn for spiritual inspiration and moral guidance?

Disappointment swept through the pews into society, specially among Negroes. In 1848 Wendell Phillips saw religion as "the most productive, . . . efficient . . . idea, and the foundation of American thought and institutions." Yet for the next 15 years religion ignored blacks, who suffered abuse. Ex-slave Frederick Douglass saw scant productivity and truth in America's churches. He said: "Between the Christianity of this land and the Christianity of Christ, I recognize the widest possible difference."[52]

A great gulf separated Christ's teaching and the moral action of professed Christians. Those presumed followers of Christ who indulged in slavery were split from His righteousness. From the stance of American churches, bridging that chasm faced the demand of selfish pride and barriers of human doubt. So churches found it difficult to deal with the complex problems of slavery and racism; they participated in its beginning, and they preferred to live in the *status quo*.

Chapter 5

Some Problems That Faced Evangelical Antislavery

Sharp controversy continued between abolitionists and their Protestant opponents. These church leaders had long admitted slaveholding might be favorable to sin and against the best public interest. Yet they resisted the idea that any institution sanctioned in the Bible must be viewed as intrinsically sinful.

Henry Clarke Wright noted in his journal that the New England clergy also feared when reformers attacked a specific embodiment of sin. Then "that sin will assume such an importance that everybody will think nothing is necessary to make them Christians but abstinence from that particular sin." The Calvinists specially, rejected any attempt to impute complete evil to abstract "essences" or groupings such as slaveholding and bodily punishment, pondered apart from the mixed good and evil of all human relationships.[1]

Even so, belief in the total depravity of the human heart— shared by most evangelicals—upheld the abolitionist argument that vast power opens access to every forbidden desire and conceived transgression. Most Quaker and Anglican abolitionists moved warily toward the stand that having the power to do evil also meant doing evil. By 1830, American abolitionists pinpointed black slavery as a microcosm of the sinful human condition.

The Northern conscience embraced the Second Awakening's blending of "modern Puritan" evangelicalism and patriotic idealism. Though most churches balked at joining the antislavery cause, they acted as pioneers. As the antislavery movement increased, many auxiliary organizations of mainstream Protestantism became centers of concern. The faction-ridden national antislavery societies were replaced by church groups. An antislavery "social gospel" made advances, winning new leaders, to bring conflict or schism.[2]

The ideals of proslavery Christianity and a Christian abolitionism clashed in the heart of Protestantism. The slavery fight became muddled by opposing interests in its inner structure. Two political issues and two ecclesiastical parallels, with a religious issue set the area of conflict. These five points are:

(a) Whether churchmen might any more than politicians jeopardize the unity of the nation in pursuit of freedom for the slave. (b) At what point the solidarity of national religious and benevolent societies became less important than a clear witness against human bondage. (c) Whether the proper role of the churches in a democratic society was to regulate individual conduct or to impose Christian principles upon social and legal institutions. (d) Whether in disciplining individual conduct the central or the local governing bodies of the sects should act, and by what procedures. And (e), whether Christians might do violence for loving ends.[3]

Most evangelical ministers thought the nation's chief mission was to cradle the Christian faith and convert the world. Unity stood paramount to them, like the churchly ties by which they hoped to fully Christianize Americans. Speaking of slavery in 1848, a Baptist home missions evangelist asked, "When shall this stumbling-block in the way of the world's evangelization be removed?" Yet he next cried, "If this nation shall make shipwreck on the rocks of disunion . . . who, *who* will be held responsible but American Christians, holding . . . the balance of moral and political power?" God charged them with this country's civil and spiritual destinies, and also "the master work of evangelizing Foreign Nations."[4]

Many Methodist Episcopal churchmen who opposed slavery saw urgent danger. A spokesman, Nathan Bangs, warned New England congregations that their church was "the chief religious, and, in a sense, the chief social tie between the Northern and Southern states."[5] Yet, the witness against human bondage was fading.

In the *Christian Advocate and Journal* (December 5, 1834), Dr. Bangs confronted the divisiveness of abolitionism. He wrote:

At the time he [Christ] made his appearance . . . slavery existed all over the Roman Empire, not excepting even the . . . land of Judea . . . about one-half of the population . . . were in . . . civil bondage. . . . When Jesus Christ sent out his Apostles to preach, did he give them a command to denounce those masters because they held slaves? and to tell them that unless they let those oppressed go free, they could not repent and enter the kingdom of heaven? Nothing of this.[6]

Also, Dr. Wilbur Fisk, and others, in *Counter Appeal*, said, "Christianity spread in a land where slavery existed as cruel and licentious as ever existed in this country." Noting Ephesians 6:5-9, they claimed, "it places it beyond debate or a doubt that the Apostle did permit slaveholders in the Christian Church." Citing Colossians 3:22, they declared:

> ... this text proves . . . that, in the . . . Church at Colosse, . . . with the Apostolic sanction, the relation of master and slave was permitted to subsist. The slave is . . . continuing a slave, the master permanently a master; the former is exhorted to obedience, the latter to justice and equity in the exercise of his authority. Who can assert, . . . that no slave-master . . . can be endured in a Christian Church?[7]

By 1857, Abel Stevens, following Bangs in guarding a moderate stand in the church on slavery, scorned the "abstractionists" who thought good men should decide on social issues apart from results. He argued that effects are the first gauge by which duty is proved. Christian reformers, who weigh issues on a moral scale only, should support compensated emancipation. This program promised economic and moral force against the evil. But, an antislavery Baptist editor chided abolitionist Theodore Parker for smashing "with a huge battering ram against all the bulwarks of society," when he had no intent to rebuild what he eagerly destroyed.[8]

This second major problem of evangelical abolitionism grew. A parallel fear for the unity of national religious organizations hindered any antislavery path which churches or societies might choose. The danger lurked not simply because proslavery beliefs flourished among Southern members. The religious attack called slavery a sin and proposed ousting from fellowship all whom it had soiled. This alienated thousands who opposed the institution, yet events entrapped them to temporarily maintain it.

But in the Northern sections—Congregationalists, Unitarians, Universalists, and smaller groups like the Freewill Baptists and Wesleyan Methodists—could denounce slavery without offending many of their members. Since the Congregationalists had no central government, their local decrees and views on slavery caused no structural crisis. Methodists, Lutherans, Episcopalians, and New School Presbyterians labored under opposite conditions. Interdenominational societies like the Evangelical Alliance, the Y.M.C.A., and the American Tract Society were "of the same mind."

Though having national scope, the Baptists escaped turmoil by founding sectional missionary boards and by strongly insisting on congregational order. "One of the brethren" of the Philadelphia Association protested in 1857 a Boston editor's claim that their group had not reproved slavery. He insisted they had, quoting resolutions of 1789 and 1805 for proof. But, he added, "The churches of the body select their own ways to seek the removal of an evil, the existence of which, . . . they unanimously deplore."[9]

In contrast, the Methodists usually spoke with a united voice. Yet the fear of schism stifled the voice of the General Conference at every stage of the slavery dispute. Though the bishops tried, as the church divided in 1844, only haggling saved for the North the "border" conferences in Maryland, Kentucky, and Missouri. It became the Northern bishops' policy to keep them in the church.[10]

American Methodists copied John Wesley in two related traits, making a unified stand of the antislavery strife unlikely. The church was rigidly organized, so disputes were formally resolved or generally agreed to be petty. Methodism was not theologically aligned (as Presbyterianism), but it stressed visible discipline. These factors made the church alter Wesley's first ruling against slavery as its membership grew in the South. By 1843 there were 1,200 Methodist preachers owning about 1,500 slaves, and 25,000 members with about 208,000 more. For almost 50 years, church unity hinged on strict silence or neutrality on the slave issue.[11]

At the gathering of 1844 the delegates argued for almost two weeks over two distinct but inseparable issues. First and basic was the slavery question: how decisive a stand would be taken, and how firmly would that line be held in Methodist discipline? Also related was the problem of explaining the church's constitution adopted in 1808: how "democratic" was the church? Were the bishops responsible to the General Conference, and disposable by it?

Bishop Andrew's slaveholding case and the ensuing debates joined the two issues. The Southern delegates favored a strong episcopacy. As the conference voted on sectional lines 111 to 69, that Bishop Andrew "desist from . . . his functions," Southerners argued that his resignation would show that the church should be divided. Northern delegates also stood firm, making it impossible to avert division or even to postpone the controversy until 1848.[12]

The Southern delegation posed a plan of division so the two churches could retain fellowship. After approval, a nine-man commission was appointed to complete the plan. Three days later the council offered proposals for the annual conferences in the slaveholding states (with Texas) to approve. Two general conferences would replace the one, state boundaries would be viewed in church extension, clergy could choose affiliation, and the publishing concern and other assets would be fairly divided.

May 14, 1844, this preamble and resolution was introduced:

In view of the . . . subject of slavery and abolition, and . . . the difficulties . . . in the present general Conference, on account of the relative position of our brethren North and South on this perplexing question; therefore,

Resolved, That a committee of three from the North and three from the South be appointed to confer with the Bishops, and report, within two days, as to the possibility of adopting some plan, . . . for the permanent pacification of the Church.[13]

May 18, Bishop Joshua Soule reported for the Committee:

that, after a calm and deliberate investigation of the subject submitted to their consideration, they are unable to agree upon any plan of compromise to reconcile the views of the Northern and Southern conferences.[14]

Peter Cartwright expressed dismay that the General conference had power to divide the church and to form a division line. Ministers from either side must not cross to preach salvation to fellowmen. Forcing the members on either north or south, to hold their membership in a division not of their choice, was despotism:

. . . the very ministers composing the General conferences who, . . . with their fellow-laborers . . . had praised the Methodist Episcopal Church as the best Church in the world, and had taken . . . into said Church the hundreds of thousands that composed her membership, assumed to themselves the power to divide said Church, . . . and say to preachers and members, "Thus far shalt thou come, and no further."[15]

Greatly saddened by the Southerners breaking from the church, Bishop Leonidas Hamline seemed to express the prevailing sentiment; "God forbid that they should go as an arm torn out of the body, leaving a point of junction all gory and ghastly! Let them go as brethren beloved in the Lord, and let us hear their voice . . . claim us for brethren." The conference was adjourned.[16]

The Southern delegation reconvened to draft an address to their 14 annual conferences, to send delegates to Louisville, Kentucky, May 1, 1845. Their vote formally organized the Methodist Episcopal Church, South. The South had ruled the episcopacy to favor slavery in the discipline; constitutional changes were few. The church in 1846 had

459,569 members (124,961 "colored") and 1,519 traveling preachers. In 1848, the Southern body sent a fraternal delegate to the Northern General Conference.[17]

The spirit of brotherly separation soon departed the Northern church. The boundary settlement ignored some "Northern" conferences which extended into "slave" states. By 1848, a "gory and ghastly" border warfare had begun. Since the actions required to divide the publishing concern miscarried, the Southern church then took legal action in 1851. In 1854 the Southern church gained a *pro rata* division. The Northern church did not redress its actions of 1848 by sending a fraternal delegate southward until 1872.[18]

Many Northerners sided with the bishops' decree of silence on the slavery issue, arguing the church could be antislavery without saying so. In 1852, Charles Adams, *Zion's Herald* editor, asked: "What am I in . . . being a Methodist?. . . I am the cleanest-sweeping . . . abolitionist under heaven." Yet he said the General Conference need not make more statements against slavery, than against "theft, adultery, bigamy, murder, or any . . . of the other vices and crimes unseparated . . . from the horrible slavery of this country."[19]

A preacher from rural Vermont retorted that the people should expect a statement on slavery from the General Conference, if only to deny the charge of compromise. He claimed that the assembly membership was more moderate than the church as a whole. Safe men were most likely elected as delegates, those who loved more than their duty "the honor of a seat in so dignified a body—rich breakfasts, sumptuous dinners, exhilarating teas, good smokes . . . downy beds . . ." Against such weaklings, he noted, were veteran delegates from the border conferences, muting public arguments.[20]

Even with grumblings the "silence" policy prevailed. The pastoral address issued by the General Conference in 1856 declared the debates that year "brought out . . . that none of the members . . . entertained proslavery sentiments" and that "little or no mercenary slaveholding" existed in the church. The address continued, "The effect of such action upon the interests of the border conferences probably alone prevented a constitutional majority from voting to recommend a change of our General Rules on the subject."[21]

New England Methodists and those from upstate New York opposed "border conference politics." A Providence, Rhode Island, minister, wrote in 1857 that societies the missionary board backed as "vanguards of liberty" contained proslavery members. Clergymen had household slaves—the titles often kept by their fathers-in-law! Cynics saw the difference between the Northern and Southern Methodists not as one of precept, but of degree.[22]

Interdenominational benevolent societies shared such straits. In 1846 Stephen Olin wrote Abel Stevens from London, at the first meeting of the Evangelical Alliance, that he wanted to "counterwork the detestable system" of slavery. Olin added, "I do not see how this great object can be forwarded . . . by attempting to complicate our plans for Christian union with it." When the conference heeded such thinking, an American and Foreign Antislavery Society delegate said such a course muted reform's voice in America. Churchmen chose brotherly love toward one another over love for the Negro.[23]

When the Y.M.C.A. began its national and international organization in 1854 and 1855, a similar slavery compromise prevailed. Abel Stevens, spokesman for the American delegation at Paris in 1855, convinced that assembly to adopt a constitution forbidding statements on the subject. He hoped that would prompt the antislavery associations in America to abandon free discussion here.[24]

Such motives moved the Executive Committee of the American Tract Society to exclude mention of slavery in its publications. This distorted the rule that its tracts must be judged "to receive the approbation of all evangelical Christians." In the early 1850s some Congregational Associations joined *The Independent* in trying to get this policy reversed. In 1856 the directors appointed a study committee of 12 notable churchmen, such as: George H. Stuart, Mark Hopkins, Francis Wayland, Albert Barnes, and S. S. Schmucker. After one meeting, they urged the society to publish against the evils of slavery, as distinct from the institution, or mode of its abolition, or concerning communion with slaveholders. The publishing committee said it could not find one manuscript which even on this point would meet the approval of all Christians! A stalemate held until 1858, when many of the directors withdrew.[25]

The benevolent societies of the nation, as many of the church denominations, were head-quartered in New York City, where the cotton trade was king. There, advice of "Christian" capitalists easily prevailed, whose growing wealth numbed their passions for reform.[26] But Albert Barnes, of Philadelphia Presbyterian First Church, wrote in 1856, "There is a spirit abroad in the land," and "a voice uttered everywhere against slavery so . . . clear that it will ultimately be regarded." George H. Stuart, a very religious Philadelphia banker, thus gave his life to evangelical missionary agencies. His and other Christian philanthropy grew from the piety stemming from the "businessman's revival" of 1857-58. [27]

A third major problem of evangelical abolitionism sprang from a belief that the correct role for churches in a democratic society was the control of private conduct. Yet some denominations debated about disciplining members for owning slaves. American churchmen took seriously the separation of church and state. They backed the "voluntary system," but avoided partisan support. Wilbur Fisk warned Methodism was evangelically powerful because it had remained politically neutral. Albert Barnes urged for 20 years that if the churches would eject slaveholders from their numbers, the evil would leave also from society. All options of teaching and plea were used to stir their consciences before excluding them.[28]

Whenever the various churches tried to regulate the relation of their members to slavery, protests arose. Even in the most episcopally governed bodies, the separate divisions—dioceses, synods, presbyteries, annual conferences, and associations—could best handle the question. Many denominations developed a framework of polity parallel that of the nation. Religious "states rights" grew up alongside that political concept.

In Baptist conventions, both North and South, popular tension mounted. Before 1844 ended, both mission boards faced decisions thrust upon them by the South. That October the Home Board declined to appoint a missionary nominee of the Georgia Baptist Convention, James E. Reeves, who was a slaveholder. Two months later the Foreign Board took the same stand when petitioned to state its policy by the Alabama Baptist Convention.[29]

Disturbed by the Home Board's neglect of the South and Southwest, leading Southern Baptists used the slavery issue to plan a distinct connectional polity. The Virginia Baptist Foreign Mission Society acted, calling "all our brethren, North and South, East and West, who are aggrieved by the recent decision of the Board in Boston." May 8, 1845, in Augusta, Georgia, advisors met to decide the type of organization to be formed, and 293 delegates from nine states convened. Soon, the Southern Baptist Convention framed a constitution and a "provisional government." Dr. W. B. Johnson became president of the organization he labored to found. After December 27, 1845 the convention became chartered under Georgia laws. In 1846 the first triennial session at Richmond, Virginia, ratified the action and began consolidation and extension.[30]

The Southern Convention was a diversity for American Baptists. It was frankly denominational in spirit and scope, designed by men who spoke of the Baptist "Church" in the singular. The convention could propose tasks and organize boards as it saw fit. It thus exposed what was latent in the Southern Baptist tradition—what its historians called a "centralizing ecclesiology." Yet the long-term basis must be considered for the hierarchical and authoritarian modes of social organization. These were produced both by slavery and its major rational defenses. The same penchant is shown in the Southern Methodist struggles over church polity, and to a lesser degree, by the strict polity views of the Presbyterian Old School.

Theologically, the Southern Convention differed from a Presbyterian synod, the Episcopal House of Bishops, or a Roman Catholic provincial council. It adopted the functions of all of these and came to wield authority equal any of theirs. In the remaining antebellum years these constitutional innovations became a divisive factor. After the slavery issue was banned from convention debate, growth ensued. In 15 years the Southern Convention's membership grew from 351,951 to 649,518 on the rolls.[31]

Meanwhile, the old General Convention became refashioned under President Francis Wayland's leadership. It had contrasting beliefs which showed the extreme congregationalism intensified by the Great Awakening and expressed by the New Hampshire Confession of 1833. This "American Baptist Missionary Union" included individual members only, with provisions to exclude proslavery members.

The Congregational Church polity did not bring such questions as slavery before their conferences to decide any rule relating to terms of Christian fellowship. Congregations separately decided such issues. Churches throughout the country, as well as in New England, for a time agreed on the slavery question.

Whether any general or local church governing units acted, many alternative procedures offered themselves—each with its own problems. Should only ministers, or all communicants, or simply bishops, be forbidden to hold slaves? Was any distinction to be made between mercenary and paternalistic slaveholding? If the church did not exclude them, should it discipline masters for unchristian conduct of their duties? Could enslaved church members testify in such cases, when the civil courts forbid it? Were those who supported abolitionist groups or served on the Underground Railroad, subverting the laws, to be condoned, or punished?

Rising problems of church procedure may be seen by the tangled action and inaction of New School Presbyterians. When some presbyteries in East Tennessee, Kentucky, Virginia, and South Carolina adhered to the denomination on doctrinal grounds, in dividing from the Old School, matters became complex. The General Assembly refused to curtail discussion. As early as 1839 it voted to refer all memorials back to the synods and presbyteries "to take such order thereon as in their judgment will be the most judicious and adapted to remove the evil."

But the 1845 Assembly voted 92 to 29, that "the system of slavery, . . . in the United States . . . is . . . an unrighteous and oppressive system." Yet the delegates did not try "to determine the degree of moral turpitude . . . of individuals involved in it." Rather, they urged their "beloved brethren" to "remove it from them as speedily as possible, by all appropriate means." They must avoid "all divisive and schismatical measures tending to destroy the unity and disturb the peace of the church."[32]

The meetings of 1848-54 showed a roused Northern conscience, asking the Assembly to vote to urge, or to require presbyteries to bar slave masters from communion. A committee faced a charge in 1855 to decide if the national body might legally take such action. Next year, though having the right, it made no decision. The Lexington, Kentucky, Presbytery said many of its clergy and members owned Negroes "from principle." The *status quo* policy could not keep the church united. Only presbyteries in antislavery territory took a stand, leaving slavery elsewhere unchecked and active.

The General Assembly condemned the Lexington unit, asking it to alter its stand. Southern delegates saw this as an "indirect" exscinding act like that which in 1837 drove the New School synods from the parent church. The next year 21 border presbyteries withdrew to form the United Synod of the Presbyterian Church, taking 15,000 members. They bypassed the Old School communion, viewing its principles as unclear in defense of slaveholding![33]

For 20 years abolitionist William Lloyd Garrison cried "war" but refused to fight, and the proslavery clergy answered "peace" when there was no peace. Evangelicals dared not forsake either the slave or the Golden Rule. Nor could they hold the hope Wilbur Fisk advanced, against the Methodist abolitionists of New England, that love would destroy evil unaided. Men like George Barrell Cheever believed that however much the law of love contradicted human bondage, that law would prevail only as men bore a cross for it.[34]

In 1857 the editors of Boston's Baptist newspaper said, "It seems . . . idle to talk longer of the existence of sound views among the great body of

Southern Christians." Moderate Northern men were "deceiving themselves, and inflicting fatal injury on the cause of righteousness, by such a pretence." Southern churchmen were not asking that slavery be conceded "to be no sin, nor an evil, but a blessing to both races . . . consonant with Christianity, and a providential institution for the conversion of Pagan Africa." True believers must not let Christ's decree of love to be broken, or fail, but rebuke its traducers. They must declare in united voice

> that slavery tramples on the great law, "Thou shalt love thy neighbor as thyself"; that it is inconsistent with the spirit of the gospel of Christ; and those who . . . perpetuate a system of oppression forfeit their title to the name Christian.[35]

Entering this void in 1852 was a profound ally to antislavery "social gospel," Harriet Beecher Stowe's *Uncle Tom's Cabin.* She was the wife of a Congregational professor of Old Testament—and an able lay theologian, herself. She confronted the divided nation with a novel that featured the evils of slave life. The book depicted the vice of slavery to any American who could read, and it was also dramatized in theaters throughout the North.

Challenging Southern leaders to deny the truth of the novel, Harriet Beecher Stowe also strongly warned:

> Christians! every time that you pray that the kingdom of Christ may come, can you forget that prophecy associates . . . the day of vengeance with the year of His redeemed? . . . Both North and South have been guilty before God; and the Christian church has . . . to answer. Not by combining together, to protect injustice and cruelty . . . is this Union to be saved—but by repentance, justice, and mercy; for . . . injustice and cruelty shall bring on nations the wrath of Almighty God![36]

In 1842 in the case of *Prigg V. Pennsylvania,* the Supreme Court held the concept that presumed any black was slave even if found in a free state. Thus, by *Prigg,* a Negro could be taken by a bounty hunter from a non-slave state to a slave state. The non-slave state could not require a judicial hearing to ascertain whether the black was in fact a slave. The Supreme Court did rule that state officials need not assist in the return of fugitives.

Meanwhile, both Negro and white members of the Underground Railroad acted. Lewis Hayden of Boston, who had escaped slavery and hid many fugitives in his house, placed two kegs of dynamite in his cellar and said he would blow up the house rather than let slave catchers enter. Abolitionist Wendell Phillips told a Boston meeting: "Law or no law,

Constitution or no Constitution, humanity shall be paramount." Some
Ohio Quakers vowed aid to runaways "in defiance of all enactments of all
the governments on earth."[37]

As Congress had the Kansas-Nebraska debate, the Congregational
Church 1854 General Conference heard a speech to abolish slavery.
Many of those ministers joined the 3,050 clerics of New England, who
petitioned Congress against the Kansas-Nebraska Bill.[38]

> The . . . clergymen of different religious denominations in New
> England . . . protest against the passage of what is known as the
> Nebraska Bill, or any repeal of . . . the legal prohibitions of
> slavery . . . it is proposed to organize into the territories of
> Nebraska and Kansas. We protest against it as a great moral
> wrong, as a breach of faith . . . unjust to the moral principles of
> the community . . . full of danger to the peace and . . . existence
> of our beloved Union, and exposing us to the righteous
> judgments of the Almighty . . .
>
> Boston, Massachusetts, March 1, 1854 [39]

A few weeks after the New England clergymen sent their protest to
Congress, 25 ministers of Chicago and the Northwest also sent a similar
challenge. The Chicago document was identical with that of New
England, except for the added words, "as citizens," and the difference in
locality. Sent with this protest, several resolutions expressed the opinions
of the protestors.[40]

Meanwhile, a Troy, New York, Methodist Episcopal Conference
resolution, proposing the exclusion of all slaveholders, failed. Antislavery
conferences like the Oneida, Maine, and Erie joined those in border
territory, rejecting it because a person might accept or retain ownership of
a Negro as a merciful act. Four years later an Iowa Conference committee
opposed a similar memorial that hindered good Methodists from buying
slaves to free them.[41]

Thomas Johnson, a Methodist Episcopal Church, South, Indian
missionary, founded in eastern Kansas the Shawnee Methodist Mission
and Indian Manual Labor School in 1830. Rev. Johnson became a rich
slaveowner by educating Negro slaves and Indian children. He received
$1.00 from the church and $1.00 from the government for each child, and
tried to make Kansas a slave state. August 6, 1854, a Boston *Journal*
reporter traveling on the frontier wrote:

> We passed the house of the Rev. Thomas Johnson, the present
> Pro-Slavery delegate in Congress. His house is beautifully

situated . . . The wilderness here already begins to "blossom as the rose." It is slave labor, however, upon which he depends, for in open violation of the law of 1820, he has for years owned and worked a large number of Negroes.[42]

Rev. Thomas Johnson was killed the night of January 2, 1865, at his home. He had renounced his early Southern training, held loyalty to the Union, and his oldest son was fighting for the Union. The violent action was by a remnant of Quantrill's band.[43] This isolated event within the realm of church ministry marks the internal strife in dealing with entrenched slavery.

Abraham Lincoln assailed slavery in the new territories and newly admitted states. He said slavery was like a snake; one attacked a snake on the prairie differently from one found in bed with his children. Slavery firmly fixed in the South should be faced one way, but in Kansas or Nebraska another way. In 1856 he said, "Let us draw a cordon around the slave states, and the hateful institution, like a reptile poisoning itself, will perish by its own infamy."[44]

The Supreme Court, in 1857, made a benchmark decision in the case of *Scott* v. *Sanford*. It widened the breach between the North and South. Dred Scott was a Missouri slave whose master had taken him to live in free Illinois, and then to a fort in the northern part of the Louisiana Purchase, where the Missouri Compromise had excluded slavery. On his return to Missouri, Scott sued for his freedom on the point that residence on free soil liberated him.

The majority of the Supreme Court held Scott was not a citizen and therefore could not bring suit in the courts. Chief Justice Robert B. Taney, a Maryland slaveholder, wrote the decision:

Under the United States constitution a black man had no rights which the white man was bound to respect . . . the negro might justly and lawfully be reduced to slavery for his benefit. He was bought and sold, and treated as an ordinary article of merchandise and traffic.[45]

The Dred Scott decision, denying free blacks citizenship and banning congress from empowering territorial legislatures to deprive citizens of slave property, fixed the issues. Frederick Frothingham in 1857 said the struggle was not only "of Religion and Irreligion, of Order with Disorder, of Self-sacrifice with Selfishness, of Civilization with Barbarian . . . [but] of God with Satan." Slavery was like Goliath defying the Lord. "If David [should] fall," Frothingham warned, "the progress of mankind is turned backward, . . . and the human race for centuries to come must . . . wade through seas of blood to regain the point where it now stands."[46]

This larger question of slavery loomed: a moral issue of right and wrong. It filled the mind and heart of Abraham Lincoln, who was unchurched. He studied both sides of the issue, and asserted the North was no more righteous than the South. Each part of the country viewed slaveholding from its own self-interest and well-being. Each opposed threats to its prosperity and security, making Lincoln sure that slavery was wrong. In 1854 he wrote, slavery "is founded on the selfishness of man's nature—opposition to it in his love of justice." Though the institution's supporters believed its goodness, he said slavery is "strikingly peculiar . . . it is the only thing which no man ever seeks the good of for himself."[47]

The Kansas-Nebraska Act of 1854, the Dred Scott decision of 1857, and those eager to make slavery national and permanent pushed Lincoln toward certain decisions. Slavery must be brought to an end, else American liberty be a lie and freedom a fraud. In 1858, Lincoln again cited Scripture—"A house divided against itself cannot stand" (Matt. 12:25). He said, "I believe this government cannot endure . . . half slave and half free. I do not expect the Union to be dissolved—I do not expect the house to fall—but I do expect it will cease to be divided."[48]

Lincoln also would preside over a house of faith divided in a torn America. The havoc of bondage severely reproached the Christian churches. For part of the Church, slavery was a dreadful sin; for the other, a God-given blessing. An earnest minister freed his slaves; some other missionary held his. The most soul-searing war of America's history erupted amidst a morally confused and spiritually perplexed nation.

Chapter 6

The Faltering Church Crusade Against Slavery

Julia Ward Howe, in her "Battle Hymn of the Republic" (1861), shows a paradoxical Christ. He comes "in the beauty of the lilies" to trample "the grapes of wrath" amid the confused times. No peace appears without war; no love without hate. The New York *Christian Advocate and Journal* noted the awful "logic of events" beat the ploughshare of love into a sword. Though against radicalism, that paper by 1861 urged the immediate emancipation of the Negroes.

Boston Congregational Edward N. Kirk preached a Thanksgiving sermon to praise war, like New York *Tribune* Editor Horace Greeley. Dr. Kirk, using Psalm 101 which begins, "I will sing of mercy and judgment," said the slave would have no mercy without reprisal for his master. This patron of the peace crusade cried, "Blessed be the war." He ignored Quaker quietism and denied the myth that the God of the New Testament was not the sovereign of the Old.[1] The crusade against slavery was a spiritual warfare, but it would be fought also on bloody battlefields.

Methodist Nathan Bangs died a month after the Battle of Shiloh (May, 1862). He foretold God acting "with such retribution, on Church and State, North and South, as should . . . rebuke alike the truculence and cowardice of men." Another person wrote that the churches' agreements brought judgment on them. "The divine purpose had transferred to war the honor of freeing the oppressed."[2] If Christians had admitted the evil of slavery and freed their slaves, armed conflict could have been avoided. They failed, so God used the Civil War instead of the Church to free the slaves.

Sadly, Northern Christians entered the battle to destroy the institution of slavery, and Southern Christians fought to preserve it. President Abraham Lincoln, in his second inaugural address, saw the shadowy purpose of the Civil War. He believed sovereign Deity seized the events to punish in bloody conflict the sins of both sections and all parties. Only so could Christians fight to free the slaves—"with malice toward none; with charity for all." The judgments of the Lord stood "true and righteous altogether."[3]

Yet Lincoln's vague stand on slavery favored the churchmen's. Like them, he felt great inner tension from it, also seeking Daniel Webster's promised land of "Liberty and Union."[4] In an 1854 Peoria, Illinois, speech he rebuked slavery, saying, "I hate it because it deprives our Republican example of its just influence in the world." But he said, "Much as I hate slavery, I would consent to the extension of it rather than see the Union dissolved."[5]

But when federal bayonets in Boston enforced the Fugitive Slave Act, and Kansas bled from the Missouri Compromise repeal, Lincoln and the churchmen saw more paradox than promise in that phrase. Antislavery clergymen joined Lincoln and the Republicans on a platform that banned the extension of slavery in the Western territories. They hoped to push the institution toward extinction, but the Dred Scott Decision ordered national law against this goal. Lincoln wrote his "House Divided" speech in spring, 1858, and churchmen sought the baptism with the Holy Spirit.[6]

Political events, not preachers' cries, awakened mid-19th century America to the "slave power" menace. National debates over the Wilmot Proviso, the Compromise of 1850, the Kansas-Nebraska Act, and the Dred Scott Decision, rang like Jefferson's so called "fire-bell in the night."[7] Yet the evangelists led in answering the alarm. Their pity for mankind and hatred of sin again spoke to the nation. President James Buchanan (1857-61) wrote, " . . . above all the Christian pulpit, had been . . . employed in denouncing slavery as a sin, and rendering slaveholders as odious."[8]

The Northern cause appealed to young Dwight L. Moody. By his home traditions and strict New England training he became an ardent abolitionist. While in Boston he often heard abolitionist orators, Garrison, Wendell Phillips, and Elijah P. Lovejoy. His uncle's boot and shoe store adjoined the courthouse, where Moody was one who tried to free Anthony Burns, a fugitive slave. Moody joined the Boston Young Men's Christian Association, April, 1854, and moved to the Chicago Association. He began full-time Christian service in 1858, and later preached to soldiers and war prisoners.[9]

By 1852 many religious papers renewed their efforts against the national curse. In Boston, the Methodist *Zion's Herald*, muted for 10 years, proclaimed the antislavery theme again after Daniel Wise replaced Abel Stevens as editor. Wise declared, "We are for peace, purity, liberty, and Temperance . . . Toward slavery, . . . undisguised abhorrence. Our only business with it, . . . to seek its 'extirpation' by all judicious and prudent means; especially from the Church of Christ." Wise rated abolitionist articles by whether they would aid the spread of scriptural holiness. His editorial "The Christian as a Citizen" declared "political action is moral action" because the Lord wants our *every* act to be holy. Retreat from politics spurred the growth of evil in the world.[10]

Also in Boston, *The Congregationalist* backed the antislavery cause. The Baptist *Watchman and Reflector*, though more cautious and spiritually minded, used forceful editorials to arouse moral opinions against the South's cherished institution. *The Christian Register*, organ of all but Theodore Parker's branch of Unitarians, carried similar abolition views.[11]

Methodists in upper New York State read *The Northern Christian Advocate*. Before 1856 William Hosmer, a radical holiness leader whose group formed the Free Methodist Church, was its editor. His book, *The Higher Law* (1852), claimed slavery opposed God's laws of love, improvement, purity, and equality. "Holiness or moral purity is one of the most essential principles of the gospel," Hosmer wrote, "but slavery is a violation of that right." Christian equality was a "spiritual agrarianism," putting prince and peasant, master and servant on common ground. Since men formed a constitution that condoned human bondage, believers must defy it.[12]

A group of Hosmer's editorials appeared the next year, titled, *Slavery and the Church*, linking perfectionism with millennial hope to urge Methodists to reform. He said the Church's mission is to establish God's kingdom on earth by banishing "unrighteousness, and the introduction of universal holiness." It was essential to ban slaveholders from the fellowship. Or else, he declared, "we should only have . . . what now occurs in lesser degree, wherever slavery is tolerated in the church—a religion without holiness—gospel progress without gospel morals." Christianity would be a curse, "sanctioning and perpetuating vices which it was . . . to remove." The Scripture would be used as "chains and manacles," turning the Church into a slave pen. He cried that the gospel is "a system of holiness"—never allied to evil. The work of conversion is an all-out war against sin, "all sin—sin of every kind and degree."[13]

The Methodist conference, which in 1852 placed Hosmer and Wise as editors of their respective papers, named well-known compromiser Thomas E. Bond to edit the New York *Christian Advocate and Journal*. His supporters viewed him as best qualified to quell the tumult over laymen's rights. Yet the antislavery party held their real purpose was to retain Methodism's largest weekly to serve the bishops' concern for the border conferences.

Bishop Stephen Elliott quotes a sampling of Dr. Bond's ideas in his book, "Great Secession:"

> Slaveholding itself is no where . . . forbidden in Scripture, though the practice was general in the time of our Lord and his Apostles; yet there is no . . . prohibition to Christians to hold slaves, . . . there are . . . exhortations to slaves to obey their masters, and to make this matter of conscience.[14]

A Genesee preacher wrote in *Zion's Herald*, "Were the out and out antislavery portion of the church to withdraw, there would be no M. E. church left." He said whole conferences were pledged, "old men, strong men, young men together; and no thought of secession . . . Slavery, not we, not the North, will leave the church." Daniel Wise counseled the New England conferences that if Dr. Bond attacked them as he had New York State abolitionists, they should keep silent. "Only let us adhere to our . . . spreading scriptural holiness throughout these lands," he said, "and leave unprofitable controversies alone; thus God will bless the labors . . . and crown all our spiritual principles with success."[15]

In 1857 Edward Thomson, president of Ohio Wesleyan University, reproved the deceitful Southern grounds that Christians should hold their slaves to obey state laws forbidding manumission. The truth is, he said:

> that Christian doctrine is . . . perverted and Christian practice lowered by the Church . . . He is . . . a restorer of the Gospel, who applies it to the sins of the times. The soft . . . Christianity which disturbs no one, is not the Christianity of Christ, who brought upon himself persecutions . . . wherever he went, or of Paul, who turned the world upside down.[16]

But in New York City, a leading antislavery magazine, *The Independent*, was founded in 1848 by some strong Congregationalist pastors. Joseph P. Thompson, R. S. Storrs, Henry Ward Beecher, and George B. Cheever pledged the paper to fight the spread of slavery in the territories, urging other moral reforms by political action. Their ideas of revival featured evangelists like Albert Barnes and George Duffield, and the perfectionists of Oberlin and New York State. These pastors typified a church whose strength outside the city lay in antislavery areas—New England, the Mohawk Valley, and northern Ohio. Joshua Leavitt, abolitionist head of *The Evangelist* in the 1830s and later of *The Emancipator*, was managing editor.[17]

New School Presbyterian pastors and *The Evangelist*, the only other major antislavery weekly in New York, surveyed the internal problems of their groups. Any statements swayed the fortunes of revival

Presbyterianism in the Southern border areas. But their chief battleground with the Old School was in the city, where *The Observer* was published with Princeton Seminary nearby.

A Presbyterian analyzed in the *Cincinnati Journal* (1852) the mix that deepened prejudice of both blacks and whites. He argued:

> The prejudices of black men were bitter because those of the white men were inveterate. The one demands the equal rights of a common nature and the other refused to listen . . . He will not admit him to his table, or his parlor, he will not permit their children to intermarry, he will not employ him as a lawyer or physician, nor elect him to posts of honor . . . there is a sense of injustice, and a feeling of unkindness, and these feelings react . . . until the prejudice becomes as bitter on one side as it is . . . unreasonable on the other.[18]

Even so, some viewed it as entirely natural for a slave to try to rise up and gain a real notion of his own power.

The Independent adopted the free-soil platform, believing the institution of slavery doing "violence to the moral sense of those who maintain it" would pass away, if it were confined. Debates over the Compromise of 1850 stifled this peaceful idea. Many Northerners became more imbued with "hatred of the slave system than ever before." Editors aimed to impede its use in the South by "argument, persuasion, and Christian appeal," and demanded that it "cease forever in the District of Columbia." Fugitive slaves should be "as free as the wind when they entered the North."[19]

However, Rev. Henry Ward Beecher, referring to the degraded state of free colored people in the North, asked in an 1855 sermon:

> How are the free colored people treated at the North?... They are refused the common rights of citizenship . . . They can not even ride . . . our city railroads. They are snuffed at in the house of God, or tolerated with . . . disgust . . . Can the black man engage in the common industries of life? . . . He is crossed down . . . to the bottom of society. We tax them and . . . refuse to allow their children to go to our public schools. We tax them and then refuse to sit by them in God's house. We heap upon them moral obloquy more atrocious than that which the master heaps upon the slave. . . . The degradation of the free colored men in the North will fortify slavery in the South![20]

In January 1855, an editorial titled, "Where Are We Drifting?" declared the country was "marching as straight upon disunion as ever people did, and blindfolded." The South, to obtain peace and union, received an edge which, once secured, they would "use to goad the North to inevitable rupture." Those who once advised assent now counseled "disunion and belligerency hereafter."[21]

George Barrell Cheever became prominent on *The Independent's* editorial board. Even more than Beecher, Cheever's flaming essays on the higher law scattered the pious compromise that settled on New York. Cheever became pastor of the Church of the Puritans in 1845, providing a base for his stand. He campaigned against all forms of "evil," including Unitarianism, Catholicism, intemperance, Sabbath desecration, slavery, and the worship of wealth.[22]

Cheever's writing and preaching struck home, drawing howls of disapproval from *The New York Observer* and James Gordon Bennett's *New York World*. The partisans of bondage knew that the churchly wavering of the 1840s had ended. Abolition became the moral goal of many great preachers in the free states. New School Presbyterian Rev. Frederick A. Ross met Cheever's challenge. Ross claimed the "sin theory" to be the "only honest ground for opposition to slavery," saying that God ordained it as a positive good was its only worthy defense. This drew the battle lines of conscience.[23]

Revivalists of all churches encouraged the antislavery goal for which some editors struggled in Northern cities. In Newark, Baptist Henry Clay Fish spoke out for national liberty and human brotherhood against the slavery forces. He cried, "We are linked together, . . . flesh of the same flesh—the members of one common family." Francis Wayland told the "Nebraska meeting" in Providence that he valued the Union. Yet, he added, "To form a union for . . . perpetuating oppression is to make myself an oppressor . . . The Union itself becomes to me an accursed thing, if I must steep it in the tears and blood of those for whom Christ died."[24]

Some notables who avoided an active antislavery stance were the Methodist perfectionist associates of Phoebe Palmer. Bishops Edmund James and Leonidas Hamline, her close friends, held the policy of silence that plagued Northern Methodism. George and Jesse Peck, Nathan Bangs, Alfred Cookman, with her admirers backed the policy. Henry V. Degen, editor of *The Guide to Holiness*, noted the issues in the 1856 election and asked readers to pray for the success of God's man, but he named neither the man nor the issues. Degen said, "We have . . . little relish for politics, . . . we are not disposed to leave our . . . mission, and enter the political arena. But . . . if ever we needed divine intervention, we need it now."[25]

Mrs. Palmer's concern for the slaves led her to support the Colonization Society in the 1830s. She also hoped to spare the country from the wrath of God that she felt would come if the blacks were not freed. When it was plain colonization would fail, she refused to become an abolitionist. She also resisted the bias of other holiness patrons to associate themselves with abolition.[26]

Phoebe Palmer was titular head of the "holiness" revival, but the 1850s spawned turmoil that imperiled her work. Free Methodist strife in western New York upset matters. Benjamin T. Roberts, a Methodist minister claiming sanctification by her guidance, was tried and convicted of unchristian action in 1857. His item in *The Northern Independent* accused the chief group of worldliness and doctrinal laxity. The 1860 General Conference denied his appeal; he and more than 20 ministers and several thousand laymen joined the Free Methodist Church. The Genesee Conference membership decreased by a third in six years.[27] Roberts chafed that Palmer and other holiness teachers evaded his efforts for the slaves.

The other-worldly and spiritual aspects of Palmer's quest for perfect love subdued the impulse to antislavery reform. Her New York and Philadelphia coterie ministered to widows, orphans, and prisoners, but they did not attack persons and institutions. For them, reproving social and political injustice was a right of God. Hearing in England of the Emancipation Proclamation, Mrs. Palmer wrote an American friend that she had long expected sad days, "when the righteous Judge would chasten us" for "the cruel wrongs of the slave." She, like many "spiritual" Christians, left the issue with God, believing "that the God of battles would give us victory."[28]

An opposite approach occurred when perfectionist experience merged, as in Charles Finney, with strong social duty and personal concern for reform. The results became politically explosive, as in the late 1840s, when Mrs. Palmer's doctrines reached Methodist abolitionists in New England and upper New York. The Wesleyan Methodists developed holiness and humanitarianism together. Orange Scott wrote in 1845, "We are organized on principles that require us to stand out . . . as a class of religious and moral reformers." "Deep experience" with God was "essential to the peace and usefulness of all Christians," but specially to Christian Reformers.[29]

Beside Palmer's perfectionist group, an appeal to other-worldliness became more typical of liturgical and antirevival Christians than their opposites. *The Christian Review*, a Baptist quarterly that ignored revivalism, kept mum on slavery until the war began. The Lutheran synods, where godly fervor waned before the national conscience awakened, used their church's confessional nature to avoid conflict. Samuel S. Schmucker, revivalist of the General Synod, and the perfectionist Frankean Synod in New York State were exceptions. Note Schmucker's sermon title, "The Christian Pulpit, the Rightful Guardian of Morals in Political, No Less Than in Private Life," printed in Gettysburg, Pennsylvania, in 1846.[30]

Charles P. McIlvaine and the Low Church Protestant Episcopal bishops, generally opposed to slavery, endured the silence that High Church and Southern prelates imposed on them until war began. Then, they ignored all social issues except the sin of rebellion. They so focused on faith's spiritual and heavenly ends that a reunion with the Southern churches could occur soon after the 1865 peace. The Roman Catholic hierarchy had a similar stance.[31]

The Roman Catholic Church in the antebellum era viewed slavery as a tenet of society that was not itself sinful. Yet in 1839 Pope Gregory XVI declared the church condemned the slave trade. Bishop Francis P. Kenrick explained the church's teaching in his *Theologia Moralis* (3 vols., 1840-43). From 1851 until his death in 1863, as archbishop of Baltimore, he held the dominant post in the American hierarchy. His teaching did not clarify the differences between the American form of slavery and that which the church condoned. Pastoral Letters of the assembled bishops between 1840 and 1852 did not mention the nation's moral dilemma. During the war the church held this stance, as bishops and archbishops North and South kept contact with Rome and with each other as events allowed.[32]

Revivalist preachers proclaimed their message in different, more strident sounds. Philadelphia's Albert Barnes wrote in 1856, "There is a spirit abroad in the land," and "a voice uttered . . . against slavery so loud and clear that it will . . . be regarded." Later a Baptist paper called for church renewal in review of their relation to slavery. Indecision on "this great question should be shunned," its editors warned; "lukewarmness is intolerable." They said, "It is a time for prayer, . . . for a more earnest consecration to Christ, and . . . benevolence for the souls he came to save."[33]

The results Charles Finney and Elder Jacob Knapp had at union revivals in the largest churches of Boston, New York, Baltimore, Buffalo, and Cincinnati in 1857 and 1858 show the heart-searching. Finney states in his *Memoirs* that the winter of 1857-8 will be remembered as the time when great revival swept across the Northern states. It spread with such power that "not less than fifty thousand conversions occurred in a single week."

Daily prayer meetings ensued in Boston for several years; the previous autumn, such prayer meetings were held in New York, Fulton Street. Many Unitarians became concerned and attended them. Finney declares:

> A divine influence seemed to pervade . . . Slavery seemed to shut it out from the South. The people there were in such a state . . . of vexation, and of committal to their peculiar institution, . . . that the Spirit of God seemed to be grieved away from them . . . during this revival not less than five hundred thousand souls were converted in this country.[34]

The revivalists' tradition judged sin even as it bore its cross. In condemning all the vices of which slaveholders were guilty, they still must love them. As an antislavery magazine editor said, "God will secure the deliverance of the oppressed. Our work is to promote it by the pure Gospel of Christ, with its faithful application to all sin, . . . to the great enormities of slavery."[35] Nationwide, revivalists clung to the union and liberty which Webster and Clay sought. But they built the fire of division which those stalwart compromisers feared.

Two results of the spiritual attack on slavery are: the Bible restored as a means of reform, and insights the revivalists added to the concept of an American theocracy. Southerners used early Methodist Bible commentator Dr. Adam Clarke's comments on some New Testament scriptures to support their position on slavery. Some remarks used are on 1 Timothy 4:1 and 6:3; Colossians 4:1; Titus 2:9; and 1 Corinthians 7:24. He states on the latter passage:

> The conversion which the Scripture requires, though it makes a most essential change in our souls in reference to God, and in our works in reference both to God and man, makes none in our civil state, even if a man is called i.e., converted, in a state of slavery, he does not gain his manumission in . . . his conversion; he stands in the same relation both to the state and to his fellows . . . and is not to assume any civil rights or privileges in . . . the conversion of his soul to God. The Apostle decides the matter in this chapter, . . . every man should abide in the calling wherein he is called.[36]

Using the Holy Bible to defend slavery alarmed evangelicals. In 1845, Yale's *New Englander* challenged those who did so to

> meet the infidel on the question of the internal evidence of the divinity and truth of the Bible, . . . Prove that any book, which authorizes and commands this "Complicated villainy," as John Wesley called it, is from the God of love, if you can.

Albert Barnes charged that "all attempts to show that the Bible sanctioned human bondage" contributed "to just that extent, to sustain and diffuse infidelity in the world."[37]

Cheever, Barnes, and Joseph Thompson, of the Congregationalist New School line, and President Charles Elliott, of Iowa Wesleyan College, each published works to show the Bible was an antislavery book. Cheever wrote *The Guilt of Slavery and the Crime of Slave-holding; Demonstrated from the Hebrew and Greek Scriptures.* He held that no divine revelation could sanction "so diabolical a cruelty and crime." Yet, he said Hebrew servitude was honorable and voluntary. An 1857 study he published decided that patriarchal slavery in Israel opposed divine purpose, bringing a curse.[38]

Thompson wrote a matching volume to Cheever's called *The New Testament on Slavery.* He believed the institution thrived in the apostolic age only as a creature of Roman law. Paul never conceded its goodness in God's sight. Placing the relationship of masters and servants "under the higher law of Christian love and equality," the apostles "decreed the virtual abolition of slavery, and did in time abolish it wherever Christianity gained the ascendancy in . . . the state." Those who held the command to obey one's master approved holding men as chattels might also prove Christ's counsel to turn the other cheek gave divine approval of assault.[39]

Wesleyan College President Elliott, a leader of moderate Iowa Methodists, agreed. Paul taught on the sovereignty of God, the brotherhood of mankind, racial equality, and universal redemption, with pleas to shun sin and do good to all people, assailing the foundation of Roman slavery. Elliott also said obedience to the apostles' principles of justice, kindness, and holiness required masters to free their servants as it was within their power.[40]

In 1860 a French visitor to antislavery evangelicals noted they knew that "a revelation, to be divine, does not cease to be progressive." If God chose "to give to his people, . . . a legislation adopted to their social condition," such decrees might also be "divinely abrogated afterward." But the Gospels do not contain "a moral code, promulgated article by article" but rather a Golden Rule, with "a series of commandments, of transformations, of progression, which we have not . . . exhausted." The visitor claimed the American pastors who preached the law of love broke the slave's shackles more than those who planned to use swords to free him.[41]

Meanwhile, the revivalists' war against slavery sustained the theocratic ideal that God should rule American society. The 19th century "soul winners" fought against all sin. When a political crisis had a central moral issue, their statements became linked with public issues. Preachers of hell-fire and damnation voiced divine judgment, promoting God's law more than any other group. They applied such precepts to divorce, the alcohol trade, vice, corrupt politics, secret societies, Sabbath-breaking, and love of money. After 1850, graduates from Andover, Yale, Oberlin, Connecticut Wesleyan, and Union Theological Seminary held sway for the dogma of God's authority over American laws and institutions.[42]

The preaching of Gilbert Haven, Methodist abolitionist, who after 1872, became a bishop, depicts evangelical influence. It also shows John Wesley's fervor for American reform into the 19th century. Haven's home training in Malden, Massachusetts, molded into his character holy living and abolition. While at Connecticut Wesleyan University, Wilbur Fisk as president, he taught a Sunday School class of young women at the Negro church in Middletown.

Young Haven's sermon on "The Higher Law," during the debate over the Compromise of 1850, spoke of devotion and rebuke that marked his later preaching. He declared, "In Christ, not in the Constitution, must we put our trust . . . On his law should we meditate, not on that which nails him . . . to that fatal cross." Next year, in his first pastorate at Northampton, Massachusetts, he expressed similar views. Haven wrote that his community Fast Day sermon was "to the great joy of the Abolitionists, and the great rage of the Websterian portion of the audience." [43]

Three years later Gilbert Haven stated his views on race to a Wilbraham, Massachusetts, congregation. He said caste feeling based on skin color was the crux of American slavery. Yet "the Bible . . . proclaims the absolute oneness of the race of man, in Adam, Noah, and Christ." Christians working to destroy the institution of slavery should also welcome the Negro to their homes, and accept the biblical consent of interracial marriage.[44]

Facing the war, Haven said America would triumph though it took "all our sons, all our treasure, all our generation" to crush the enemies within and without. Other nations would see "the image of . . . Christ shining in our uplifted face." America would govern the earth, "not in the boastful spirit of national pride, but in the humble spirit of Christian love." Only then we can be "members of an equal, universal, happy family, the family of Christ." Haven urged Methodist preachers to seek that goal, purging "all the old leaven of malice and wickedness" that they might become "a new lump, sanctified and set apart for the Master's use."[45]

This replied to such comments by Rev. Orville Dewey, pastor of the New York City Unitarian Church of the Messiah. He cued the antislavery hopes of racial idealism in 1844, saying that the "inferiority" of the Negro meant "that his nature is . . . childlike, affectionate, docile, and patient . . ." Such "inferiority," Dewey argued, became "an increased appeal to pity and generosity." "Is it," he asked, "the part of . . . Christian people to oppress the weak, to crush the helpless?"[46]

Theodore Parker, liberal Unitarian minister and militant abolitionist, took a different tack. The early settlers of Massachusetts Bay, he declared in 1854, had in them

> the ethnologic idiosyncrasy of the Anglo-Saxon . . . to . . . conquer . . . his haughty contempt of humbler tribes . . . to subvert, enslave, kill, and exterminate; his fondness for material things, . . . his love of personal liberty, yet coupled with . . . respect for peaceful and established law. [47]

The revivalists were at the head of the religious attack upon the Negro's slavery. Evangelists saw God coming to issue mercy and judgment through the providence of history, and to pour out the Holy Spirit to cleanse America of its sin. This vision enabled them to break the barriers of conservatism and other-worldliness, of skin-color prejudice and economic interest that so long checked the American churches from a wholehearted fight against slavery.

In 1858, *Northwestern Christian Advocate* editor T. M. Eddy, from southern Indiana, preached at a camp meeting in White Pidgeon, Michigan, and a local newspaper censured him as a "Black Republican Reverend." The following year Eddy urged readers to join in the nominating process so the proper men might be elected to office. He delighted in the large Republican rallies in 1860, but criticized the "proslavery" stance of Rev. Peter Cartwright, a loyal Democrat who supported Stephen Douglas.[48]

The spiritual awakening of 1858 prompted the national soul-searching, implying Abraham Lincoln's election. Perhaps it also hastened the Civil War. The New York *Independent* (October 17, 1861) reported the annual session of the General Association of Congregational Churches held at Binghamton. A committee on the "state of the country," with Rev. J. P. Thompson, J. Butler, and H. N. Dunning, reported on some resolutions. They declared that slavery, "as the original cause . . . of our national troubles—as the serpent of evil . . . entered our garden of liberty, to beguile us into sin and ruin, should not be left untouched by the nation in this . . . crisis."[49] Six months earlier, Southern forces seized Ft. Sumter in Charleston harbor. They believed God offered this chance to strike a fatal blow on slavery.

Whatever geographical, economical, or political concerns sparked the Civil War, the antislavery forces became obvious. As noted earlier, the first move against slavery in America arose from religious communities that highly regarded the brotherhood of mankind. It began among the Quakers in pre-revolutionary times, with united Christian action inspired by the teachings of Christ. But not all professed Christians opposed the slave system.

Meanwhile, from 1845, The Methodist Episcopal Church, South, did missionary work among the slaves on many plantations. Without the tumult of Northern antislavery foes, Southern Methodists developed a missionary strategy that did not menace the institution of slavery. In the fearful wake of Nat Turner's slave rebellion, many whites sought to control the religious ideas given to blacks.

During the last decades before the war this stress on missions to the slaves was strong among Southern Methodists. They gave $1.8 million to the cause between 1844 and 1864. The growing influence of Bishop William Capers of South Carolina promoted this mission. In the year of his death (1854), Southern Methodists spent $25,000 for this effort. The 25 plantation missions served by 32 preachers then had 10,000 black members, and 1,000 white.[50]

Newcomb's Encyclopedia of Missions, for 1858, totals the number of converts in missions at around 250,000. Such missions were among the heathen nations conducted by Protestant Christian churches in Europe and America, reaching to Asia, Africa, Pacific Islands, West Indies, and North American Indians. In contrast, the converts in the slave states were reckoned to number 465,000.[51]

David Christy presents the Christian proslavery defense:

Thus, while the larger number of religious men, throughout Christendom, have been denouncing American slavery as incompatible with African evangelization; a handful of pious men, in the slave States, . . . have labored for the salvation of the slave, with a success nearly double that . . . of all the other missionaries throughout the heathen world.[52]

The *New York Observer* of 1859 notes some church extracts:[53]

In the Presbytery of Charleston, South Carolina, 1,637 out of 2,889 members, . . . are colored. In the whole Synod of South Carolina, 5,009 out of 13,074 are colored members. The

Presbyteries of Mississippi and Central Mississippi, of
Tuscaloosa and South Alabama, of Georgia, of Concord and
Fayetteville, . . . In the whole of the above-mentioned bodies,
there are 9,076 colored out of 33,667 communicants...

The *Mobile Daily Tribune*, telling of the religious training of slaves,
declared:

Few persons are aware of the efforts . . . in the various Southern
States, for the moral and religious improvement of the negroes;
of the number of clergymen, of good families, accomplished
education, . . . who devote their whole time and energies to this
work; or of the many laymen . . . slaveholders themselves—who
sustain them by their purses and . . . as catechists, Sunday-school
teachers, and the like.[54]

The paper also cited a "candid admission" from the *Philadelphia
Inquirer:*

The introduction of African slavery into the colonies of North
America, . . . brought about by wicked means, may . . .
accomplish great good to Africa;... Hundreds and thousands have
already been saved, . . . who otherwise must have perished.
Through these and their descendants . . . civilization and
Christianity have been sent back to the perishing millions of
Africa.[55]

Yet Christianizing slaves did not ruin the evil institution sheltered by
the South. No one voiced any intent that Christianity should sponsor
freedom for the slaves. The slaveholders would quickly halt all religious
instruction of their slaves if such intimations were made. Betterment for
the Negroes was only within the slave system, with no preparation to
enter a free society.

Southern Christians felt convinced of their duty to evangelize the
slaves, but they could not dismiss the slaves' longing for freedom. The
moral blindspot that allowed the bondage of a people could not be atoned
by efforts to convert them. The massive sore wounding America could
never heal unless the slaves were freed. Nor could a civil war guarantee
the restitution of all things.

A see-saw battle persisted within the Church against the factions that
favored slavery. Most churchmen hoped the crusade against slavery
would remain a "spiritual" warfare, shooting only volleys of words at
slaveholders and prayers to God. Often silence ensued within the church
because of uncertainty. The pros and cons of slavery became exhausted.

Christians and humanitarians still faced the bleeding moral issue that no verbal argument could blot out. No amount of restraint used in dealing with slavery would prevent the Church from becoming a Civil War casualty.

Chapter 7

Churches, Clergy, and President Lincoln

Abraham Lincoln portrayed a typical American view of slavery for the middle third of the 19th century. Even facing the urgent moral issue of slavery, Northern people hesitated to confront the South's "peculiar institution." Most Christians never championed the abolitionist cause. As Lincoln opposed slavery, he did not imagine an American society where freed slaves lived and worked alongside whites. Yet, his Emancipation Proclamation in 1862 began the process of freeing the slaves.

If Lincoln did not oppose slavery on "religious" grounds, a "religious sense" molded his feelings. He believed the existence of the United States stood crucial to liberty worldwide. So he sought a policy to end slavery but allow Southerners to rejoin the Union as brothers. Lincoln never viewed the Civil War as a Northern crusade, but as divine punishment on the entire nation and people for their indulgence to slavery. He believed the war would only be fruitful if reconciliation surpassed the enmity.

Lincoln's "religious sense" began and formed from his mother's influence. Nancy Hanks Lincoln, a hard-shell Baptist, read the Bible morning and evening. On Sundays she gathered her children and read to them Bible stories, and prayed with them. After becoming president, Lincoln, speaking of his mother, said: "I remember her prayers, and they have always followed me. They have clung to me all my life."[1]

As early as 1843, Lincoln's religion, or lack of it, had hurt his political aspirations. He admitted he was not a member of "any Christian Church." Yet he believed the truth of the Scriptures and never spoke in disrespect of religion in general or of any denomination of Christians in particular. He declared he could not support any man for political office who would be "an open enemy of, or scoffer at, religion."[2]

Events in Lincoln's life further shaped his spiritual life. His broken engagement to Mary Todd in 1841 caused him spiritual anguish. A friend gave Lincoln a new Oxford Bible, which Lincoln declared was "the best cure for the 'Blues' could one but take it according to the truth." Abraham Lincoln and Mary Todd at last married November 4, 1842, bringing him to an organized church, since Mary attended the Springfield, Illinois, Episcopal Church.[3]

In 1846, Lincoln became the candidate for Congress from the Sangamon District, against Democrat Peter Cartwright, noted Methodist backwoods preacher. Abe Lincoln gained election by a record majority of 1,511 votes. Before the "Compromise Measures of 1850," Lincoln told his law partner, Mr. Stuart: "The time will come when we must all be Democrats or Abolitionists. . . . my mind is made up. The slavery question can't be compromised."[4]

From 1854 on, the Repeal of the Missouri Compromise roused Lincoln from his law office to the political arena again. His writings and speeches show willful strength of thought. On the slavery issue, he was beset by the abolitionists who wanted to drive slavery out of the country. Also, he faced those working to extend slavery. Lincoln searched for legal authority and political precedent because he believed "the Fathers" of the nation had put slavery on "the course of ultimate extinction."

Yet, Lincoln saw two basic dangers in the spread of slavery, beside the injustice of slavery itself. One was slavery's evil influence on the country's political freedom; the other was its bad effect on the free labor system set as an inherent part of democratic government. Lincoln often told people that "the white man's charter of freedom" will become worthless if the Negro is denied "life, liberty, and the pursuit of happiness." Closing an appeal in 1854 in Peoria, Illinois, he warned: "In our greedy chase to make profit of the negro, . . . beware lest we cancel . . . even the white man's charter of freedom . . . "[5]

Though Lincoln once said he did not remember a time when he was not against slavery, some believe he took this stand only by the stress of war. Yet, in 1855, Lincoln's letter to George Robertson of Lexington, Kentucky, clearly projects the violent course the slave power would take. Lincoln writes:

My Dear Sir: . . . [you] . . . spoke of "the peaceful extinction of slavery" . . . we have had thirty-six years of experience; . . . there is no peaceful extinction of slavery . . . When we were the political slaves of King George, . . . we called the maxim that "all men are created equal" a self-evident truth; . . . we have . . . lost all dread of being slaves . . . become so greedy to be *masters* that we call the same maxim "a self-evident lie."

That spirit which desired the peaceful extinction of slavery has itself become extinct with the . . . Revolution. . . . The Autocrat of all the Russians will resign his crown and proclaim his subjects free republicans, sooner than will our American masters voluntarily give up their slaves.

Our political problem now is, "Can we as a nation continue together permanently—forever—half slave, and half free?"[6]

(The prophecy that the Russian czar would free his serfs before the South did happened in 1860; Lincoln was elected president.)

Before Lincoln's presidency, the moral issue of slavery moved his religious formation. His views of morality stemmed from his own beliefs. He said that without the revelation of the Scriptures people could not discern between right and wrong. He declared, "In regard to this Great Book, . . . it is the best gift God has given to man. All the good the Savior gave to the world was communicated through this book."[7]

Speaking in Chicago, July 10, 1858, on America's commitment to the tenet of equality, Lincoln applied a scriptural standard:

> . . . It is said in one of the admonitions of the Lord, "As your Father in Heaven is perfect, be ye also perfect." The Savior . . . did not expect that any human creature could be perfect as the Father in Heaven . . . He did set that up as a standard, and he . . . attained the highest degree of moral perfection. So I say . . . all men are created equal: let it be as nearly reached as we can.[8]

During the 1860 campaign, Newton Bateman, superintendent of Public Instruction for the State of Illinois, had quarters opening into Lincoln's executive chamber at Springfield. As Lincoln studied a voter canvass of Springfield, he called Bateman to go over the lists with him to see how the city's ministers might vote. After careful study, Lincoln said to Bateman:

> Here are twenty-three ministers, of different denominations, and all of them are against me but three; . . . I am not a Christian—God knows I would be one—but I have carefully read the Bible . . . These men well know that I am for . . . freedom everywhere as free as the Constitution and the laws will permit, and that my opponents are for slavery. . . . and yet, with this book . . . in the light of which human bondage can not live . . . they are going to vote against me . . . .[9]

Bateman said that Lincoln struggled to retain his composure. Then, he spoke with a trembling voice and cheeks wet with tears:

> I know there is a God, . . . he hates injustice and slavery. I see the storm coming, . . . his hand is in it. If he has a place and work for me . . . I am ready. . . . I know I am right, . . . liberty is right; for Christ teaches it, and Christ is God. I have told them that a house divided against itself can not stand; and Christ and reason say the

same; and they will find it so. . . . God cares, and humanity cares, and I care, and, with God's help, I shall not fail. I may not see the end, but it will come, and I shall be vindicated.[10]

William Herndon, Lincoln's longtime law partner, disputed Bateman's account. Joshua Speed, a friend of Lincoln during the early Springfield years, wrote that Lincoln "was skeptical as to the great truths of the Christian religion." Lincoln's first law partner, John Todd Stuart, deemed him an infidel. Isaac Cogdal, a Menard lawyer in the central Illinois circuits, said that Lincoln gave no credence to "the orthodox Theologies of the day." Mary Lincoln said her husband "was not a technical Christian."[11] One can make a decision from Lincoln's speeches and writings.

Lincoln's election in 1860, and the breakup of the national structure as one Southern state after another seceded from the Union, impacted his spiritual life. The difficulties of "getting rid" of slavery became overwhelming by the time Lincoln assumed the presidency in March, 1861. A series of events worked what Lincoln called a "process of crystallization" in his mind.

President Lincoln thought the nation derived its strength from the people. The defense of the Union was in them. "When the people rise . . . in behalf of the Union and liberties of this country, . . . 'The gates of hell cannot prevail against them.'" Of secessionists, he said, "In their views, the Union as a family relation would seem to be no regular marriage, but rather as a . . . 'free-love' arrangement, . . . on 'passional attraction.'"[12]

When the United States Congress convened December 2, 1861, Republicans saw changes in the war objectives. With political expediency, military necessity, and moral urgency, an adroit leadership, launched an onslaught against slavery. Congressmen offered resolutions calling for emancipation; and they introduced a drastic slave confiscation bill in the Senate.[13]

Midwestern Republicans appealed for emancipation, declaring slave confiscation and liberation would smash the Confederate war effort, save the Union, and punish the South. Though some reproved slavery as a sin against God, humanity, morality, and natural rights became lesser issues. Representative Owen Lovejoy of Illinois, whose words on slavery echoed Puritan views, assured the house members that he did "not wish the inference to be drawn . . . that we are for making the war directly upon slavery."[14]

The Republican party then used voluntary Negro colonization as its official policy. The blacks who received freedom and agreed to leave would be sent outside the United States. President Lincoln's message to Congress in December of 1861, urged that slaves seized under a confiscation act passed earlier and those who might be freed by state action be removed to "some place, . . . in a climate congenial to them." He also asked the lawmakers to include free Negroes who wanted to depart.[15]

The colonization view blended racism and humanitarianism, as rooted in the American heritage. Most who favored deportation thought by the nation's past that inborn racial contrasts—mainly of color rather than slavery—caused the race problem. Senator James R. Doolittle of Wisconsin, a colonization patron, stated, "the *question of race* is a more troublesome one than the question of condition [slavery] in the truth."[16] This attitude also expressed the thinking of Northern ministers and churches.

The editor of the American Missionary Association's antislavery monthly wrote in January 1862, "The new year will . . . be a momentous one." Every child of God and "lover of his race" must hold "himself, and all that he has, consecrated . . . to the master's service, to be used, . . . for the establishment of his Kingdom of peace and righteousness in our land and throughout the earth." Blending a sense of impending judgment with millennial ardor and social realism occurred commonly in wartime revival appeals.[17]

The blend of antislavery idealism and racism held by leading Republicans in 1862 showed their followers' grassroots religious ideas with political bias. Midwesterners often mixed their dislike of slavery, pity for the slaves, and aversion for the Negro. Senator John Sherman thus said, "The great mass of this country are opposed to slavery— morally, socially, politically." He also stated that Ohioans—people of the Midwest—were "opposed to having many negroes among them"; colored people were "spurned and hated all over the country North and South."[18]

A blatant expression of this feeling appeared in a leading Republican paper, the Springfield, *Illinois State Journal*:

> . . . the nigger is an unpopular institution in the free States. Even those who are unwilling to rob them of all the rights of humanity, . . . willing to let them . . . to live and to labor . . . do not care to be brought into close contact with them. . . . we have . . . with nineteen twentieths of our people a prejudice against the nigger . . . [19]

Yet, Abraham Lincoln stood in the moral strife over slavery —the central figure in the Civil War. His hatred of the slave system matched the moral fervor of the abolitionists. Lincoln's antislavery zeal was tempered by respect for private property, by his constitutionalism, desire to hold the loyal slave states, and by knowing the problem of two free "races" coexisting in the same society. He grasped Northern attitudes toward Negroes, but his slavery policy struggled in indecision and doubt. It moved with the secular and religious feelings of Northern people, with his own morality, sensible statesmanship, and political expediency.

Lincoln wanted to push slavery toward extinction without taking the powers of national government beyond the Constitution. In December, 1861, speaking to Congress, Lincoln urged the states to move voluntarily toward gradual emancipation with compensation for those owners who freed their slaves. He asked Congress to give financial aid to states using that plan, and to provide some means of colonizing the freed Negroes, with those already free, who wanted to leave. His antislavery program became a voluntary state emancipation with compensation and colonization.[20]

Beyond these plans, Lincoln had a fateful policy for dealing with Confederate slavery, believing war to be the emancipator. He chose to let the purging of battle uproot slavery, as God willed, without special congressional or executive action.[21] The idea that war alone would abolish slavery, flourished in the North, especially early in the war.

Lincoln tried to prepare the people for emancipation by an education campaign in the press, stating that sterner measures might be needed to save the nation. Meanwhile, only the needs of the Union guided him. Horace Greely, New York *Tribune* editor and spokesman of the abolitionist press, in his "Prayer of Twenty Millions," lectured Lincoln for being too easy on slavery. The President countered, August 22, 1862, saying:

> My paramount object in this struggle is to save the Union, and is not either to save or to destroy slavery. If I could save the Union without freeing any slave, I would do it; and if I could save it by freeing all the slaves, I would do it; and if I could save it by freeing some and leaving others alone, I would do that.[22]

September 13, 1862, in talking with two Chicago ministers, who offered memorials calling for national emancipation, Lincoln refined his views. Comparing the advantages and disadvantages of freeing the slaves, he claimed he could legally proclaim liberty. He viewed this as a "practical war measure," which he had under consideration. He promised to do whatever appeared to be God's bidding; slavery was the "root of the rebellion or at least its *sine qua non*"[23] —"without which not."

Before the interview was published, the Army of the Potomac drove Lee's Confederate army out of Maryland. Lincoln used this victory to issue his Preliminary Proclamation of Emancipation, September 22, 1862, and he asked Congress to give financial aid to states adopting gradual emancipation. Work for colonization would continue. Yet, the proclamation was a drastic change. It said that slaves in any "state, or designated part of a state" still in rebellion January 1, 1863, would be considered free.[24]

Lincoln's statement to the ministers, that slavery was the cause of the *sine qua non* of the rebellion was a main point in the abolitionists' creed. Like some radicals, he believed that he was the instrument of a righteous God who ordained him to destroy slavery. As Lincoln said, his action on slavery would depend on whatever appeared to be God's will. When the President later stated he would issue the preliminary proclamation, he told his cabinet that he had made "a vow." If God made the Union Army victorious in Maryland, he would view it "an indication of Divine will, . . . it was his duty to move forward in the . . . emancipation . . . God had decided . . . in favor of the slaves . . . ."[25]

As President Lincoln gave the January 1, 1863, proclamation, it set his liberation course, proclaiming all slaves free held by Confederate control. Yet the Emancipation Proclamation did not indict slavery. Note the moral end of his order: "And upon this act, sincerely believed to be an act of justice, warranted by the Constitution, upon military necessity, I invoke the considerate judgment of mankind, and the gracious favor of Almighty God."[26]

The proclamation evoked praise by Republicans for a righteous act; they believed God decreed emancipation. His prophet, Abraham Lincoln, obeyed Him. An Iowa newspaperman said Lincoln just carried out the Lord's command. The Chicago *Tribune* editor viewed the rebellion as God's scourge sent to punish the nation for the institution of slavery. The Lord said, "Let my people go," and Lincoln made the Emancipation Proclamation. Once defaming him, he now cried, "Let us thank God for Abraham Lincoln, and pray that through him the other nine plagues may be averted." He also wrote that the North no longer based its efforts to subdue the South "upon the entities of political growth, but upon the eternal verities of God and men, we must succeed."[27]

The tactics and avowals of antislavery people, shaped by sincere religious convictions or by political crisis, showed the basic racial attitudes of most Northerners remained unchanged by the war. Critics of slavery were more humane and informed toward the black race than the Democrats. Some hoped for a change in the Negroes' political, legal, and economic status everywhere, but they did not advocate full equality of the "races."

In early 1863, Northern life would not be basically changed by the abolition of slavery. Antislavery spokesmen scorned the old Negro exclusion laws and fought any new ones, praised the conduct and ability of the freedmen, and urged the enlistment of black soldiers. Yet, they opposed miscegenation, intimacy between whites and blacks, and Negro immigration, while claiming the superiority of Caucasians.

In May, 1863, Senator John Sherman told an Ohio audience, "I am not in favor of negro equality, but because you and I are . . . more favored in intellect . . . are we to be the masters of those who were made in the Lord's image?" John Wentworth, a Democrat joining the Union party, in Chicago scoffed at the idea "that the negroes would crowd out white labor at the North. The inferior race could never encroach upon the rights of the superior." A Republican editor said the Democratic newspaper in Dubuque, Iowa, was anti-Negro. It lacked "confidence in . . . its supporters to resist the attractions of the darkies, and . . . hates a negro more than it does a 'rattlesnake.'"[28] Even the best advocates of emancipation—churchmen wanting a righteous war, men loyal to antislavery—withheld fellowship to the Negro.

Yet through the churches or the humanitarian associations such as the Contrabands' Relief Commission, Western Freedman's Aid Commission, many midwesterners gave time and money to provide aid and education for Southern Negroes. As federal forces struck into the Southern heartland, increasing numbers of Negroes rushed into the Union lines. They gathered around Union camps, hampered military operations, often living in privation and disease. In early 1863, General Ulysses S. Grant called the situation in west Tennessee and northern Mississippi "serious" and "troublesome." Lincoln named the Negro refugee problem "a difficult subject—the most difficult with which we have to deal."[29]

Iowa's radical governor, Samuel J. Kirkwood, wrote General-in-Chief Henry W. Halleck that he would not regret it if at the end of the war they found, "that a part of the dead are niggers and that not all are whites." He later stated publicly that he "would prefer to sacrifice the lives of niggers rather than those of the best and bravest of our white youths."[30]

Some "men of God" found this reasoning a total match with their theology. During an emotional antislavery discourse a Minnesota Congregationalist cried, "Why should we send our sons and brothers to perish by thousands, when the slave population is ready to aid the government, if we will give permission?"[31]

Moral feelings deepened as the tragic conflict reached the lives and homes of those far from the battlefield. In Fremont, Iowa, Sara Ann

Crandall Beals composed a poem on the death of her brother, Harvey Crandall. A casualty at Vicksburg, Tennessee, he died July 23, 1863. My great-grandmother wrote:

> He went to fight his country's foe
>   And to set free the slave
> But the scorching fever burnt his brain
>   But you laid him in the grave.
>
> Away from home and friends so dear
>   From those who loved him best
> My brother sleeps in uniform
>   But his spirit is at rest.
>
> Though low and hard his dying bed
>   His brothers gathered round
> To hear his last, his parting words
>   And catch the last faint sound.
>
> So faint and low, so feebly spoke,
>   Tell them I am going home
> Where there is no hunger, pain, or strife
>   To make poor soldiers mourn.
>
> But hark, the Saviour's calling me,
>   Poor soldier come away
> And rest with those that's gone before;
>   This voice I must obey.
>
> No more the sound of fife or drum
>   Shall wake me from my sleep,
> But be left alone to mourn,
>   In solitude to weep.
>
> Hunger and pain can't reach me there,
>   No more the cannon roar
> Disturbs the weary soldier's rest
>   On Canaan's happy shore.

The verses contain patriotic, antislavery, and religious elements that marked growing Northern fervor.

Moved by the religious and patriotic currents sweeping in the wake of Gettysburg and Vicksburg, more people viewed the war as a fight for liberty. They claimed the antislavery policy endowed the Union with moral supremacy, helping to conquer the South and purge the national character of its remaining defect. Then, to those who saw the rebellion as divine punishment for wrongdoing, the recent war success signaled that God approved liberation. He would lift His curse once slavery became abolished.

By mid-1863, most of the large religious organizations of the North and many leading pastors served as the spiritual arm of the Republican party. While they preached the antislavery gospel to reveal the vision of freedom's holy war, they blasted the disloyal Copperheads and canonized the Lincoln administration and its policies. In December of 1863 the Chicago *Times* voiced a common complaint of the Democrats saying:

> A fair share of the pulpits are . . . devoted to [the Negroes'] cause; the African and him in bondage being the theme, instead of "Christ and him crucified;" . . . the elect and abolitionists, natural depravity and democracy, the devil and Vallandigham [notorious Ohio congressman], the New Jerusalem and negro equality, are . . . used as synonymous.[32]

Some people with Democratic views left their churches to avoid antislavery preaching and harrassment. Northern clergy rallied support for Republican-Unionist candidates with sermons and decrees during the elections of 1863. Methodist preachers in Cincinnati told their members to vote "the unconditional Union ticket," accusing Democrats of opposing the war and the "Church of God." In October, 1863, the Cincinnati *Catholic Telegraph* editor Rev. Edward Purcell endorsed the Union party slate. That December, he rebuked the Democratic party as a proslavery body.[33]

Editor Purcell's attack melded racism with antislavery zeal. He believed freedom would clear the Negroes out of the North, ending the strife between blacks and whites. He declared:

> We desire to see . . . no partnership between the two races. We have no desire to see them intermingled, neither working together . . . The natural superiority of the white race ought to be . . . preserved. This is impossible so long as slavery exists, because the poor white man is just as much . . . in the power of the rich planter as the slave.[34]

Many church and political leaders stressed the philosophy that the war was a divine judgement sent to punish the nation for using slavery. The curse would end when people cast out the evil institution. President Lincoln popularized this concept. His letter to a Kentucky newspaper editor in 1864, told of submission to a righteous God's will when he confessed that He alone could claim credit for the state of the nation. "If God now wills the removal of a great wrong, . . . we of the North as well as you of the South, shall pay fairly for . . . that wrong, . . . history will find . . . cause to attest . . . the justice and goodness of God."[35]

Iowa Representative James F. Wilson ventured the exuberant optimism and moral urgency of the antislavery movement as he called for abolition. In Congress, he declared:

> Providence has opened up the way to that higher Civilization and purer Christianity which the Republic is to attain. Our Red Sea passage promises to be as propitious as . . . God's chosen people when the waters parted . . . their escape from the hosts upon whom those waters closed and . . . the burial appointed by Him who had declared, "Let my people go."[36]

Many churchmen thus spoke of Christian people as they atoned for their sins by opposing slavery and slaveholders, helping the enslaved, and proving the gospel of the brotherhood of mankind. Abolition would unite the divided nation, giving freedom to a land. As righteous Americans fulfilled their "holy mission," they offered a haven for the burdened peoples of Europe, and spread Christianity and republican institutions around the world.

At the 1864 General Conference of the Methodist Episcopal Church in Philadelphia, representing nearly 7,000 ministers, and a million members, an address was presented to President Lincoln. Joseph Cummings, chairman of the Committee on the State of the Country, prepared it. The Conference voiced "the loyalty of the Church, . . . to the interests of the country, . . . sympathy with you in the great responsibilities . . . in this trying hour . . . "

> We pray that . . . this shall be truly a . . . free country, in no part . . . State or Territory, shall slavery be known. The prayers of millions of Christians . . . daily . . . that you may be endued with . . . wisdom and power. . . . our prayers . . . for the preservation of our country undivided, . . . triumph of our cause, . . . a permanent peace, gained by the sacrifice of no moral principles, but founded on the Word of God, . . . righteousness, liberty, and equal rights to all.[37]

May 18, Lincoln wrote:

> Gentlemen,—In response to your address, allow me to . . . thank you, . . . for the sure promise it gives. Nobly sustained as the Government has been by all the Churches, . . . the Methodist Episcopal Church, . . . is . . . the most important . . . sends more soldiers . . . more nurses to the hospital, and more prayers . . . than any. God bless the Methodist Church . . . all the Churches—and blessed be God, who, in . . . our great trial, giveth us the Churches![38]

During 1864, in an essay on the "moral results" of the war, to promote the United States Christian Commission, Rev. Robert Patterson said, until the conflict, Christians "never dreamed of the rough combat with the powers of darkness which an earnest effort to convert the world demands." American religion had acquired a "respectable burgess" character; he wrote, "fat, well clad in broad cloth, with gilt Bible, Gothic church and organ," while an "underground class" it bypassed grew larger in the great cities. Churches needed a revival to sweep the army, one that met both the social and the spiritual needs of men. Only thus would America be ready for the "last great struggle between freedom and slavery, truth and error," as gathered by the Lord.[39]

We are entering . . . upon a period foretold by prophets of old . . . the overthrow of despotism, and the down-fall of anti-Christ. . . . Christians . . . gird yourselves for this great undertaking . . . wrestle with God for a revival, and we shall see such an outpouring of the Spirit as will convert the army, revive the church, and regenerate the nation.[40]

This required more than to free the slaves and defeat the rebels. The Chicago *Tribune* called for repeal of the "infamous Black Laws." The paper claimed, "The safety of the white race lies in doing justice to the blacks, for God has declared against their oppressors." To win God's blessing and the war, Secretary of the Treasury Salmon P. Chase wrote in May, 1864, that Lincoln must "let the black loyalists have a fair chance . . . come into the army on . . . equal footing as to pay, . . . promotion, and right to vote on the soil which they help recover from rebellion." The Cincinnati *Western Christian Advocate* editor also applied this theory to the North. Depicting the conflict as "God's warfare for man," he warned, "[We] shall be used as His instruments to scourge the oppressor and to open prison-doors, till the American people, North and South . . . *recognize the essential manhood of the negro*, and . . . equality before the laws and in the sight of God, with the proud and cultivated Saxon race."[42]

Such promptings urged government, religious, and charitable organizations to rehabilitate the slaves, providing them with Christian instruction, land, education, federal aid and protection, and a Freedman's Bureau. The Republican consensus held that all men should have racial harmony, justice, and prosperity. Some clergymen, editors, and politicians sought other ways to win more respect and tolerance for Negroes. They compared the pleasing conduct of colored soldiers and civilians with that of Democratic "traitors." Yet, these attempts tried to reduce racism, with appeals to religious and class prejudice, charging that only the Irish and "poor whites" had Negrophobia.[42]

Belief in white racial superiority survived both the antislavery crusade and the rhetoric of equal rights. The casual efforts of eastern abolitionists to confront this creed had little effect on such thinking. To most midwesterners of all parties, experience and science still pointed toward the innate inferiority of the blacks. Yet, they admitted that Negroes had the ability to live under freedom. While crusading for equality, many politicians, church leaders, and humanitarians still voiced the usual midwestern attitudes about the inferiority of Negroes.

A minister from Ohio addressed the General Conference of the Methodist Episcopal Church in 1864 on a proposal to organize Southern Negroes into separate jurisdiction within the church. He preferred no distinction in the Church, but he did not favor amalgamation. Perhaps the Africans would "find homes and liberty in a warmer climate than ours." He suggested the government send Negro troops to Mexico, "and the mongrel population of that country will have nothing to fear from amalgamation."[43]

Indiana congressman and religious freethinker Robert Dale Owen blended egalitarianism and pragmatic racism that often thrived in the psyche of midwestern radicals. Early in 1863, Secretary of War Edwin M. Stanton appointed him head of the American Freedmen's Inquiry Commission. His final report, in June, 1864, was a "Radical Blueprint for Reconstruction." He decried racial prejudice, urging the creation of a federal bureau to protect the freedman. He backed civil equality for Negroes, and held the Southern states from readmittance into the Union until they guaranteed equal rights to all of their inhabitants.[44]

Democrats said God, or nature, had ordered the black race to eternal degradation, but the commissioners viewed Negroes as inferior to whites in some ways and superior in others. "The Anglo-Saxon race, with great . . . character, much mental activity, . . . spirit of enterprise, has . . . a stubborn will . . . moderate geniality . . . Its intellectual powers are stronger than its social instincts . . . a race . . . better fitted to do than to enjoy." The Negro race: "Genial, lively, docile, emotional, the affections rule . . . It is a knowing rather than a thinking race . . . little given to stirring enterprise, but . . . to quiet accumulation. It is not a race that will ever . . . lead in the material improvement of the world; but it will make . . . respectable positions, comfortable homes."[45] The Negroes had more of the Christian graces of meekness and long-suffering.

However, this report does not represent a totally Christian viewpoint. Charles Darwin's evolutionary theories and the higher criticism come against the biblical fundamentalism of American Christian thought. Many held a literal explanation of the Bible and attacked science as the spawn of Satan. Moderates shifted toward a social gospel, and liberals of the Protestant movement drifted into various systems of "freethought."

Amid the various opinions most Unionist churchmen believed slavery was both a moral evil and a source of national conflict. If there were those who would not wage a war only to abolish slavery, few would mourn its passing. Whatever their motives, a majority of Northerners sealed their commitment to emancipation when they voted for the party of abolition in the 1864 elections.

In January, 1864, President Lincoln wrote:

How to better ... the colored race has long ... attracted my ... careful attention; ... I am clear ... what course I shall pursue ... as a religious duty, as the nation's guardian of these people who have ... vindicated their manhood on the battlefield, ... to save ... the republic, they have demonstrated in blood their right to the ballot ... [46]

After the lame duck Congress reconvened, House Republicans reconsidered and passed the proposed Thirteenth Amendment January 31, 1865. The response of the Midwestern press to congressional approval of the antislavery amendment split along partisan lines. Bitter frustration shared by some Democrats soon peaked in a caustic editorial of the Dubuque, Iowa, *Democratic Herald*:

EXCELSIOR, SAMBO!

At last the abolition millennium is about to dawn. The incubus of slavery which weighed down our country for over eighty years, ... foisted upon us by those slave-driving nabobs, Washington, Jefferson, Jackson, and others ... is about to be removed, and our disenthralled country ... will spring into the fore rank of civilized progress, amid the shouts and songs of the freed, the twang of banjo, the ... "fantastic heel and toe," and most palpable odor.[47]

Yet, the Springfield *Illinois State Journal* praised Congress for passing the most vital act in its history. It sent " joy to the hearts of the friends of freedom throughout all Christendom." The Chicago *Tribune* stated, "This gigantic stride in our progress towards national purity, universal liberty, and a righteous peace will be hailed with ... religious gratitude by our liberty-loving American people ... [The congressmen] have removed ... the last moral stain ... the only disgrace from our flag."[48]

At Lincoln's second inauguration in March 1865, the military outcome seemed clear. Yet the moral issue remained vague, and permeated Lincoln's words in taking the oath of office. "Neither party expected for the war the magnitude, . . . duration, which it has . . . attained . . . Both . . . read the same Bible, and pray to the same God; and each invokes His aid against the other . . . The prayers of both could not be answered; that of neither has been answered fully." He said that between God's purposes and humans doing them, there is a difference—not pleasing to all people. Writing to Thurlow Weed, Lincoln said that to deny any difference "is to deny that there is a God governing the world."[49]

The words of Lincoln's Second Inaugural Address (March 4, 1865) remain essential:

> If . . . American slavery is one of those offenses which, in the providence of God, must needs come, . . . He now wills to remove . . . He gives to both North and South this terrible war, as the woe due to them . . . shall we discern therein any departure from those divine attributes which the believers in a Living God always ascribed to Him? . . . fervently do we pray—that this mighty scourge of war may speedily pass away. Yet, if God wills that it continue, until all wealth piled by the bond-man's two hundred and fifty years of unrequited toil . . . until every drop of blood drawn with the lash, shall be paid by another drawn by the sword, as was said three thousand years ago, so still . . . "The judgments of the Lord are true and righteous altogether."
>
> With malice toward none; with charity for all; with firmness in the right as God gives us to see the right, let us strive on to finish the work we are in . . . [50]

That same year, bishops of the Methodist Episcopal Church, South, sent a pastoral letter to their clergy, stating:

> . . . We must express with regret . . . that a large portion . . . of Northern Methodists have become incurably radical. . . . They have incorporated social dogmas and political tests into their church creeds. They . . . impose conditions upon discipleship that Christ did not impose. Their pulpits are perverted to . . . questions not healthful to personal piety, but promotive of political and ecclesiastical discord . . .
>
> The conduct of certain Northern Methodist bishops and preachers in taking advantage of . . . a state of war to intrude themselves into several of our houses of worship, and . . . hold these places against the . . . protests of the congregations and rightful owners,

. . . They are not only using, . . . churches and parsonages which we have built, but . . . set up claim to them as their property . . . [51]

Yet, out of national suffering came true understanding—as brothers fought to the death, it begat brotherhood. Every moral, religious, and political ideal of a free people became imperiled, whether by peace or by war. Both church and state suffered a crisis of conscience and conduct. Neither the rhetoric of revivalists nor the claims of politicians could cloud the issues or dim the promise of truth.

At the war's end a contributor to the newfledged magazine, *The Nation*, wrote hopefully of "The One Humanity." He said God placed before the country this issue of race, as the stone of stumbling that would make or break "our Israel." The Christian state's "lofty ideal, its divine mission" was "to help all the weak, to lift up all the fallen, to raise to the highest culture of which he is capable, every son of Adam."[52]

But the agitation of the Reconstruction era prevailed. Many churchmen shared in the rantings, revealing the shallowness of commitment fostered by the conflict. What is called the "reunion and reaction" of the 1870s portended the return of the nation, like many Christian converts, to the slough of privilege and prejudice. That slough's appeal remains. After well over a century we still bypass the promise of brotherhood.

Chapter 8

The Church and Biased Reconstruction

The church became an agent in splitting the nation. John C. Calhoun prophesied of the snapping of church cords in a Senate speech March 4, 1850. Church divisions showed that the nation's moral conscience acted awry. Church historian William W. Sweet said, "There are good arguments to support the claim that the split in the churches was not only the first break between the sections, but the chief cause of the final break."[1]

Henry Clay on the eve of his death in 1852 believed this: "I tell you, this sundering of the religious ties which have bound our people together I consider the greatest source of danger to our country."[2] By 1864 Professor R. L. Stanton, of Presbyterian theological school at Danville, Kentucky, held that idea in his book *The Church and the Rebellion*. He claimed the South's revolt against lawful authority started "In the Church of God." He also accused Northern "doughface" preachers, who by guarding "Southern rights," encouraged the growth of secessionism.[3]

More recent research supports such conclusions. Professor James Silver wrote in the middle of this century:

> As its greatest social institution, the church in the South constituted the major resource of the Confederacy in the building . . . of civilian morale. . . . Southern clergymen were responsible for a state of mind which made secession possible, . . . they sustained the people in their long, costly and futile War for Southern Independence.[4]

On the Northern side, a different line of duty formed. In April 1865 at a Thanksgiving service after the fall of Richmond, Virginia, Rev. Phillips Brooks, the future Episcopal bishop of Massachusetts, offered the victors' prayer:

> We thank Thee, O God, for the power of Thy right arm, which has broken for us a way, and set the banners of our Union in the central city of treason and rebellion. We thank Thee for the triumph of right over wrong. We thank Thee for the loyal soldiers planted in the streets of wickedness. We thank Thee for the wisdom and bravery and devotion which Thou hast anointed for

Thy work and crowned with glorious victory . . . And now, O God, we pray Thee to complete Thy work.[5]

President Lincoln, shot by an assassin on Good Friday, died Saturday April 15. By May 26 all Confederate armies laid down their arms. Yet the "close of the Rebellion" awaited declaration by President Andrew Johnson on August 20, 1866, and the act of Congress March 2, 1867. The war caused 1 million casualties, with 600,000 dead. People did not understand why so many had suffered and died. The two sections grieved differently over the war. The grief of the South became more deeply etched, while that of the North seemed soothed by victory and apparent grounds of hope.

Father Abram Ryan, a free-lance chaplain to Confederate troops, whose spirit, as one remarked, shall "keep watch over the Stars and Bars until the morning of the Resurrection," wrote these lines a few days after Lee's surrender.

> Furl that Banner! furl it sadly!
> Once ten thousands hailed it gladly,
> And ten thousands wildly, madly,
>   Swore it should forever wave;
> Swore that foeman's sword should never
> Hearts like theirs entwined dissever,
> Till that flag should float forever
>   O'er their freedom or their grave!
>
> Furl that banner, softly, slowly!
> Treat it gently—it is holy—
>   For it droops above the dead.
> Touch it not—unfold it never,
> Let it droop there, furled forever
>   For its people's hopes are dead![6]

Many Southerners hold this fervent resignation to fate. They sought to regain personal status, but their hearts remain with the "Lost Cause," thinking of military valor and some mythic past. The Confederate flag yet has official status in the states of Alabama, South Carolina, Georgia, and Mississippi. A major religious result of this sentiment clings to the evangelicalism of antebellum days, but ignores the relevant issues raised by modern events.[7]

In the decade following Lincoln's death, malice more than mercy typified reconstruction in the South. It spawned Northern exploiters—"carpet-baggers," and Southern renegades—"the scalawags." The Civil War's desolate aftermath of bitterness became inflamed by fraud, plunder, and corruption. The Southern economy crumbled, with many leaders in prison or exile, and education lay in a shambles. Poverty crippled all the Confederacy, while Northern manufacturing, banking, and mining progressed.

At Lincoln's death, Vice President Andrew Johnson became sworn in as president, April 15, 1865. Like Lincoln, Johnson received questions about his religion. Some accused him of Catholic ties, or being atheistic. Though Johnson joined no church, he said: "So far as the doctrines of the Bible are concerned, or the great scheme of salvation, as founded and taught and practiced by Jesus Christ, I never did entertain a solitary doubt."[8]

Religion, politics, and practics became a tangled mess after a few months of the Johnson administration. Emancipation of slaves soon forced the nation to consider Negro suffrage. These freemen without voting rights stood, like slavery, against the American ideal. Equalitarians, both white and black, launched the Negro suffrage movement to counter this defect.

Churchmen supported Reconstructionists in Washington, and church channels tried to aid the newly freed blacks. Many relief associations started in Northern cities and towns by 1861. The United States Commission for relief for the National Freedman formed in 1863, merging five of the large city organizations. The American Freedman's Union Commission began in 1866, founded for a range of societies. After 1869 Congress managed reconstruction and freedman's aid. Church societies like the Northern Presbyterians organized their freedmen's committee in 1864; and Methodists began their Freedman's Aid Society in 1866. Other churches followed.

The commitment of most Northern Protestant churches to the Congressional radicals became very intense. Even a dubious effort to impeach the president in 1868 won sweeping support. Northern Methodists stood nearly convinced that Southern Methodist church property should be seized. Yet reconstruction indecision and scandal became so common that even ardent and capable reform leaders lost sight of the "Southern question."

Most white Southerners thought reconstruction meant only one thing: to put back the pieces so far as possible like they stood in 1860, *status quo antebellum*. This bias remained, amounting to a highly personal and unresigned distortion of judgment. They began at once to assert that black freedmen proved incompetent to exercise the right of suffrage. One Northern Presbyterian editor declared, "They stacked their arms but not their principles."

The Northern churches remained active with their support for radicalism and aid to the freedmen. The Methodist, Baptist, and Presbyterian churches that divided over the slavery issue wanted to dismiss the Southern branches of their denominations. Since the Southern "schismatics" held slavery as God's will with more unity than the Northern churches who opposed it, they became spurned. The *Independent* issued a majority view July 27, 1865: "The apostate church is buried beneath . . . divine wrath; its hideous dogmas shine . . . like flaming fiends; the whole world stands aghast at its wickedness and ruin. The Northern church beholds its mission."[9]

In early summer of 1865, Virginians said the freed Negroes should be protected like immigrants, infants, and women, but they could not vote. Arkansas conservatives also denied that Negroes had any political rights. The Florida State Constitutional Convention of 1865 decreed that their laws should be enacted by the white race alone. That year South Carolinians agreed that Negroes should have all privileges vital to their new condition, except suffrage, for which they lacked the mentality and virtue to understand. Voting was not a right but a privilege entrusted by the community to responsible persons.[10]

The Louisiana whites claimed the freedmen remained protected by the state's black code. Suffrage was not, as many Northerners thought, needed for the self-defense of blacks. If colored people voted and representation remained based on population, anarchy and revolution would result. Furthermore, the right to vote was not a "natural right," else women and children, excluded on the grounds of mental incompetence, would possess the right. They stood much more intelligent than Negroes. If any tests became necessary, the test of color, distinguishing as it did between the ignorant and the intelligent, defined the most accurate test.[11]

Meanwhile, the blacks looked for some political power. A group met at the Norfolk, Virginia, First Baptist Church, December 1, 1865, and drew up these resolutions:

> . . . the stories . . . That we are . . . preparing for insurrection and riotous . . . are vile falsehoods designed to provoke acts of unlawful violence against us . . .
>
> . . . we have faith in God and our Country and in the justice . . . of the American people for redress of all our grievances . . . we will . . . labor in all lawful . . . ways for equal rights as citizens until finally granted.
>
> . . . we appoint [a committee] . . . to Washington to urge upon Congress such legislation as will secure . . . protection to

ourselves of life, liberty, and property . . . granting . . . the right
to testify in the Courts and of equality of suffrage the same as to
white citizens. . . .[12]

President Johnson's reply to a delegation of black leaders in February
1866 dismayed the few blacks who held faith in him. At an exchange of
views in the White House, Johnson claimed to be "a friend of humanity,
and especially the friend of the colored man." He would serve as their
Moses to lead them from bondage to freedom, but he would not lead them
to the ballot box. Their voting power risked their freedom and a race war.
Pledging to government by consent of the governed, he defined that
maxim to mean that white people in each state should resolve the black
suffrage question.

During this "Presidential Reconstruction" no state of the Deep South
allowed Negroes to vote. Mississippi rejected the Thirteenth Amendment,
like Kentucky, fearing it would set Congress to empower the freedmen.
Alabama, Florida, and South Carolina attached riders to their approval.
But the first series of Reconstruction Acts, passed in February, March, and
July, 1867, divided the South into military districts, ordering constitutional
conventions, with Negro suffrage. Radicals also forced the adoption of the
Fifteenth Amendment, binding the South to universal suffrage.[13]

By May, 1868, political furor gathered to impeach Johnson. The
Methodist Episcopal Church, in general conference in Chicago, became
detered from adopting a resolution for an hour of prayer for his conviction
only by an aged member, who reminded ministers of the sanctity of an
oath. Bishop Matthew Simpson side-stepped the issue by calling for an
amendment for an hour of prayer "to save our Senators from error." This
passed unanimously.[14]

President Johnson stood acquitted May 17, and he finished out the
term. Johnson was not nominated for the office in the upcoming election.
The Democrats chose Horatio Seymour, and the Republicans nominated
Ulysses S. Grant. In the 1868 presidential election the Republicans
gained needed support from the South. Without the 450,000 votes of
Negroes for him, Grant could have faced defeat.[15]

The Republicans moved to prevent Southern whites from striking the
equal suffrage measures from the state constitutions, to bar the Negro
vote. The Republicans proposed a constitutional amendment that a
citizen's right to vote should not be denied by a state or national
government because of race or color. Sent to the states in February, 1869,
the measure became ratified on March 30, 1870, as the Fifteenth
Amendment.

Taking the name Conservative, white Southerners resented the Republican-Negro regimes. Southern hostility fed in part on fear of "Negro domination." Seeing former slaves holding high public office and parading in the militia became like wormwood and gall to the taste. A number of conservatives joined secret orders like the White League of Louisiana. They said that the founders of this government intended "that this should be a white man's government, as far as our efforts go, it shall be."[16]

The best known of these covert groups was the Ku Klux Klan. It began in 1865 at Pulaski, Tennessee, as a band of mischief-makers bent on a good time. Yet by the spring of 1867 the Klan became an organized movement, spreading across states, to combat the "Loyal League." The Klan would waylay any Negro who persisted in defying its orders. Some form of corporal punishment struck—whipping, tar-and-feathering, or lynching. This might befall white Republicans or whites who fraternized with Negroes.

Amid the ebb and flow of political currents, the Christian Church faced the problems in Southern reconstruction. But church reserves, like college funds, became drained by the war efforts and the Southern political ruin. Denominational schools closed, publishing houses tried to survive, and church bodies struggled to regain organization. Northern churchmen offered personnel and funds, seeming like political "reconquest." Righteous vengeance so saturated some Northern efforts that bitterness sank deep into the Southern soul. The Northern gauge marked that when "treason" became properly repented of, Southern sin would be forgiven.

Southern whites searched their grief for the meaning of the war. Usually the theological beliefs of the "crusades" sufficed, rooted in "the old-time religion." The learned also believed the assigned categories of judgment and punishment remained enough. Yet the victorious North invoked these with even greater assurance. Even so, the cast-iron grave markers of the Confederate army cried out for divine vindication, with the motto, *Deo Vindice.*

Robert Lewis Dabney (1820-98) became a fervent and articulate theologian of Southern Presbyterianism. A professor before the war, he served as adjutant under General Stonewall Jackson. For nearly two decades, Dabney spoke for his denomination in Virginia and Texas. His views appeared in lectures, sermons, and published works. Dabney believed the war was "caused deliberately" by abolitionists who "with calculated malice" goaded the South to violence to revolutionize the government and "gratify their spite." "I do not forgive," he said of the Northern Presbyterians. "What! forgive those people, who have invaded our country, burned our cities, destroyed our homes, slain our young men, and spread desolation and ruin over our land!" He craved a "retributive Providence" that would destroy the North and smash the Union.[17]

Henry Ward Beecher, a molder of the Northern view, stood moderate compared to Dabney. Beecher counseled compassion for Southerners in general. Yet he issued a strong indictment:

> I charge the whole guilt of this war upon the . . . plotting political leaders of the South . . . God will reveal judgment and arraign these mighty miscreants, . . . and every maimed and wounded sufferer, and every bereaved heart in all . . . of this land, will rise up and come before the Lord to lay upon these chief culprits of modern history their awful witness . . . And then these . . . remorseless traitors, these . . . cultured men with might and wisdom . . . shall be . . . plunged downward forever and ever in an endless retribution.[18]

With Beecher's picture of the Last Judgment, focused on Southern leaders, arose the common view that the region deserved God's wrath. Theodore T. Munger, noted Congregational pastor-theologian of New Haven, combined liberal doctrines of progress with a belief that divine punishment was realized. In his essay on "Providence and the War," written 20 years after Appomattox, Munger explained the "divine logic" which punished the South "for its sins," with the North as the "sacrificing instrument."[19]

Other men sought broader theological grounds for discerning America's ordeal. Unsure about God's purposes, they saw the ambiguity of historical events, and doubted their region's moral purity. These men tried to view the entire tragedy—its triumphs and its defeats—as meaningful for American people as a national whole. They called all Americans first to penitence and reform, and then to reconciliation. One such noted thinker was Northern Congregational minister, Horace Bushnell, Munger's hero.

Bushnell stressed the social nature of human existence. This required an understanding of the war as a single experience of one corporate body. It was a *Volkskrieg*, a people's war, in which the nation purged itself and realized its unity. Through meditation on the nature and meaning of expiation and vicarious sacrifice, as in Christ's crucifixion, he sought to understand the suffering and sacrifice of war. He thought that in both cases, the expiation of corporate sin and guilt opened the way for atonement (at-one-ment). Bushnell wrote his treatise *The Vicarious Sacrifice* as the nation bled in battle. He believed the war could be good in a similar manner that Good Friday was in saving mankind.[20]

Despite a surface healing, the very word "Reconstruction"—referring to the decade right after the Civil War—misstates what took place. The length of the Reconstruction period is indefinite. Some say it lasted from 1865 to the 1890s. Actually it began in 1867 and ended in some states as early as 1870. In all states it ceased by 1877. So-called Reconstruction followed—after 1865 to 1867—a time when the Southern states passed "Black Codes" to annul Lincoln's Emancipation Proclamation in all but name.

Even so, right after the war, it seemed the ex-slaves might now have the fruits of democracy. The United States Congress aided the former slaves by passing laws that granted military control of the South, gave blacks equal rights, and cancelled the power of ex-Confederate leaders. Congress passed the Fourteenth Amendment to the Constitution, (1868), making the former slaves citizens. The Fifteenth Amendment (1870) gave all black men the right to vote.

Blacks began to move into the public arena, and became elected to public office all over the South. Hiram Revels, a Methodist preacher, and Blanche K. Bruce became United States Senators from Mississippi. Pinckney B. S. Pinchback became lieutenant governor of Louisiana. John R. Lynch, a Methodist, Speaker of the House in Mississippi won election to the U.S. House of Representatives. Also blacks served as superintendents of education, treasurers, judges, sheriffs, other local posts, and could join the military.

Rev. Revels, the first black Senator from Mississippi, expressed the feelings of many blacks about what course white Methodists should take to treat newly freed blacks with justice:

> When the Methodist Episcopal Church—our church—during and after the war—turned her attention to the . . . poor and ignorant colored people of the south, I greatly rejoiced . . . about four millions of human beings, emerged from slavery . . . and knowing . . . they never could be . . . useful citizens, without . . . literary, moral and religious instruction; she chose the southern states as a part of . . . future operations, and sent some of her ablest ministers to her new work, . . . there are in Mississippi and other southern states hundreds of regularly organized . . . churches, in which thousands of colored people . . . worship God, and receive . . . instruction from preachers . . . advancing in mental culture . . . [21]

After the Civil War, racial bias persisted in all areas of American cultural and social life—even the church. Two-thirds of the black members of the Methodist Episcopal Church, South, left during 1860-1866. They joined the African Methodist Episcopal Church, the African Methodist Episcopal Zion Church, or churches organized from the mostly white Methodist Episcopal churches. Black Methodists in the South, like their Northern brethren in pre-Civil War years, learned that justice could best be obtained through organizations in which they had a strong voice.[22]

Meanwhile, the American Baptist Missionary Convention faced trouble. The convention leaders sought to make a missionary of every pastor in the South and a mission station of every Negro church, no matter its age, or strength. The convention made other attempts to bring every church and pastor under the new structure's control. The group wanted the American Baptist Home Mission Society (white) to accept them as a distributing agent for their funds in the South. This was bitterly refused.[23]

Rev. R. L. Perry reports: "At their twenty-sixth Anniversary at Richmond, Alabama, August, 1866, this body united with the Northwestern Convention." Named the "Consolidated American Baptist Missionary Convention," they worked mostly in the South. Diverse opinions occurred on management and jurisdiction at Richmond in 1876, setting the stage for future disruption.[24]

The Consolidated American Baptist Missionary Convention, organized in 1866, united the efforts of most Negroes in all sections of the country. In the annual meeting held in New York City, November, 1876, the report shows that 46 schools were aided and 18 new schools became organized with over 500 baptisms. Delegates came from Pennsylvania, New Jersey, Connecticut, New York, North Carolina, South Carolina, Georgia, Florida, Alabama, Mississippi, Louisiana, Texas, Arkansas, and Kansas.[25]

However, 1876, the nation's centennial year, witnessed both a tumultuous celebration and the great sellout of Reconstruction. So-called reconciliationism prevailed; the freedman pursued his own rueful efforts alone. The country's "moment of truth" regarding the racist issue became defered for another century. Lincoln's Union of an "almost chosen people"—made "more perfect" in the Constitution and given a new birth in the agonies of war—taking the moral burden assigned by the Almighty—faced abortion.

From 1865 to 1872, the Freedman's Bureau became the federal government's answer to the question: "What's to be done with the Negro?" The bureau mediated between the former master and ex-slave, providing medical aid, education, and work training. Even before the war ended, many major denominations assisted freed persons with food and clothing. Churches set up Sunday Schools, other schools, and orphanages, augmenting the government's work.

Official policy called for integrated schools, but that varied in local cases. Missionary teachers instructed poor whites as well as blacks. A clash occurred in Beaufort, North Carolina, because H. S. Beals, an educational officer of the American Missionary Association, held a separate school for poor whites. A co-worker opposed it. Beals defended such schools; he thought they adapted to white feelings and to the urgency to educate any child, white or black, who came to them. He warned that to integrate the white school would "scatter that school in a day."

> We are right, but the . . . sentiment of the white people *here*, is *wrong*. Shall we . . . convert them . . . before we give them what . . . will secure that conversion . . . poor white children are crying out for this life giving influence. Is it our . . . principle, to hold this multitude, clamoring for intellectual light . . . . till we force them to adopt our ideas?[26]

In 1867 the South was the only settled section of the nation without a public school system. Only wealthy whites got even an elementary education. Reconstruction governments founded the first Southern public schools. Northern churches, benefactors, and the Freedman's Bureau helped with funds for the Reconstruction state legislatures. Yet when plantation owners were taxed for education, they called it "stealing." Many teachers came from the North, with various single women enlisted by churches and missionary societies.

Most Northern teachers acted by religious or humanitarian desires to uplift the Negroes and to rebuild Southern society. A Freedman's Bureau inspector depicts them as "a band of missionaries who have come from the Christian homes of the land—following the example of the Divine Master—going about doing good."[27]

Many Yankee teachers urged the Negroes to demand the rights of free men. A courageous Quaker, Cornelia Hancock, strove against the "violent rebels" of South Carolina. She accused President Johnson of shielding the "secesh" (secessionists) from punishment, and flayed the Freedmen's Bureau for grants to untrue Southerners. She demanded that Negroes be given the franchise to vote and hold office, and protected.[28]

Southerners soon rejected the Northern teachers as tenants. Any family that offered them shelter faced the threat of being burned out. The teachers had to live in public buildings and churches. Even churches rebuffed them, and storekeepers refused to sell them food or raised the prices. On the streets, teachers often faced insults. Some Lexington, Virginia, college students called a missionary teacher that "damned Yankee bitch of a nigger teacher." Mobs like the Ku Klux Klan, attacked the freedman's mentors, whipped many, coating some with tar and cotton.[29]

In the presidential campaign of 1868, the abuse of teachers increased. After the Radical victory of that year, Southerners began to terrorize the missionaries. Maria Waterbury had to use a railway car in Jackson, Tennessee, moving it as a fortress from district to district. In North Carolina, teachers had "as much to undergo, as if they were in Turkey." One night in Bastrop County, Texas, terrorists dragged a teacher from his home, tied him to a tree, and whipped him severely. His schoolhouse was burned.[30]

By 1870 most of the Northern teachers had left the South, working until the Radical governments could begin free public school systems. The missionary teachers' schools had enrolled only a small portion of the Negroes during a brief time. But they began the education of freedmen, as a nucleus to develop a colored public school system, and founded a number of colleges. These became the chief source for Negro professionals, especially teachers.[31]

The most active church agency for freedmen became the American Missionary Association. It began at Albany, New York, in 1846 as some small Congregational church societies merged. Their missionary pledge to nonwhite peoples had a strong antislavery mood. By 1860 its 112 abolitionist home missionaries outnumbered its workers abroad. At the war's end, 528 missionaries and teachers lived in the South. After the war the AMA helped to found and staff schools in the South. They raised funds to aid thousands of teachers and administrators working among the Southern blacks.

Right after the war, the American Missionary Association, backed mostly by Congregationalists, started important industrial and agricultural schools in the South. By 1870 some 20 schools, including major institutions like Fisk (Tennessee) and Hampton (Virginia), became founded by this group alone. The Freedman's Aid Society (Methodist) and the American Baptist Home Mission Board also financed increased educational opportunities for the Negro.

With the Radical rise, the issue of mixed schools fired debate in every Southern state. Alabama's Radical constitution called for schools that all children could attend free. The legislature in 1870 decreed separate schools unless parents approved integration. The Arkansas convention ruled that all children should have free instruction, and the legislature set a "separate but equal" school law. The Georgia convention declared free education for all children; the legislature decreed "separate but equal" schools. The 1870 Mississippi legislature opened schools to all youth, without distinction. Officials construed the law to allow separate schools with "equal advantages." In Louisiana, segregated public schools became banned, but only a few became really integrated.[32]

In 1873, Mrs. Jennie Culver Hartzell, wife of the presiding elder of the New Orleans District of the Methodist Episcopal Church, South, met the plight of black women there. She formed programs for women in all 15 black churches around New Orleans. She sent "women missionaries into . . . [their] homes . . . meetings for mothers and young women, train . . . for Sunday School work, give religious instruction; teach . . . home industries, urge attendance upon Church and . . . lead all to Christ as their Saviour."[33]

Further efforts progressed to organize more work on behalf of the women. After the adjournment of the 1880 General Conference in Cincinnati, June 8, 50 women met to hear Mrs. Hartzell's plea to create a women's home missionary society. A constitution for such a society stood adopted July 10, 1880. Its purpose was: " . . . to enlist and organize the efforts of Christian woman in behalf of the needy . . . women and children of all sections of our country without distinction of race, and to co-operate with the other . . . agencies of the Church in educational and missionary work."[34]

During the whole period of Reconstruction, Northern Protestant churches bolstered the Radical program. When the conflict ceased they became the main moral support for the political leaders who pledged to prevent any compromise with the South. This involved the churches in the Republican strategies to prevent or delay the rise of a politically strong South. Yet, the freedmen's great needs and resolve to reform the South best explain why churches made Reconstruction a continuation of the antislavery crusade. A potent church paper, the *Independent* of New York, challenged its 70,000 subscribers: "These venomous [Southern] masters should be put under tutors and governors till the time appointed. A freedman's bureau is less needed than a rebel's bureau."[35]

The racial impasse that aroused armed conflict also prevented a just reconstruction. A unique time of testing found the nation wanting in wisdom and integrity. Like it or not, this "tragic era" is of great importance to the moral and religious history of the American people.

Many historians have been apologetic and evasive in treating the period, with its more recent ramifications. The mind-set of *status quo* was the ultimate winner of the Civil War.

Common church-historical accounts, as well as the political historiography on the era, need truthful changes. The prevailing explanation in both cases is twisted because it was shaped amid a resurgence of crusading "Anglo-Saxonism" during the turn-of-the-century decades. Northern Protestant historians stood devoted to temperance, Sabbatarianism, nativism, and immigration restriction. They became swamped by the same concerns that Kenneth Stampp ascribes to the historical profession generally. Their basic views on ethnic and racial issues "were *precisely* the ones that southern white men had been making about Negroes for years. And . . . the old middle classes of the North looked with new understanding upon the problems of the beleaguered white men of the South."[36]

The Grand Old Party saw that social structures, old folkways, and the legacy of slavery could not be changed by governmental fiat or by mere civil servants. Despite the ruin and despair, agrarian recovery and industrial advance occurred. The Bureau of Refugees, Freedmen, and Abandoned Lands, begun in 1865, won over President Johnson's veto (1866), failed the freedman's hope to get "abandoned lands." Like other noble plans, the Bureau became a victim of political meddling, weak leadership, and racist surmises.

The 25,000 troops assigned to control the South—and guard the Mexican border—did not halt the Klan attacks. No courts convicted the Klan members who killed many skilled Negro leaders. "We are in the hands of murderers," wrote 300 Vicksburg voters in 1875, "They say they will carry this election either by ballot or bullet." After the massacre of 30 Negroes at Meridian, Mississippi in 1871, Congress passed a law to end the Ku Klux Klan menace. Other groups sprang up to take the Klan's place.[37]

More serious matters assailed the Reconstruction governments. They faced charges of fraud and misuse of public funds. Corrupt officials defiled all levels of government: city, state, and federal. This "Tragic Era" saw the Credit Mobilier scandal, the Whiskey Ring, the salary grab, and the Tweed Ring. In New York City during 1867, the Tweed Ring stole $100 million from the city government. Meanwhile, members of President Grant's Cabinet fled the country to escape prosecution for the misuse of public funds.

Social and political problems arose so fast in the North the Reconstruction became a task that was "let go." Both political parties repudiated the graft of "Grantism" at their conventions in 1876. They nominated two moral presidential candidates. The democrat, Samuel J. Tilden, became cleared of a Tweed ring link. Former major-general Rutherford B. Hayes, the Republican, used Ohio's anti-Catholicism while running for governor there.

Hayes stood named as president, in a disputed election, over Tilden by one electoral vote. For accepting the "whisker-win," Hayes promised his rival that he would stop troubling the South about blacks, withdraw the Federal troops, and permit the South to deal with the "Negro" problem on their own terms. These moves brought the compromise of 1877, breaking the promises of emancipation, which soured the fruits of Reconstruction.

An important church-historical corollary applied to Stampp's previous observation. The churches remained the major institutional context in which the antislavery impulse could thrive during the war and Reconstruction. By the time of the war with Spain (1898), all zeal for reform cooled. Strangely, the social gospel almost forgot the South and the freedmen. This happened despite its debt both in method and theory to the antislavery movement. The plight of blacks became its worst in the "Progressive Era."[38]

Gradually, the size of the task, the hostility of Southern whites, and the loss of fervor among leaders of the church agencies curtailed many projects. This trend increased as the Freedmen's Bureau waned, ending official reconstruction in 1877. Then, some Supreme Court rulings in 1883 made crucial sections of the Civil Rights Act of 1875 unconstitutional. It ruled the Fourteenth Amendment forbade states, not individuals, from discriminating.

While blacks lost that mandate support, schools such as Lincoln University in Pennsylvania, Morehouse College and Atlanta University in Georgia, Talladega College in Alabama, Tougaloo University in Mississippi, Hampton Institute in Virginia, and Fisk University in Tennessee, survived. These all became founded or financed by the churches. Prior to 1900, most of "the faculty members of Southern Negro colleges were idealistic educational missionaries who had been educated in Northern colleges."[39]

The South went its own religious way; the chief new church progress in this era meant neither reconquest nor reunion of the estranged regions. Rather, it meant the growth of Negro churches, mostly Baptist or Methodist. These churches became vital during Reconstruction when the Federal army, the Freedman's Bureau, and the Union Leagues used them to brace Radical Republican power. After 1877 they yielded to the "Southern solution" (segregation, subservience and tenantry), not becoming a "radical" social force until the 1950s. By later 19th century gains, such churches formed a distinct religious ethos which historic denominational loyalty could not submerge or alter. For over a century the black churches survived as chief bearers of the African-American heritage.

Facing the shame of slavery, the toll of war, and the snarls of Reconstruction, churches thrived within the Negro community. The Negro church, legal before the Negro family, surpassed local business. During the 19th century the church connection of blacks increased from 5 percent to 30 percent of the people. The church became a house of worship, a social and educational center, and the ministry offered the Negro his best professional chance. To the thousands in the pews, churches gave security, status, and spiritual food. The God of Abraham, Isaac, and Jacob had rescued them from Egypt's bondage.[40]

Yet, their full inheritance in the Promised Land became far removed. Over a century after Appomattox brought freedom, the mournful splendor of the Negro spiritual remains.

> Deep river, my home is over Jordan,
> Deep river, Lord, I want to cross over into camp-ground
> O don't you want to go to that gospel feast,
> To that promised land, where all is peace?
> Lord, I want to cross over into camp-ground.[41]

Chapter 9

Postwar Churches: Religion, Science, and Racism

Appalled at the ignorance and moral incapacity of the "black race," Protestant Episcopal Bishop T. U. Dudley, of the Kentucky Diocese, declared in an 1885 issue of *Century Magazine:*

> Instinct and reason, history and philosophy, science and revelation, all alike cry out against the degradation of the race by the free comingling of the tribe which is highest with that which is lowest on the scale of development. The process of selection which nature indicates as the method of most rapid process indignantly refuses to be thus set at naught.[1]

Dudley's words reveal the manner in which society, both North and South, religious and secular, kept seeking a suitable solution to the "race" issue. Managing logic, the new insights of science became used to bolster the *status quo.*

From the Second Awakening (1790s) to the war with Spain (1898) was a century of an "ordeal of faith" for churchgoing America. The religious impulse known as "liberalism" spanned the century. Ideas of academic liberty faced the social, moral, ecclesiastical, and theological issues in the Civil War and its aftermath. Liberalism like Dudley's so dealt with the issues that its advance seemed gradual. Yet, viewed as a whole, liberal theology stood as an intellectual movement that affected all of American life.

The so-called "golden age" of liberalism was not golden for everyone. A profound social change put the traditional content of biblical preaching and teaching under duress. With these problems were the intellectual hurdles provoked by scientific discoveries, critical religious scholarship, and shifts in moral and religious attitudes. New disputes arose from increased scientific certitude and the critical examination of Christian biblical beliefs.

As Charles Darwin's *Orgin of Species* burst upon world thought in 1859 his evoutionary concepts gripped the minds of many people. Already contrary views flared among Christians as to whether Scripture condemned or condoned slavery. Various church groups split over that issue. Historical research posed basic questions about the Bible, the history of doctrine, and the world religions. Darwin's theory of evolution through natural selection became the century's principal idea. In 1871 he published *The Descent of Man,* including the human species within the same general hypothesis.

Rising positivistic naturalism challenged Christian thought, pressing for modern methods to acquire knowledge. From physics to biblical criticism, myth and error began to be dispelled. Forget what to do about the Negro problem. Are all moral standards and religious beliefs only behavioral changes of mankind—the most astute of vertebrates? Are the Bible, Christian faith, and the Church to be understood as existing only in history? Such issues moved some alleged Christians to adopt the unbiblical solutions of romantic subjectivism and idealistic pantheism to keep their faith.

The issue of the Bible's infallibility loomed large. Contrary views set the "fundadmentalists" against the liberal "modernists." Many Christians tried to admit both the Bible and science without denouncing either. Transcendentalism was one such religion. This "Free Religion" movement gained continuity through its impact on Unitarian tradition. Former Unitarian Theodore Parker became Transcendentalism's hero-martyr in 1860.

Many Christians opposed Parker's accepting German critical studies of the "historical Jesus," and his claim that Christianity did not rely on Jesus Christ's actual existence. The crucial issue was biblical authority. In 1853 the Unitarian Association's executive committee, "in a denominational capacity," removed itself from the errors of Transcendentalism. The committee declared its faith in "the Divine origin, the Divine authority, [and] the Divine sanctions of the religion of Jesus Christ."[2]

From 1865 to 1872 the Parkerites became excluded from the newly formed National Unitarian Conference. After 1887 many of them joined the Free Religious Association, with a properly Unitarian stand, and they adopted evolutionary doctrines and Social Darwinianism. It was a continuation of the *laissez-faire* (do nothing) movement after it adopted the Darwinian phrasing of "struggle for existence" and "survival of the fittest." By 1885 the theological faculty at Harvard was of their persuasion.

Members of the Free Religious Association, at their first convention in Boston in 1867, elected Octavius Brooks Frothingham (1822-95) as president. The movement acquired a semioffical weekly journal when Francis Ellingwood Abbot founded the *Index* two years later. Abbot

(1836-1903) graduated from Harvard in 1859. While there, and later as a Unitarian minister in Dover, New Hampshire, his rationalistic and antiauthoritarian "scientific theism" took form. Abbot is veiwed as the first American theologian to develop a system of religious thought in accord with Darwinian evolution.[3]

The decade of the 1870s contained harsh interfaith controversy on the church-state question. Abbot's target was the evangelical National Reform Assocation that began work toward a new Christian preamble to the federal Constitution. Robert G. Ingersoll (1833-99), whom Abbott called "the Dwight L. Moody of Free Religion," became a scourge of churches. Though the son of a minister, he devoted his mature life to agnosticism. People paid to hear his attacks on the clergy, the Bible, and the Christian faith. By 1880 he became known as the nation's most outspoken infidel.

The *Independent,* a religious paper with over 6,000 clergy subscribers, also regarded evolution. Its review of *The Origin of Species* inferred that the book moved the Creator from "the animated universe," but noted its ample scientific material. The book stood for "the careful study of theologians" and scientists. By the late 1860s attempts to square evolution with Scripture arose. If "the Bible does not assert that species were created distinct by an authoritative fiat we may be allowed to hear . . . the speculations of zoologists," said a writer.[4] By 1880 the *Independent* reversed itself and published polemics on behalf of evolution.[5]

Two decades after the introduction of Darwinianism, changes occurred among some conservative periodicals.[6] The *New Englander,* an important forum of Yankee clergymen which first charged Darwin with reviving "an old, exploded theory," in an 1883 article, granted the frenzy of some Christian apologists. "A fresh source of conviction," claimed the writer, "is opened to our anticipations of immortality. It is . . . inconsistency for an evolutionist to deny the probablity of a higher future life."[7]

After 1869 the full impact of Darwinianism struck American churches. At first most clergy failed to grasp the dramatic change in world view that evolutionary theory proposed. During the 18th century, Western Christendom pondered the Enlightenment, including Newtonian physics, rationalism, and deism. But the firmament was made to declare the glory of God. Since all creation originated as a hymn to God's gracious rule, the natural religion of the philosophes found lodging in even the revivalistic evangelical theologies. Any Christian could see God's marvelous handiwork.

From Darwin, nature revealed a war of mankind struggling for existence not only against insects, but against other people, other human races. The fittest triumphed. As resistance to evolutionary beliefs arose, Unitarians, avowing the goodness and dignity of man, stood with conservatives. Charles Hodge, of Princeton Seminary, wrote an orthodox denial. His *What Is Darwinianism?* (1874) named the essential factor, natural selection, and denied it stood for a variance to belief in an omnipotent, omniscient Creator. Hodge declared Christians must regard scientific facts in some other way.

Puritanism was the major factor in America's moral, religious heritage. The Church's concern shaped society. The Second Great Awakening and the "theocratic" revival campaigns of the Evangelical United Front renewed this goal. Antebellum revivalism became roused for social reform and for sanctified citizens, so this republic was a model for the whole world. Lyman Beecher and Charles Finney so held this vision that they agreed to the "new measures" in revivalism. Unitarians and Transcendentalists also had a reforming spirit. In the 19th century, teachers of Christian morals and political economy in American colleges and universities taught that social, economic, and political theory rightly adjoined Christian ethics. The social gospel reaffirmed this.

Abolitionism, with its hymns, slogans, and prophetic zeal, was a crucial prelude to the Social Gospel. Both held a desire to harness the churches and a mood to put every other interest of the church under the great national issue of the day. The line from abolitionists Theodore Weld and Elijah Lovejoy to social gospelers Washington Gladden and Walter Rauschenbusch should be noted.

Liberalism prompted complacency and self-satisfaction among the socially conservative classes of people. For many, the "golden age" became, as one calls it, the "Age of Excess." The social gospel arose as a prophetic impulse to the public, becoming a powerful minority in the early 1920s. Yet its intradenominational battles became often bitter and futile. Social gospelers usually stood with theological liberals, but the reverse did not hold true.

The social gospel faced the American's basic contempt for poverty. This "hard shell of sanctified realism," fostered by the Puritan ethic, embraced both its pious and secularized forms. Such an attitude did not stem from the ancient theory that some poverty was inevitable, or from the idea of a Great Chain of Being that made lowly people a basic element to the Creation. The Puritan doctrine of work evaded a static exegesis of the Lord's words, "The poor you will always have with you"

(Matt. 26:11). Since God called no one to mendicancy or idleness, those who begged and did not work either now suffered or should be punished for their sins.

In the 1870s Henry Ward Beecher, amid the complex urban surroundings of New York, made that proposition axiomatic:

> Looking . . . through city . . . village and country, the general truth will stand, that no man in this land suffers from poverty unless it be . . . his *sin*. . . . there is enough . . . if men have not enough, it is . . . the want of provident care, and foresight, and industry, and frugality, and wise saving.[8]

In this gilded age of industry Social Darwinianism gave the stock ideas of the Puritan ethic added force and "scientific" support. Herbert Spencer declared Darwinian theories brought development to human societies, and became known as the founder of Social Darwinianism. In the United States he won over William Graham Sumner, the Broad Church Episcopal minister of Morristown, New Jersey. In 1872 Sumner left the pulpit to teach at Yale, where he exchanged liberal Christianity for conservative Spencerism. Sumner's evolutionary determinism viewed any hope for mankind only through a work-confirmed moralism and the evolutionary process.

William Sumner was a political economist of strong *laissez-faire* concepts before he became a sociologist. On the political side Sumner advocated Social Darwinianism and was a conservative. On the scientific side, he believed that folkways and mores gave societies stability, also making social change hard to achieve. His desires for the *status quo* led him to say that no attempt should be made to change the folkways and mores.[9]

Sumner swayed social science concepts on Southern problems, specially the Negro issue. The "folkways and mores" theory spread from the scientists became in Southern educated classes a political *credo*. The description of something as "folkways" or "mores," or the stereotype that "stateways cannot change folkways," became used in Southern literature on the Negro as a formula of mystical importance. It appeared couched whenever a precept claimed that "what is, must be" without giving full, factual reasons.[10]

William Sumner further declared:

> . . . we cannot go outside of this alternative: liberty, inequality, survival of the fittest; not-liberty, equality, survival of the unfittest. The former carries society forward and favors all of its

best members; the latter carries society downwards and favors all its worst members.

Thus people's optimism defied the realities of social struggle. Human "natural rights" were not in nature; their humanitarianism, democracy, and equality were not eternal verities. They were only the passing mores of a stage of social evolution. Sumner preached the predestination of the social order and the salvation of the economically elect through the survival of the fittest.[11]

By 1901 William Lawrence, the Episcopal bishop of Massachusetts, said: "Godliness is in league with riches."[12] The "gospel of wealth" became two "positive principles:" "that man, when he is strong, conquers Nature," and that "in the long run, it is only to the man of morality that wealth comes." Beyond this lay "the privilege of grateful service" and Christ's "precepts on the stewardship of wealth."[13] Only as people called this attitude into question did American Protestantism produce the social gospel.

The creed of competitive individualism merged into Social Darwinianism. Since social progress and individual justice consist in the *bellum omnium contra omnes,* —the law of the tooth and claw— it meant an endless war to find the survival of the fittest. This creed condoned a merchant trying to crush a competitor or to exploit wage earners and consumers. For every businessman who cited "the survival of the fittest," perhaps 10 others confirmed their style by talking about the "right to manage."

Liberal theologians claimed that many advocates of evolution, like Joseph Leconte; James Dwight Dana, American geologist; and James McCosh, president of Princeton University and the semi-official voice of American Presbyterianism, stood as Christian men. They became personal symbols of adapting religion and science. Darwin and Spencer brought Congregationalist Henry Ward Beecher, a ranking American preacher, into the evolutionary fold. Through Beecher's *Christian Union,* a circulation of 100,000, and the *Outlook,* edited by Lyman Abbott, his successor at Plymouth Church, the tolerant bias of Beecher's new theology became widespread.

Beecher's main method to square the Christian religion and science was to discern between the science of theology and the art of religion. Theology would be corrected, enlarged, and freed by evolution. Yet religion, as a spiritual force in human character, remained. "A cordial Christian evolutionist," Beecher resolved the design problem with business idioms, such as "design by wholesale is grander than design by retail."[14]

Lyman Abbott (1835-1922), and Beecher, denied the traditional concept of sin, which shamed God as well as mankind. Abbott's evolutionary view saw immoral acts as a lapse into animality. Sin was odious, but the libel on God implied in original sin dogma would not be.[15] Abbott's book, *The Evolution of Christianity* (1892), held that "in the spiritual, as in the physical, God is the secret and source of light." It inferred the evolution of the Bible, the Church, Christian society, and the Soul.[16]

By the 1880s religion had to share its traditional authority with science, both physical and social. American religious thought became greatly secularized. Churches adapted evolution, and few renowned Protestant theologians disputed it. Some put evolution into divine purpose, and deft preachers imbued Christianity with this authoritative concept from science. Old foes joined to resist any pessimism about the promise of American life. Ministers said that American atheism had not produced one "champion of . . . national reputation."[17] (Ingersol was an agnostic).

Phillips Brooks, rector of the Boston Trinity Episcopal Church, explained, "The spirit that cries *'Credo quia impossibile,'* the herioc spirit of faith, is too deep in human nature for any one century to eradicate it."[18] Like Beecher told his Plymouth Church congregation, "The moral structure of the human mind is such that it must have religion." He continued:

It must have supersitition, or . . . intelligent religion. It is just as necessary to men as reason is, as imagination is, as hope and desire are. Religious yearning is part . . . of the human composition. And when you have taken down any theologic structure . . . man would still be a religious animal, would . . . go about and construct some religious system for himself.[19]

Most people of this "Gilded Age" agreed with such sentiments.

While evolution became favorably received among the ministers and members of the liberal Protestant churches, many devout persons, Protestant and Catholic, remained unmoved by Darwinianism. Perhaps the most popular religious leader of the "Gilded Age" was Evangelist Dwight L. Moody. Most of his followers either ignored or denied the validity of the troublesome questions raised by the new science. The resolve of Christian fundamentalism into the 20th century signaled an incomplete Darwinian conquest.

During the Civil War Moody worked in the Northern army camps as an agent of the Christian Commission, giving aid to the wounded and guidance to the confused. After the war, he returned to the Chicago slums to direct relief and found missions. His reputation for advancing the Christian cause spread through the Young Men's Christian Association. While in England on business for the YMCA in 1872, they asked Moody to preach in London. From 1873-75, some 4 million people heard him preach. In 1875, after his successful evangelistic meetings in Great Britain, Moody returned to America.

D. L. Moody's revival circuit in America ran from Brooklyn to Philadelphia, from New York to St. Louis, and to the Pacific coast. His message was a simple blend of American optimism and evangelical Arminianism. Raising his Bible, he told people that eternal life was theirs for the asking—to "come forward and t-a-k-e, TAKE!" To those who came, his guidance quickly moved to the point: "Join some church at once." Which church didn't matter. This simple gospel and approach changed the lives of many across the country.[20]

Since his hearers shared no common religious training or intellect, Moody wanted "teachers who shall teach and show what the gospel is." In 1879 he founded a school for girls near his old home at Northfield, Massachusetts; the Mount Hermon School for boys opened two years later. In 1889 he turned Chicago's Evangelization Society into a coeducational religious school, later known as Moody Bible Institute. From such centers, his revival campaigns, and his supporters, Moody's name and message became widespread.[21]

Harper's Weekly said of Moody in the crisis year of 1896: "He is the enemy of sectionalism and all hostility of class to class. His mission is to arouse the conscience and awaken the spiritual side of men, to make them patient, long suffering, dilligent."[22]

D. L. Moody's gospel preaching focused on God's saving act in Jesus Christ, to convert and save the sinner. The Church was only a fellowship of the saved. Persons being saved improved public morality. Yet Moody's message did not reach those vexed by the moral problems of industrialism, racism, or the rational dilemmas of the closing century. He believed that individual conversions would solve every personal and social issue. Charitable works also reached needy people with God's Word of salvation.

Another noted evangelist traveled nationwide within the same time-frame. Like Moody, Samuel Porter Jones lacked education. The Civil War interrupted his schooling, and he never went to college. Yet he became admitted to practice law in 1868, at age 21. Jones was converted and delivered from drink by the dying testimony of his father and the preaching ministry of his grandfather.

Called to preach in 1872, Samuel P. Jones became ordained an elder of the Methodist Episcopal Church, South, in 1876, by Bishop George F. Pierce. Baptists, Presbyterians, and Congregationalists also supported Sam Jones in city campaigns led by the Ministerial Alliance. His revival circuit ran from his home state of Georgia across the South, to the Pacific Coast—Los Angeles, Sacramento, and San Francisco. He preached in New England—Brooklyn, Boston, and Baltimore; the Midwest—Toledo, Cincinnati, Indianapolis, Chicago, Minneapolis, Omaha, Kansas City, and St. Louis.[23]

Mrs. Laura Jones said her husband preached to the colored people nearly everywhere he went. She described Houston as one of the greatest of such meetings. "He talked to them in a very plain, practical way, creating wonderful enthusiasm, and presenting the truths that they should know, in a way that the humblest and most ignorant colored person could understand."[24] He then urged them to live sober lives, to be true in their homes and look to Jesus Christ as their only hope now and hereafter. Jones gave Negroes thousands of dollars for building their churches and schools.[25]

Until his death in 1906, Sam Jones evangelized for 25 years, fighting the liquor industry, saloons, theaters, gambling, and Sabbath-breaking. His Scripture-based sermons offered salvation through Jesus Christ. Christianity required more than church membership; one must turn from sinning to righteous living. Yet facing the subjection of blacks, he said the Christian gospel was their only hope—not politics. Any hope for betterment rested on personal Christian morality—both black and white.

Preserving Sunday as a day of worship and rest became a major crusade. Violating its observance attacked the crowded city, the factory, and the witless immigrant as ruining "the very foundations of public morality and private virtue." Opposing such, pietist churches faced the assault of Sunday newspapers, Sunday sports, and all Sunday business. Conservative churches supported labor's struggle for a six-day work week, hoping that religion could better find a place with rest and relaxation. Rev. Josiah Strong, Congregationalist minister, declared, "there is . . . no better index of general morality than Sabbath observance."[26]

Strong held faith in universal progress (both material and moral), and in the future of the Anglo-Saxon race. Speaking for the Evangelical Alliance, Strong joined his stake in urban problems and home missions, urging the nation to Anglo-Saxonize mankind. "My plea is not, Save America for America's sake, but, Save America for the world's sake."[27]

By 1898 such thinking provided a pious major premise for the logic of a war with Spain. It also moved America into the world's commercial and political affairs.

After the Civil War, American fears of subversion turned against the Southern "Redeemers" rather than against Catholics and foreigners. The Gilded Age quaked at growing immigration and the gathering of untrained minorities (specially blacks) in the cities. This caused an upsurge of nativism. Three reasons relate why the new forms of countersubversion were often less theological and more crassly racist: (1) As the old Puritan roots of antipopery were supplanted by cultural compromises and liberal theology, nativism's doctrinal intention became a function of folk Protestantism or secular prejudice. (2) The influx of evolutionary thought added scientific support to ideas of "Nordic" superiority. Such changes pushed Northern racial attitudes closer to those formed earlier in the South. (3) Acceptance of Jim Crow laws against blacks joined a growing consensus as to the "errors" of radical Reconstruction.[28]

This rise of Anglo-Saxon racial pride, hostility and fear prompted diverse acts. America's "idigenous foreigners," the Indians were among the first under the "white man's" power. Then there came more than 4 million Negroes, most of whom were freed slaves. Though most stayed in the South, frightening numbers moved North. Proslavery theorists predicted that without the healthful control of slavery, African-Americans would not long survive.

Meanwhile, Rev. D. Clay Lilly urged his fellow Southerners to recall the lesson of history that their Negroes were mere children. They labored well for others under humane discipline but failed to meet the serious duties imposed on them by freedom.[29] Because of fundamentalist beliefs, Southerners looked for arguments grounded in religion to support slavery. They sought divine favor for racist views, and looked for the will of God behind "the voice of Nature." Thus, Senator Garrett Davis of Kentucky declared that "the great God who created all races never intended the negro, the lowest," to have equal power with the highest, the white race.[30]

These concepts impacted church congregations in both the South and the North. If God had made the races unequal, then rancor toward the Negro was an "instinct of manhood, the elevation of the soul, the pride and dignity of race which God Almighty has implanted in the breast of every reasonable creature."[31] Since the law of nature and God's law declared and determined it, Negroes must work as bootblacks, cooks, farmhands—as mere laborers.

Leaders later urged common schools to prepare colored people for proper entry of their duties as citizens. Rev. Edgar Gardner Murphy, for example, favored Negro education because an ignorant class "cannot exist in a popular government without finally bringing it to disorder, distress, and ruin." He further stated:

> . . . there comes the danger of political disintegration among the whites, and a consequent disposition to call in the Negro vote as umpire. Shall we keep him in the condition which best fits him to follow vile leaders, . . . to bad government; or shall we guard against that day by educating him enough to make him amenable to the influence of reason and right?[32]

Southerners had routinely adjusted the idea of white supremacy *laissez faire* economic doctrine. The ideology of white supremacy and the social order of which it was both a cause and result became fully developed around 1900. White men being superior, gave them the right to rule blacks, creating the caste system as a successor to slavery. In the North or South, white command over resources led to command over persons; command over persons led to command over resources. Likewise, with political power came control over social and economic policy. Controlling social and economic policy gave whites a monopoly of political power.

Christianity sometimes moved against the social order, but from 1900 clergymen generally absolved the "Southern way of life." They refined the system by critcizing cases of individual cruelty and by urging their congregations to deal fairly with black people. They said whites should give openings to blacks, but Providence required segregation in church, school, and society, with political supremacy for whites. Yet their program to improve the lot of Negroes did not include one iota of social equality.

Churchmen saw support for a type of white supremacy in the apostle Paul's charge to the servant to be obedient to his master. No precise reproof of caste in the New Testament showed that this institution conformed with Christianity. Also, they said, Christ never cried out against slavery, then brutally practiced in the Roman empire. The long tradition of placid dualism between divine and secular law made caste systems acceptable within the natural order of fallen human nature. Evolutionary concepts also backed the humanism that emerged among materialists and atheists of the Enlightenment. So, when the clergy condemned unkindness and lack of love by any person to another, black or white, they were not condemning the social order. Many Christian

Southerners felt right in both believing in slavery, and in the post-Civil War caste society. Brotherly love did not mean equality for all mankind.

From 1900 until after World War II Negroes received little hope from white churches in the South. Their racial dogma offered little valid reason, much emotion, and used group images that kept a fixed social distance. In 1914, Dr. Thomas Pearce Bailey, onetime dean of the Department of Education at the University of Mississippi, gave as a scientific study, the Southern orthodoxy affecting the Negro. This race attitude was "not so much a code of cases as . . . a part of their morality and of their religion."

In his book, *Race Orthodoxy in the South and Other Aspects of the Negro Question,* Bailey summarizes this creed: [33]

Blood will tell.
The white race must dominate.
The Teutonic peoples stand for race purity.
The negro is inferior and will remain so.
This is a white man's country.
No social equality.
No Political equality.

In matters of civil rights and legal adjustments give the white man, . . . the benefit of the doubt, and under no circumstances interfere with the prestige of the white race.

Let there be such industrial education of the negro as will best fit him to serve the white man.

Only southerners understand the negro question.

The status of peasantry is all the negro may hope for, if the races are to live together in peace.

The foregoing statements indicate the leadings of Providence.

Meanwhile a kindred spirit coursed through the Northern churches. It stemmed from a different base, but produced similar results, feeding on religious impulses. In 1881 the American Board of Foreign Missions declared: "That which is good for communities in America is good for the Armenians and Greeks and Mohammedans of Turkey." Josiah Strong spread similar ideas in 1885, as secretary of the American Home Missionary Society in Ohio. In his book, *Our Country,* Strong declared Anglo-Saxons above all other races were champions of "a pure spiritual Christianity." The Anglo-Saxon was schooled for "the final competition of races," in spreading his civilization worldwide. "And can anyone doubt that the result of this competition of races will be the 'survival of the fittest'?"[34]

Religious faiths became stirred by the social gospel preached by men like Jewish Rabbi Stephen S. Wise and Washington Gladden, a Congregational minister. Besides his pastoral duties, Gladden served on the Columbus, Ohio, city council. In 1903, he declared that industrial education for Negroes was not enough, that they should be given higher education equal to the whites. The time approached, he hoped, "when the Christian church will be able to discern and declare that simple truth that Religion is nothing but Friendship; friendship with God and with men."[35]

The social gospel movement arose as evolutionary theory began changing the progressive clergy. Persons like Walter Rauschenbusch (1861-1918), Baptist pastor and later Rochester Seminary professor, proclaimed the use of Christian principles in American social and economic life. If religion has power, use it for a moral social order. For "the religious spirit . . . enlarges hope, unfetters daring, evokes willingness to sacrifice, . . . Under the warm breath of religious faith, all social institutions become plastic."[36]

Rauschenbusch further wrote:

Translate the evolutionary theories into religious faith, and you have the doctrine of the Kingdom of God. This combination with scientific evolutionary thought has freed the kingdom ideal of its catastrophic setting and its background of demonism, and so adapted it to . . . the modern world.[7]

Churchmen focused their attention on the human condition. Progressive politicos took cues from religious reformers. A Kansas minister, Charles M. Sheldon, influenced Christian social thinking. He wrote a novelized tract, *In His Steps* (1896), telling the social practices of a small-town congregation that tried living by Jesus' precepts. Fictional Rev. Henry Maxwell announced from his pulpit:

What I am going to propose now . . . ought not to appear unusual or at all impossible of execution. Yet . . . it will be so regarded by a large number, perhaps, of the members of this church. . . . I want volunteers . . . who will pledge themselves . . . for the entire year, not to do anything without first asking the question, "What would Jesus do?" And after asking that question, each one will follow Jesus as exactly as he knows how, no matter what the result may be.[38]

Sheldon's volume sold around 23 million copies by 1925.

Some pioneers of the social gospel forsook the general social uses of evolution. Influenced by individualism, or fearful of socialism, they modified the free workings of competition, turning from Manchesterian economics and the social fatalism of the Spencerians. Rev. A. J. F. Behrends wrote, "Christianity cannot grant the adequacy of the 'laissez-faire' philosophy, cannot admit that the perfect and permanent social state is the product of natural law and of an unrestricted competition."[39]

George Herron (1862-1925), Minneapolis Congregational minister and professor of Applied Christianity at Iowa (Grinnell) College, attacked self-interest and strife as bases of social organization. He deplored Sumner and Spencer for their appeal to self-interest. Assuming that competition is the law of life and development was, to Herron, "the fatal mistake of the social and economic sciences." Cain was "the author of the competitive theory."[40] The balance to the competitive principle was the rule of Christian ethics and the dicta of Christian conscience. As Herron declared, "the Sermon on the Mount is the science of society."[41]

Churches held the secular conscience, but they neither led nor followed. From the late 19th into the 20th century, movements to reform the economic and political systems heard similar arguments from the pulpit as from other rostrums. The social gospel clergy were a minority in every Protestant denomination. Fundamentalists and other "conservative" churchmen—socially as well as theologically—refused to interject the Church into political reform. Yet, basically the liberal and conservative clerical positions on social reform were alike. Both reflected mundane values of society rather than imposing any more elevated spiritual purpose upon it.

After the Spanish-American War in 1898, President William McKinley insisted that Spain should cede Puerto Rico to the United States. Senator Thomas C. Platt of New York wrote McKinley after a tour that nine-tenths of the people wanted to keep the Philippines. Spain's holding of any part of the archipelago meant "our failure to discharge the greatest moral obligation which could be conceived." The *Baptist Union* cited general missionary efforts: "A still higher obligation rests on us. . . The conquest by force of arms must be followed up by conquest for Christ."[42]

> More than a year after President McKinley concluded to keep the Philippines, he received the General Missionary Committee of the Methodist Episcopal Church, an active expansionist group. He told them he had not wanted to keep the Philippines, declaring: I went down on my knees and prayed Almighty God for light and guidance more than one night. And one night it came . . . that there was nothing left for us to do but to take them all,

> and to educate the Filipinos, . . . civilize and Christianize them,
> and by God's grace do the very best for them, as our fellow-men
> for whom Christ also died.[43]

These good words faced America's own domestic needs. But protests became quelled by cries that Filipinos and Negros were inept.

Social Darwinianism seemed to decline after 1900. The attacks of Christian literalism also eased against the theory of evolution. Only a simple relationship between mankind and God could be intelligible to earnest Protestants of many denominations. Under the name of "fundamentalism" there arose an effort to simplify the old creeds to basic articles of faith that a theologically unlearned generation could understand. *The Fundamentals,* a series of 10 pamphets published in 1910, gave the movement its name.

The Fundamentals condensed Christianity into five points. First was the literal infallible authority of the Bible, the base of the other four—the virgin birth of Jesus Christ, His substitutionary atonement for mankind's sin, the Resurrection, and the Second Coming. *The Fundamentals* resolved from this creed that "no possible points of contact" could exist between Christianity and Darwinism. Fundamentalism engaged Baptists, Methodists, and other evangelicals, but also Presbyterians and Episcopalians became drawn into the turmoil of the 1920s by this change. Fundamentalists thought they stood as champions of the true orthodoxy.

To the liberal Reinhold Niebuhr, the "frantic orthodoxy" of the Fundamentalists showed their need to whitewash the anxieties and unbelief of the world. Presbyterian J. Gresham Machem, a leading theologian of fundamentalism, agreed. People became weary of the Church, riddled by "the turmoil of the world," seeking a faith whereby they could "forget . . . all those things that divide nation from nation and race from race, to forget human pride, . . . the passions of war, to forget the puzzling problems of industrial strife, and to unite in . . . gratitude at . . . the Cross."[44]

Yet fundamentalists denounced modernist clergymen as worthless hypocrites, seducers of the young, and agnostics. A crusade in the 1920s moved to oust the teaching of Darwinian evolution from public schools. "Old-time" religionists scorned liberal reformers as well as natural science and biblical criticism. The anti-evolution laws passed by eight Southern states were as democratic as any "liberal" regulation of the progressive era. Darwinianism was banished in Arkansas by popular referendum. Yet the test of the Tennessee statute in 1925 was the trial of John T. Scopes, a biology teacher who taught the process of evolution.

William Jennings Bryan, the populist Democrat and spokesman for biblical literalism, debated against the liberal and agnostic Clarence Darrow—and lost.

The war with Spain ended the post-Civil War era, as American gains in the Caribbean and the Pacific prompted the nationalization of Southern attitudes on race. The freed Negro's plight reached its nadir as other domestic issues moved ahead. Besides evolution taught in public schools, there was industrialism, urban political corruption, the "new" immigration, and Prohibition. The Progressive Age induced Southern and Northern Protestantism to meet the need for an "evangelical united front." Yet racial attitudes and the state within major churches in the South remained hostile to integration. "Jim Crow" laws increased. "Denomination mattered little, for support for the racist creed ran the gamut from urban Episcopalians to country Baptists."[45]

Religious liberalism and critical scholarship had too few champions, and only a small group in the South. For decades, the Fundamentalist controversy remained a Northern affair. By 1927 only 4 percent of the Southern Methodist clergy were seminary graduates, only 11 percent had college degrees, while 32 percent had only an elementary education. The Baptist situation was similar. Negro church pastors had little training. Fundamentalism dominated most church colleges and seminaries throughout the South. Rural and small-town citizens made Southern churches the citadels of social order and thinking that tended to be anarchistic.

These churches controlled public opinion by enforcing forms of the Puritan ethic that had a Southern tone in the early colonial period. What one said of the Baptists may be applied generally: "Their significance in Southern life consisted not in their power to mold their environment . . . [but] in . . . perpetuating the standards prevailing in society at large."[46] In joining forces with Northern Protestants, Southern churches became powerful. Nationalism and war urgencies (as against Spain or Germany) could divert popular notice, veil facts, and defer the looming racial crisis. Yet, a 20th century rendevous stood pending.

Appallingly, the theory of evolution's impact on Christianity, or the response of liberal theology, and Fundamentalism's rebuttal, none offered relief for the Negro. Evolution did not cause racism, but it offered shelter for racial bias via the principle of the survival of the fittest. Most so-called scientific findings of the era denied that blacks deserved equal social standing. Liberal theology, in adapting orthodox theology to the Enlightenment and to science, kept the *status quo* about the Negro. Also, the social gospelers, though concerned with human relationships and improving social conditions, never seriously dealt with the root cause of much social blight—racial prejudice. Even Fundamentalists, who believed all of the Bible, who carefully set the main points of the gospel, ignored a basic law of Christ—love your neighbor as yourself—second only to loving God with all heart, mind, and soul.

American churches remained too anxious about their own social status. Without the consent, or silent assent of the Church, the "Jim Crow" laws could never have restrained blacks from equal standing in society. Emancipation from slavery meant freedom from a master, but it ignored acceptance and full inclusion in American society. By the mid-1880s 13 states adopted civil rights laws, but the actual racial patterns of segregation remained unchanged. In the North assent grew among the white population to "the Southern Way" of solving the race problem, and a tendency to practice it.[47] The freed blacks became tethered by a new bondage.

Chapter 10

How the Church Befriended Jim Crow

Negro scholar W. E. B. DuBois complained in 1897 that while sociologists gleefully counted his prostitutes and bastards, vast despair darkened the black man's soul. Though blacks could accept the prejudice based on just analysis, DuBois became sick of the "systematic humiliation, the distortion of fact . . . the cynical ignoring of the better and boistrous welcoming of the worse, the all-pervading desire to inculcate disdain for everything black."[1]

White supremacists claimed that after the Civil War Negroes had greater freedom in religion than in other affairs. Yet the creation of Negro churches seemed to produce a spiritual decline, further proving that the ex-slave was unworthy of independence. When taught by their masters, the slaves were sober Christians. After becoming self-directed, they yielded to their fervid natures, pursued excess, and often reverted to heathenism. Ethics became divorced from theology; thieves and adulterers went uncensured.[2]

A congressman who wrote a piece on such heathenism in Liberty County, Georgia, alleged that Northern papers refused to publish it because Northern people would think it came from the prejudice of Southern white men.[3] But in the *Century Magazine*, Bishop T. U. Dudley reached a Northern audience, declaring that the Negroes' "religion is a superstition, their sacraments are fetiches, their worship is a wild frenzy, and their morality a shame." The remedy was renewed white control despite objections by black ranters.[4]

White Southerners held that miscegenation was unchristian. During radical Reconstruction they cringed before the hybrids who distorted them, claiming that Providence imposed the station which black men would occupy.[5] Twenty-five years later, reviewing the evils of Reconstruction, they clothed the South in righteousness and denounced the "wicked defiance of the law of Almighty God to divide human beings into distinct races, and the institution of the beastly system of mongrelism usually called social equality."[6]

The constitutional amendments and civil rights acts of the Reconstruction period merely offered black freedmen legal equality in the

courts and at the polls. The states, like the federal government under the
original Bill of Rights, could not "deprive any person of life, liberty, or
property, without due process of law," to deny him "the equal protection
of the laws," or to abridge his "privileges and immunities." Neither state
nor federal government should deny a citizen's right to vote "on account
of race, color, or previous condition of servitude."[8]

The white South settled its former slaves into a form of the old racial
caste. Though legally the freedmen could move about, most of them
remained as peasants in the plantation regions. Few went beyond the
nearby cities of the industrialized "new South." Few basic social
advantages accrued from legal freedom. Churches and lodges were the
main Negro communal organizations free of white surveillance. A black
farmer's wife and children could no longer be taken from him and sold. Yet
the uneasy tenure of a share-cropper or laborer left a family's livelihood as
exposed to the whims of landlord or employer as under slavery. This held
sway until World War I, when Northern demand for labor and the Southern
farming depression first induced many Negroes to relocate.

From Reconstruction days into the 1890s Southern white factions
controlled the Negro vote. When that failed, they disenfranchised him by
devious requirements. He must prove his literacy or pay a poll tax—from
which white men usually stood excused. Both state and municipal
lawmakers imposed on the Negro physical segregation. This became
enforced in trains, streetcars, sidewalks, parks, theaters, hotels, hospitals,
libraries, schools, and cemeteries. "It took a lot of ritual and Jim Crow,"
a Southern historian said, "to bolster the creed of white supremacy in the
bosom of a white man working for a black man's wages."[9]

The judicial and executive abdication of the "original understanding"
of the constitutional amendments caused Frederick Douglass in 1889 to
wonder whether

> American justice, American liberty, American civilization,
> American law, and American Christianity could be made to
> include and protect alike and forever all American citizens in the
> rights which have been guaranteed to them by the organic and
> fundamental laws of the land.[10]

For decades after Appomattox, a strong majority in the South stood
against Negro suffrage. The most militant men urged violence to break up
the Negro electorate, until other means were devised. An Alabamian
prophesied, Negro suffrage "is upon us in 1870, and, in the absence of
civil commotions, it will be upon us in 1970."[11] A Georgian, Father
Abram Ryan, thundered: "this is a white man's Government, and upon

this doctrine future political contests must be fought until the question is finally and irrevocably settled."[12]

Southerners clung to the basics of proslavery thought, and to the wrongs it masked. They viewed the Fifteenth Amendment as that "great iniquity," that "boldly, daringly . . . revolutionary . . . universal savage suffrage amendment."[13] Fearing social equality was the result of political equality, a Virginian put his fealty to the white man's party: "I hain't no objection to the Republican party . . . it's the niggers . . . it's the NIGGERS."[14]

Many Southerners, horrified by lynchings, condemned brutal force against the Negroes. Writer George Washington Cable opposed the violence and objected to white supremacy. Though many "silent Southerners" were of like mind, they did not comment. Critics like politician Walter H. Page; Southern Methodist Rev. Atticus G. Haygood; scholar William P. Trent; and Episcopalian Rev. Edgar G. Murphy, upheld white supremacy while denouncing violence.[15]

In 1881, Haygood, then a professor at Emory College, Oxford, Georgia, later a bishop in the Methodist Episcopal Church, South, wrote a book, *Our Brother in Black, His Freedom and His Future*. Southerners read that Negroes would stay, that they were free, so a new attitude must be developed toward them. Haygood viewed slavery as a dead issue. Both North and South received warning to "cool off and recognize the truth of things." He foresaw the relation of whites and blacks as a "national race problem," and said Negroes were neighbors and members of the community.[16]

Rev. Murphy, of Arkansas, a graduate of the University of the South and Yale, founded the Southern Society for the Consideration of Race Problems, with its first conference in Montgomery, Alabama, in 1900. He also published two books, *The Present South* in 1904 and *The Basis of Ascendancy* in 1909. These works dealt with the basic precepts of social progress, and the problems in social thinking and planning which a bi-racial civilization entailed.

Yet between 1889 and 1898 there were 1,351 recorded lynchings in the South compared with 139 in the North and 110 in the West.[17] Besides the mob, the hangmen, who fired public feelings, people of wealth and respectability, the press and the pulpit, who created and upheld public opinion, also had responsibility. The North colluded with the South in founding white supremacy—nationwide. They both held Africans in contempt.[18] The Negro was an inferior being, held in serfdom by the lordly Caucasian, from scientific, scriptural, and historical accounts.

These were basic to black-white relations from the Civil War until 1900—and beyond.

A rung of legal hope for blacks was cut from their ladder toward success in 1896. Homer A. Plessy, a Negro, challenged a Louisiana law ordering railroads to provide "equal but separate accommodations" for whites and blacks. The Supreme Court, by an earlier Massachusetts case, upheld Louisiana's act, approving the "separate-but-equal" doctrine. The Court decreed a state's right to pass a law supplying separate railway carriages for the white and colored races.[19] The majority view also implied states could order separate school and other aids for blacks and whites, saying:

> . . . we think the enforced separation of the races . . . neither abridges the privileges or immunities of the colored man, deprives him of his property without due process of law, nor denies him the equal protection of the laws, within the meaning of the Fourteenth Amendment. . . . [20]

By this the "Jim Crow" system of laws gained constitutional support with respect to travel, and in all areas of public life.

The phrase "Jim Crow" dates to the 1830s. On holidays such as Independence Day and Christmas, slaves were allowed to have a dance. Even without fiddles, they would "pat guba." To "dance Jim Crow" was one of their favorites:

> Once upon the hill top,
> And then upon the toe,
> An'ev'ry time I turn around
> I jump Jim Crow.[21]

Yet by 1838 the Negroes hated the term "Jim Crow." Blacks used "Jim Crow" to mean whatever discrimination they faced in America.

In 1883 the Supreme Court revoked the last of the civil rights laws (1875) passed by Congress after the Civil War. The "Jim Crow" movement grew stronger after the Court's ruling, setting new laws requiring separate public facilities for Negroes and whites. After 1890 a segregation wall held blacks to separate hospitals, schools, and neighborhoods, rest rooms and drinking fountains, train and theater accommodations, and separate cemeteries—a cradle to the grave system of racial segregation.

This "Jim Crow" era debased Negroes in magazines, newspapers, nursery rhymes, popular songs, cartoons, movies, and jokes. In 1887, a Southern white wrote, "Southerners will call a Negro 'Senator Smith,' or 'sheriff Smith,' or 'Colonel Smith,' to escape addressing him as 'Mr. Smith.'"[22] A St. Louis Bible society published a book by Charles Carroll, entitled, *The Negro a Beast or in the Image of God?* (1900). It declared people of color had no soul, and sold thousands of copies.

White Southerners defended the "Jim Crow" laws as a means to ensure better necessary relations between the races. Yet, such measures actually sparked lawlessness against blacks. The new laws ignored the old conservative method to distinguish between classes of the race, to encourage the "better" element, and to draw it into a white alliance.

Americans in every section were liable for Jim Crow's spread. The churches befriended Jim Crow by holding the Negro *status quo*. Their silent apathy allowed, and moved to take citizenship rights from blacks. Federal government policies and actions copied this apathy. After 1890, the presidency continued such a policy while Congress repealed most of the Reconstruction laws. Apathy spread under President Rutherford B. Hayes (1877-1881). He withdrew the last federal troops from the South, ending protection of freedmen.

President James A. Garfield, Hayes' successor, did appoint a few blacks to public office before his assassination in 1881. Frederick Douglass was made marshal of the District of Columbia, John Mercer Langston became minster to Haiti, and Congressmen Blanche K. Bruce and Robert B. Elliot received posts in the Treasury Department. Chester A. Arthur followed in the White House. He saw the Independent revolt in the South as an opportunity to split the white vote and restore Republican power in the region. President Arthur withdrew his support from Negro leaders and sought to place Southern whites in command. During Democrat Grover Cleveland's first term (1885-1889), he appointed several blacks to office in the South.

Yet the federal government failed to enforce the Fourteenth and Fifteenth Amendments to the Constitution, to protect the civil rights of blacks. This helped white Southerners to keep most Negro voters from the polls. Under all-white Democratic rule, the South drew a curtain of silence around the "Negro question." Their writers said the South was a land of charm and chivalry, of magnolia blossoms, white lace and mint juleps. They depicted Negroes as happy, childlike, cared for by kind, generous and heroic whites. Such gloss hid the harsh reality of Southern resolve to keep blacks subdued. Republican President Benjamin Harrison (1889-93) dodged the "Negro question" to draw Southern whites.

In the booming industrial and commercial cities through the North and West, Protestant churches became the preserve of the middle and upper classes. "Go into an ordinary church on Sunday morning," one clergyman said in 1887, "you see lawyers, physicians, merchants, and business men with their families . . . but the working man and his household are not there."[23] What was true of the white laborer was also true about blacks in white churches—not there.

Church folk did assert that the poor themselves were wrong if they were both poor and unchurched. If men who were laborers had been churchgoers, "instead of giving so much of their time and earnings to saloons, or to labor associations," the Congregational weekly advised in 1894, "they would find themselves less frequently pinched by poverty and less in want of real friends than they are now."[24] A clergyman who probed the fiscal status of Pittsburgh Protestants concluded that "evangelical Christianity pays!"[25]

Severed from political life and limited in the world of work, the postwar Negro turned to the church, his traditional pillar of hope. The faded great expectations of Reconstruction prompted blacks to look to the church for encouragement. The Negro church in the South began a larger role than in antebellum days, because the Civil War freed black churches from the white control enforced during slavery, by a white preacher and white observer.

Also, the war caused a separation of white and Negro churches in the South. Racial theories held by most white Southerners, that urged them to set "Jim Crow" practices in secular life, dampened any welcome of Negroes into their churches. The few whites who were willing to retain Negro members favored them only if they would sit in the galleries formerly for slaves and not enter the church's social or business affairs. Blacks refused such terms.

Southern Protestantism divided into all-white and all-black denominations. In 1866 Negro Baptist congregations in South Carolina, Georgia and Florida held their own association. Within 14 years, a South-wide convention of Negro Baptist churches met in Montgomery, Alabama. By 1880 white and black Baptists traced their own separate ways in the South. The National Baptist Convention became organized in St. Louis, August, 1886. In 1893 at Washington, D.C., the Baptist National Educational Convention formed.

Other denominations experienced a similar separation. Late in 1870 the Colored Methodist Church in America organized, an offshoot of the Methodist Episcopal Church, South. Negro Methodism in the South became stronger after the Civil War by the coming of the African Methodist Episcopal Church and the African Methodist Episcopal Zion Church, which until the Civil War worked largely to the North. By 1896 the AME church had 452,725 members and the AME Zion 349,788 members. Both churches surpassed the Colored church of Southern Methodist lineage, with 129,383 members, and the Northern Methodist church's Negro Conference of 246,249 members.[26]

Despite the Negro exodus from the Methodist Episcopal Church, South, the 1894 *Discipline* carried the point with regard to the "Testimony of colored People," first adopted in 1867. It says:

> Ought the testimony of colored persons to be received in our Church trials? The answer made and approved is that, in view of the altered civil condition of the colored people within the recently slaveholding States, and in view of the late General Conference of the Methodist Episcopal Church, South, in respect to their ecclesiastical status, the testimony of said colored people ought not to be excluded from Church trials, in cases where it is obviously applicable, said testimony being weighed according to its merits. (1867.)[27]

Like the Methodists, Negro Presbyterians in the South began to form their own churches. Over two-thirds of them started by 1870. Yet, not until 1898 did the General Assembly of the Presbyterian Church in the United States transfer its Negro units to a newly organized African-American Presbyterian Church.[28]

By 1900 Christians divided along the color line even more markedly than ever before. Although some churches in the North still kept their doors open—like the 10,000 to 12,000 Negro Presbyterians in white churches in 1900—Southern churches were almost completely segregated. W. E. B. DuBois wrote in 1907, "There may be in the South a black man belonging to a white church today, but if so, he must be very old and very feeble."[29]

DuBois also wrote that the census of 1890 showed nearly 24,000 Negro churches, with a total membership of over 2.5 million. There were 10 church members to every 28 persons, and in some Southern states one in every two persons. Besides these, many, while not enrolled as members, attended and took part in church activities. "There is an organized Negro church for every 60 black families in the nation, and in some States for every 40 families, owning, on an average, a thousand dollars' worth of property each."[30]

The Negro churches sparked economic cooperation among blacks, published effectual periodicals, and aided Negro education. The churches stood as a strong refuge in a hostile world. The church became a surrogate for nationality, meeting diverse social needs and providing an arena to develop leadership, as well as religious needs. After 1877, as "Jim Crow" laws, harassment and political repression mounted, the church helped preserve racial solidarity.

The denial of the Negroes' civil rights increased from the 1870s. The plantation owners and their advocates did not legalize the Jim Crow system at once. Short of a quarter century of Negro suffrage, and less than a decade when the black vote functioned, the South began to disfranchise blacks with constitutional amendment. In 1890, the Mississippi Constitutional Convention met that summer to handle the suffrage issue. Southerners viewed this convention as a guide to other states, saving them from Republican conspirators in Congress who sought to place Southern states under the control of their Negro population.

The Mississippi Constitutional Convention chairman, noting two distinct and opposite types of mankind in their state, posed the manner to arrange it so they might live together amiably. Telling blacks of their good white friends, the chairman told how God made each race desire to control the other but gave the white race the edge, since white rule "always meant prosperity and happiness to all races." White rule, thus, "may be said to be a law of God."[31]

Five years later, South Carolina copied the Mississippi Plan. It required that every elector "be able to read any section of the Constitution . . . be able to understand the same when read to him, or give a reasonable interpretation."[32] Then in 1902, Virginia joined the list of states disfranchising Negroes "legally." Carter Glass, author of the constitutional disfranchising clause, said: "Discrimination! . . . that is . . . what this convention was elected for—to discriminate to the very extremity of permissible action under the limitations of the federal Constitution, . . . to the elimination of every Negro voter who can be gotten rid of."[33]

By 1910, blacks in the South became as totally disfranchised as they were under slavery. Disfranchisement subdued Southern Negroes to their base status. Without political power they only watched their former masters use the state government against them in every social area. Such action construed the conditions and discipline to maintain a quasi-slavery, which tolerated lynch mobs and other random violence. Without suffrage, blacks could not help govern the society as they did in Reconstruction. Nor could they curb those measures designed to hold them as a usable black caste. The so-called redemption of the South and disfranchisement were acts of racial prejudice to perpetuate white control over blacks.

Southerners held the serfdom of Negroes was inevitable. Every person of knowledge, they declared, expected this result. Captured

Africans shipped to America as cheap labor for proud people were and always would be a subservient and inferior race. Southern whites simply made intelligence subdue ignorance. Noting the spoils of the Spanish-American War, Dr. E. E. Hoss of the *Christian Advocate* asked: "If intelligence and property were to rule in the Pacific islands, why not in American commonwealths?"[34]

Yet, the year 1895 held important changes in American Negro life. The Supreme Court heard the case of Mr. Homer Plessy, a black who broke the Jim Crow railroad laws. (The Court decision in 1896 made segregation legal in America for the next 58 years.) Lynchings increased and Southern states rewrote their constitutions to discard Negro rights. Booker T. Washington tried to conciliate the whites and mediate between them and the Negro people. His 1895 speech at Atlanta aroused approval by most whites and many blacks. In his "Atlanta Compromise," he declared:

> . . . To those of my race who depend on bettering their condition . . . who underestimate the importance of cultivating friendly relations with . . . their next-door neighbor, I would say: 'Cast down your bucket where you are' . . . in making friends in every manly way, of the people of all races . . .

> To those of the white race . . . I would repeat what I say to my own race: 'Cast down your bucket where you are.' Cast it down among the eight millions of Negroes whose habits you know, whose fidelity and love you have tested . . . Cast down your bucket among these people who have, without strikes and labor wars, tilled your fields, cleared your forests, builded your railroads and cities, and brought forth treasures from the bowels of the earth. . . .

> The wisest among my race understand that . . . progress in the enjoyment of all the privileges that will come to us must be the result of . . . constant struggle . . . It is . . . right that all privileges of the law be ours, but it is vastly more important that we be prepared for . . . these privileges. . ..

> . . . I pledge that in your effort to work out the great . . . problem which God has laid at the doors of the South, you shall have . . . the patient, . . . help of my race.[35]

Not all black leaders agreed with Washington. In his famous book, *The Souls of Black Folks*, written in 1903, Negro scholar Dr. William E. B. Du Bois answered Washington:

> . . . But so far as Mr. Washington apologizes for injustice, North or South, does not rightly value the privilege and duty of voting,

belittles the . . . effects of caste distinctions, and opposes the higher training and ambition of our brighter minds,—so far as he, the South, or the Nation, does this,—we must . . . firmly oppose them. By every . . . peaceful method we must strive for the rights which the world accords to men, clinging . . . to those great words which the sons of the Fathers would fain forget: "We hold these truths to be self-evident: That all men are created equal; that they are endowed by their Creator with certain unalienable rights; that among these are life, liberty, and the pursuit of happiness."[36]

Facing a black freedom movement, Southerners, looking over the course of their region's history since emancipation, declared that Northerners stood guilty of three gross errors in fostering Negro participation in politics. They erred by deeming that all men are equal, by saying that the national government must protect Negroes from their foes, and that the interests of whites and blacks were opposed. Southern whites always claimed these were basic mistakes. Northerners seemed to waive Negroes to white guardianship.[37]

For decades there was no substantial moral leadership in the legal process. The White House, the courts, schools, congresses, state governments, and often, even churches, refused to support any movement toward an open society. There was a grievous backlash in education because of the 1896 Plessy v. Ferguson doctrine. Judge Loren Miller concludes that the majority

> . . . reduced the fourteenth Amendment to . . . a pious goodwill resolution . . . [and] . . . smuggled Social Darwinianism into the constitution and had armed future . . . segregationists with the . . . doctrine that they could protect racial discrimination *through law* while preserving it against change . . . that *law* could not function in that sphere of human affairs . . . The Negro, under the court's guardianship, was reduced to . . . second-class citizenship; voteless in the South; helpless in . . . brutal aggression . . . denied access to . . . public accommodation; represented in public office by those whose very elections were dependent upon their promise to . . . redouble his [the black's] disabilities; forced to . . . scrounge for an education; segregated . . . his life; condemned to separate and unequal schools and public facilities . . . no place to turn for redress of his grievances except to the Courts that had approved the devices used to reduce him to his . . . almost hopeless degradation.[38]

In 1900, Southern newpaperman John T. Graves, backing Negro deportation at the Montgomery, Alabama, Conference on Race Relations called for urgent separation of the Anglo-Saxon and Negro races. There was "no peace, no purity, no traquil development, no durable agricultural prosperity . . . no moral growth for the white race outside of separation." While the whites claimed that they would never accept Negroes as an equal, the blacks desired to be equal to white men above them. Without deportation, Americans would see an ambitious but weak race destroyed.[39]

Negroes ignored emigration until political victories decreed official white supremacy. Then, many moved to freer places; some joined the "Exodus" to Kansas in the late 1870s. By 1891 a quarter of a million blacks moved North and West. This left the South to men who sought, by raising the states above federal government authority on civil rights, to reverse the Civil War's outcome. Douglass warned white Southerners: "Drive out the negro and you drive out Christ, the Bible and American liberty with him."[40]

However, as Dr. E. E. Hoss of the *Christian Advocate* noted, it would take generations to replace the black labor force, and "we should think it a poor exchange to swap off a million . . . negroes for an equal number of Italian Dagoes or Hungarian miners."[41] Southern Methodist Bishop Charles B. Galloway became troubled about Negroes fleeing the South. This turmoil, induced by lynchings, the separation, strangled Negro education. If Negroes continued to leave, the South faced industrial disaster.[42]

The Jim Crow code did not assign the servant group a fixed status in society—they put the Negro down. They discerned between Southern white attitudes toward blacks amid Reconstruction, and later feelings. Rev. Edgar Murphy in 1911 called one "defensive" and "conservative" and the other "increasingly aggressive" and "destructive." He wrote, "These new antipathies are . . . assertive and combative . . . ruthlessly destructive." This movement grew in aggression. "Its spirit is . . . an animus of aggrandizement which makes, in the imagination of the white man, an absolute identification of the stronger race with the very being of the state."[43]

Yet, Rev. Murphy was a Southerner who saw "the conscious unity of race" as "the broader ground of the new democracy." He believed that despite any defects it was "better as a basis of democratic reorganization than the distinctions of wealth, of trade, of property, of family, or class." Rev. Murphy praised "the deep sociological value of what has been called 'race prejudice'" though he deplored some of its fateful results.[44]

Mob violence began to rack the South, causing bedlam for blacks to endure. In 1904, the state of Georgia became gripped by a series of race riots. They began in the town of Statesboro when a mob took over a courtroom where two blacks stood convicted of murdering a white farmer, his wife, and two children. The mob dragged the two Negroes out and burned them alive, signaling sweeping violence. Many black men and women became attacked and beaten, with homes wrecked. The mob leaders went unpunished.[45]

Atlanta, in September, 1906, became rocked by fierce racial trouble. Saturday, September 22, newspapers carried stories of alleged outrages against white women by Negroes. A mob gathered to attack any black in sight. Then Negroes in the Brownsville suburb, hearing about the violence, armed for self-defense. So the police started rounding up blacks and arresting them for bearing arms. An officer shot into a Negro crowd, and they returned the fire, two whites and four blacks were killed. The whites' rampage injured many people and destroyed much property. J. W. E. Bowen, president of Gammon Theological Seminary, was struck with a rifle butt by a police officer. After days of rioting peace became restored. Some black and white citizens formed the Atlanta Civic League to improve relations and to prevent further bloodshed. Again, leaders of the lawlessness went unpunished.[46]

Also in 1906, Brownsville, Texas, faced a riot. Racial insults sparked a furor over three companies of Negro soldiers—part of the famed Twenty-fifth Regiment—fighters beside Teddy Roosevelt's Rough Riders in Cuba. In the tumult, one white man was killed and two blacks were wounded. Before a full investigation could ensue, President Roosevelt abruptly ordered the dishonorable discharge of all three companies. But after further government investigation, the discharged soldiers who were eligible could reenlist, with full pay and privileges restored. Most blacks viewed the episode as proof of the federal government's slight for their welfare.[47]

During this same period race riots also beset the North. One of the most violent riots that occurred in the North happened August, 1908, in Springfield, Illinois. Two Negroes were lynched, four whites killed, more than 70 persons injured, and rampant property damage occurred. Reporter William E. Walling wrote:

> On Sunday, August 16th, the day after the second lynching, a leading white minister recommended the Southern disfranchisement scheme as a remedy for Negro (!) lawlessness, while all four ministers who were quoted in the press proposed swift "justice" for the Negroes, rather than recommending true Christianity, democracy, and brotherhood to the whites.[48]

This bloody riot spurred the formation of the National Association for the Advancement of Colored People (NAACP).

On the centennial of Abraham Lincoln's birthday, February 12, 1909, Oswald Garrison Villard, grandson of William Lloyd Garrison, wrote, calling believers in democracy to join a national conference for "the renewal of the struggle for civil and political liberty." Among the 53 signers were social worker Jane Addams; Mary E. Wooley, president of Mt. Holyoke College; Rabbi Stephen S. Wise; and Rev. John Haynes Holmes, Unitarian. With W. E. B. Du Bois, the Negro signers were Ida B. Wells, crusader; Rev. Francis J. Grimke, Presbyterian; and Bishop Alexander Walters. In answer to the call, two meetings convened in New York. From those meetings emerged the National Association for the Advancement of Colored People.[49]

This association met the national notion of rural purity and urban corruption fed by the racial concepts of the times—to which every President from Grover Cleveland to Woodrow Wilson added. When Cleveland showed sympathy for Southerners in the Cabinet, they were forced to support a Democrat for President, to maintain the one-party system and white supremacy in their home states. President William McKinley roused racism by his foreign policies, and he rescinded an order sending Negro troops to Little Rock, Arkansas, facing local protests. Nor did the Brownsville, Texas, riot move President Theodore Roosevelt to seek justice in the racial issue. President William Howard Taft pledged not to appoint Negroes to office in any region where white citizens objected. This barred blacks from new federal jobs in locales where most Negroes lived.

President Woodrow Wilson allowed the league of segregation in several bureaus in Washington, D.C. As federal officials in the South could fire or downgrade blacks, the collector of Internal Revenue in Georgia said; "There are no Government positions for Negroes in the South. A Negro's place is in the cornfield." Many protests ensued. Yet in September, 1913, President Wilson wrote the *Congregationalist* editor: "I would say that I do approve of the segregation that is being attempted in several of the departments." Wilson argued that Jim Crow became adopted for the Negroes' good.[50]

With the reformed and Puritan legacy, American evangelical Protestantism believed the ideas and practices of revivalism were essential to its being. Puritan piety provided the theological base for this great strategy of church extension. Yet George Whitefield, the founder of American revivals, also owned slaves. After Whitefield, revivalism became promoted by the Congregational, Presbyterian, Dutch Reformed, and other strong colonial groups. No church groups did so much to take the revival spirit to every farm, village, and city as the Methodists and the Baptists.

The crucial point of revivalism was a specific conversion experience, to be a true Christian. Focus on the individual sinner led to a preoccupation with personal sins, which caused the erosion of social ethics noted in colonial times. Even the antislavery revivalism of Cartwright and Finney never fully clarified ethical views. This lack confused relationships after the Civil War. Then the rise of big business complicated the moral life of nearly every American. As typified in the preaching of Moody, Jones, and later, Billy Sunday, revivalism tended to skirt or be ambiguous to social ethics such as racism. But revivalism confronted such matters as drinking, gambling, prostitution, and the theater.

Another element that aided revivalism was Arminianism, a doctrinal bias named from a dispute of the Netherlands Reformed church against Jacobus Arminius. Its spread in America came mostly from John Wesley and the Methodists. Because of Arminius's stress on mankind's free will, an innate point to revivalism, Calvinist doctrines of unconditional election and limited atonement lost their vigor. In 1906, on readmitting the Cumberland Presbyterians after 100 years on this issue, the Presbyterian Church (North) revised the Westminster Confession to an Arminian reading. By 1911 most of the Freewill Baptists, after a longer split, found the offending doctrine too weak to prevent reunion.

Revivalists often preached to interdenominational audiences, so nearly all doctrinal emphases were "soft-pedaled." Besides the nationally known preachers, many thousands of local ministers and regional evangelists did this also. In time a concensus emerged. Its main points were the infallibility of the Scriptures, the deity of Christ, and mankind's duty to be converted from the ways of sin to live by a pietistic moral code. Such revivalism often stunted doctrinal development. The main issue of American Protestantism became "Are you saved?" Increasingly it meant, "Have you decided to be saved?" Such questions missed the whole issue: "How is a Christian to live righteous in his social world?"

This religious revivalism blended with renewed nativism that focused on Protestant Anglo-Saxons. A Gilded Age was not a time for prejudice to die or for virtue to grow. In Roger Burlingame's phrase, it was a time of "moral paralysis." The popular principles of *laissez faire* economics and Social Darwinianism made complacency a public virtue. Only "getting ahead in the world" really mattered. The "Self-Made Man" became the idol and "rags-to-riches" the vision for the American people in pursuit.[51]

Moving against this custom, yet a subtle part of it, marched a band of reformers. Their efforts peaked with the Muckrakers, the Progressive movement, the New Nationalism of Theodore Roosevelt, and the New Freedom of Wilson. Their equals in the churches became the leaders and patrons of the Social Gospel. Yet among those who conscientiously led this reform, few realized the moral effects of ethnic, racial, and religious prejudice. Few protests against bigotry or its basic assumptions appeared in the reformist literature of the Progressive and Social Gospel movements.

These principles of racism also fueled the fires of American nativism. Till this time, many people used race theories against blacks, and in apologies for the institution of slavery and the Southern way of life. However, racist notions became eased by the growing belief in the uniting and reforming power of American Protestant culture. Evolutionary optimism helped buoy this belief. Many held that emigration was a sifting process that brought the best and strongest to these shores, bolstered by Darwinian environmentalism, which saw American institutions as shaping human raw materials. Yet, white skins remained much preferred.

Thus Christian churches befriended Jim Crow laws by simply seeking to retain *status quo*. People clutched the old moral creeds and standards of individualism as they faced the drastic Industrial Revolution. Their personal problems were so urgent and complex, a religious and intelligent person might not discern the effects of his choices and behavior. The Jim Crow laws thus squelched a further social upset that imperiled the North as well as the South.

Yet, in 1918, Dr. James Dillard organized the Southern Publicity Committee. The group sent, mainly to weekly papers in small towns and rural districts, news stories of Negro attainments, and cases of cooperation between whites and blacks. This sign of good will boosted by the Commission on Interacial Cooperation met with great success, guided by Mr. R. B. Eleazer, the leader.

Later, the Commission on Church and Race Relations, appointed by the Federal Council of Churches, held conferences of whites and blacks to promote racial good will. Brotherhood is the assumed gift of the Christian Church, but its friendship with Jim Crow has muted the reality of such doctrine. Dr. Du Bois noted this truth in the *Christian Century*, stating that the Church would not remove the color line. Instead, the

Church would heed rising liberalism, but ignore the brotherhood of mankind because of time-favored *status quo* and of opposing wealth and power.[52]

Will the Church ever reach beyond the sacrosanct *status quo*? To have racial peace in our country, and throughout the world, the Church must shift its focus from social standing to brotherhood. The Church as a whole must find common ground to build bridges across the cultural and skin color gap. Individual Christians must face the massive need and courageously begin to lay the foundations for bridge-building.

Chapter 11

Racism and the Burden of Bridge-Building

The basic grist for missiological mills today includes such concepts as dialogue, contextualization, common ground, and bridging. Missions Professor David Hesselgrave declares that "religious, cultural, social, ethnic, and other barriers must be crossed if the Great Commission is to be obeyed. Scores of books and hundreds of articles indicate we are aware of this."[1] Such bridging for world evangelization remains crucial for Christian contact with ethnics in the United States. The color, cultural, and social barriers are as real here as in other lands.

Hesselgrave further cites a risk rising from a worldwide trend that exists in America. It is the danger of not going far enough—"of turning from the hard work of seeking to understand other worldviews and relating meaningfully to people who hold them."[2] While overseas mission efforts have shown some success in the care and persistence in dealing with foreign peoples, the home missionary effort in ministering to African-Americans has faltered.

Common white Christians evade building a bridge of brotherhood with the blacks. Churches seem too busy to understand the woeful heritage of the blacks and their ensuing viewpoints. In dealing with the slavery and racism, the blacks remain assigned to sub-human status. Most whites do not learn about black culture, to accept them as equal human beings—or as equal Christians.

Rev. Leroy Haynes, of the Christian Methodist Episcopal Church gives a current view. Writing from Dallas, as program director for the Eighth Episcopal district, Haynes states:

> Not since . . . Reconstruction, after the newly emancipated slaves were released, has the Black Church in America faced a greater challenge than it faces today. In all areas of life the Black community finds itself under seige. Our community is being attacked by the disintegration of the Black family, mass unemployment, Black on Black crime, poverty, functional illiteracy, inadequate housing and medical care, and a turning back . . . on civil rights gains won in the 1960s.[3]

Prior to President Franklin D. Roosevelt's relief programs of the 1930s and the poverty programs of the 1960s, the only institution blacks believed would care for their poor and stand for their humanity was "the Black Church." As the government created relief and poverty programs to stifle "authentic transformation of the American political and economic system, the Black Church found itself . . . under the pacifying effects of the government's diversion plan." Black churches began using a precept learned from white churches: "It's not our business to deal with the poor; let the govenment do it. Our business is only with spiritual matters."[4]

A new social reality formed, by structural and philosophical changes, in the American government and economy. This social reality confronts the Black Church, saying, "I will no longer feed, clothe, and shelter your poor. . . . I will not be an advocate for you against oppression and discrimination. You must do for yourself."[5] What trusts have white Christians had? What duties now face the white church? The hard answers seem obvious: Individual Christians must work Christ's "Great Commission" in this nation. The Church must renew its caring efforts to build bridges to accept this people whites have generally separated from American society.

In 1947, some radio messages broadcast by "The Methodist Hour" issued some required characteristics for bridge-builders. Of the series, was Dr. W. B. Selah's sermon "Character Is Fate." His text was: "The ungodly . . . are like the chaff which the wind driveth away" (Psalm 1:4, KJV). The major premise was that "character certainly determines the fate of the individual." Selah also said that character is fate in opportunity—in trouble—in temptation—in the judgment day. And, character is fate in the realm of government. The nation's fate depends on character.[6]

Dr. Selah's clincher was: "Character is fate in the realm of social progress." A better world cannot be built by bad men, and a friendly world cannot be formed by people who hate. A Christian world can only be built with Christlike character. Only those who will work and sacrifice for a better world are used of God to establish justice and right. Only people of true Christian character can be used to build needed bridges. Selah's prayerful remarks aim the shining truth to the present dilemma. He cried:

> Give us men who have in them the spirit of Christ and who walk close enough to Him to feel . . . His love for humanity. Give us men who . . . practice His principles, men who in business and in politics and in all their human relationships strive to do unto others as they would that others should do unto them. Give us men who love their neighbors as themselves, . . . men who will seek for others the same rights, the same privileges, and the same

opportunities that they seek for themselves. Give us men who look upon every human being, whether black or white, as a child of God—too sacred to be held in contempt, too sacred to be exploited. [7]

Also, during that 1947 series, Dr. William H. Wallace, Jr., preached a message, "Stripped for Action!" His text was:

> Therefore, with all this host of witnesses encircling us, we must strip off every handicap, strip off sin with its clinging folds, to run our appointed course with steadiness, our eyes fixed upon Jesus as the pioneer and the perfection of faith—upon Jesus who, in order to reach his own appointed joy, steadily endured the cross, thinking nothing of its shame, and is now seated at the right hand of the throne of God (Hebrews 12:1-2, Moffatt).

Many Christians go through life weighed down by the excess luggage of selfish luxury, hindered by the "lights of mental and spiritual imaginations turned low!" Christians as individuals and church groups tend to forget "the first things" about the faith and Great Commission of Christ's followers. Dr. Wallace asks:

> . . . Today is Race Relations Day . . . Isn't it . . . time that we strip some of the prejudices from our minds on this question and begin to work it out . . .? I am as white as any, . . . born farther south than the "deep south," . . . the Southern Christian white man needs to take the lead in this great problem before our nation . . . All the Negro wants or needs is . . . a fair deal. . . . I believe we must do this.[8]

A psychological whitewash covered the beliefs to explain why Negro slavery should be exempt from the demand for democracy. These reasons included three modes: the religious ("the Bible sanctioned slavery"), the cultural ("a productive democracy—like ancient Athens—must be based on unpaid labor"), and the biological ("the Negroes were biologically inferior and must be helped like children or horses; . . . never be allowed to pollute the better blood of the whites"). These reasonings gained support from current and later scholars and scientists, whose claims excused slavery. Such beliefs became used as morale builders during the Civil War. The biological reason—termed racism—became the most powerful, with profound implications for later misuse of Negroes.

Such historical facts are important for churchmen as well as sociologists, to see how the caste-segregation system developed. The full disclosure of secular history and religious practice in the American colonial and national eras would clarify the status of African-Americans.

But both secular and church historians held the popular Southern myth that racism and caste existed from the first interracial contacts and are endemic to race relations. This myth crossed the Mason-Dixon line; it spread throughout the North.

Educated Northerners also ignored the early history of slavery in some Northern states, and how castes developed there. Leading Northern historians and churchmen let Southern apologists record the history of their region during the post-Civil War years without a strict account. Both Southern and Northern historians share the bad conscience, which led them to belittle the Negro and to ascribe social traits and biological events to biological certainty. They could excuse themselves amid harsh race relations, profess Christian faith and declare the national ideals of freedom and equality. Church people were part of the racial problem—not the solution.

Still, from the early 20th century, the issue of what to do with blacks in the church and in all society, troubled the thinking and conscience of many Christians. Some whites kept calling for efforts to "keep blacks in their place." Such ideas by prejudiced whites prompted actions to disfranchise blacks in the South and to coerce them by lynchings, castrations, and other cruel acts. All white Christians had to reconcile segregation and other so-called "Jim Crow" practices with social holiness and Christian love.

Among some tragic acts of hostility were four major racial outbreaks—one in Harlem, one in Los Angeles ("Zoot Suit" riot), and two in Detroit. The most serious flared during the week of June 20, 1943, in Detroit, where racial feeling sprang from a three-year increase of 50,000 Negroes (with 450,000 whites), mostly from the South. That hot Sunday afternoon, 25 Negroes and 9 whites were killed; property losses exceeded $2 million. Detroit set up a Mayor's Interracial Committee to assuage the loss, seeking roots of the trouble, and taking needed steps toward healing.[9]

The clergy of middle- and upper-class churches tried, most of the 19th century and into the 20th century, to adjust between religion and their parishoners' material values. They felt the victory of "big business" meant their own defeat. Other rising professionals became anxious about status like those who thought they were slipping. College professors claimed "academic freedom" from the control of businessmen-trustees and changed from keeping the *status quo* to censure a culture ruled by big business.

The confusion did not cancel the Salvation Army's commitment to blacks after World War II. Salvation Army USO activities were segregated during the war—like the U.S. Army. There were separate Salvation Army USO clubs for black troops in the South; Washington, D.C.; Harlem; Junction City, Kansas; Mt. Clemens, Michigan; and in Ipava, Illinois. The Army's indoor evangelical activities also were segregated in the South in the late 1940s. Yet, the black corps had many lasting conversions recorded in them.

A traditional Army ministry became used as a bridge these years— the open-air meeting. Adjutant Vincent Cunningham, editor of the Southern *War Cry*, was the driving force behind a campaign to launch such meetings. They first met in the black districts of Atlanta, with success, and carried all over the South.

Efforts to draw more Southern blacks into the Army's ministry made no impact on racial segregation before 1950. But they acted before the national opinion shift that followed the Supreme Court school desegregation decision in 1954. Professor Herbert Wisbey, in 1949-50, saw that segregation was "not accepted by the Army with an easy conscience." In 1950 a national commission became founded along with territorial ones. The Army joined the White House Conference on Children and Youth; it was "concerned about continuing legal separation of race." Yet, the Southern territorial commission reported "an upsurge . . . of good will in a tradition-ridden area of the nation, in . . . prejudice and discrimination."[10]

By 1955 divisional and territorial activities, such as Young People's Councils, Girl Guards, and Home League rallies, were integrated throughout the South. Local units remained segregated. In Northern cities, neighborhood racial complexion combined with the desire of black Salvationists for a local center for worship and service. Some corps remained largely or entirely black, such as: St. Louis Euclid Avenue, Omaha Northside Corps, Cleveland Central Area, Harlem Temple, Brooklyn Bedford Temple, Pittsburgh Homewood Corps, and Milwaukee West Corps. Where segregation issued from past policy, divisional leaders were to clear the barriers.[11]

The decade of the 1960s brought violent and lasting change to race relations in the United States. The Salvation Army pointed its "soldiers" to a new perception of the "Brotherhood of Christ." In May, 1964, the territorial commanders issued a joint statement on "racial justice." Officership, employment, and joining The Salvation Army were open to any person regardless of race. "All social welfare services" were offered on that basis. Yet race riots in many Northern cities pushed the Army into a dilemma.[12]

The Army's willingness to open youth programs to neighborhood young people, and equal dispersion of welfare kept the movement from being viewed by blacks as just one more agency of a bigoted and hateful "establishment." The Salvation Army increased its evangelical ministry among blacks, who formed a larger ratio of the urban population every year. Since the "inner city" often meant black, some believed that the Army in the city must become what one officer called "a largely black organization" simply to survive.[13]

In 1971 the commissioners' conference appointed a Task Force for each territory to survey racial programs. These were to extend the Army's evangelical ministry. New programs included counseling, employment referral, day-care centers for working mothers, "probation, parole, and court work," medical clinics, recreational, gymnasium, camping, black studies, community planning, and vocational training. Drum and bugle corps were tried with inner-city youth.

In many ways, the religious and social work of the Salvation Army offers an example to other church denominations. Some of the Army's successful ministry points to the building of bridges that surmount racial barriers. One notable issue called for an end to forming homogeneous units. Evangelistic work by various churches had been aimed at ethnic groups, but not mixed. One exception was in some camp meetings. That form of heterogeneous worship was not set in church buildings. This fostered division of worship only widened the gap in how whites perceived blacks, and vice versa.So-called "brotherhood" could meet only at a "safe" distance.

The early 1950s signaled progress as black Americans struggled for justice and equality. In 1954, the court decision of Brown v. The Board of Education of Topeka, Kansas, reversed the "separate but equal" doctrine of the 1896 Plessy v. Ferguson case. Rev. Martin Luther King, Jr., in 1955 led the Montgomery, Alabama, bus boycott. Mrs. Rosa Parks refused to vacate her bus seat, sparking a conflict December 1, ending in 1956. Then The Methodist Church, moved by Christian conscience, faced its segregated structure.

At the 1956 General Conference, Methodists adopted Amendment IX to its constitution, to hasten the abolition of the racially constituted Central Jurisdiction. It "gave Annual conferences the right to change from one Jurisdiction to another, and a local church the right to change from one Annual Conference to another if the changes were acceptable to all parties involved."[14]

The amendment was to accomplish "voluntary integration," that all areas of the nation supported. Thurman Dodson, of the Central

Jurisdiction, said: "We realize that the Amendment does not abolish segregation. But it does move in a direction toward which this great Church of ours ought to move." He also said: "I am hoping . . . from this Conference, the world will know that The Methodist Church . . . is on its way toward an integrated society."[15]

In 1955, young Evangelist Billy Graham believed mass evangelism included all peoples. Rev. Ralph S. Bell, a black, joined the Billy Graham team as an associate evangelist in 1965. His education included training at Moody Bible Institute, Taylor University, and Fuller Theological Seminary. Later, Bell declared at a conference on urban ministries:

> When I was a student, I had heard from Evangelicals that all men were equal, but a white student was forbidden to room with me in an evangelical Bible school. I had heard that all men were equal, but I was asked to attend a black church, where I would be much happier. I had heard that all men were equal, but certain evangelical seminaries were closed to me.[16]

By the early 1960s, the civil rights movement made a solid impact on vital areas of American cultural and institutional life. Black activists grew assertive over segregation and racism, rousing the conscience of white Americans. Some segregation walls began falling, but many were still in place. Martin Luther King, Jr., and others gave black and white church people a new vision of the Church and its potential as a moral force. It must be a catalytic agent for righteous change in society.

In The Methodist Church, between 1956 and 1966, several black annual conferences used Amendment IX to transfer out of the Central Jurisdiction. A committee was appointed to study the effects and use of Amendment IX. That commission was Chairman James S. Thomas, Richard Erwin, John H. Graham, John J. Hicks, and W. Astor Kirk. They met in Cincinnati, March 26, 1961. Their report stated, "Each step taken to dissolve the Central Jurisdiction must be . . . part of an overall plan to abolish all forms of racial segregation and discrimination from The Methodist Church."[17] The Central Jurisdiction must disband, confirming the rights of blacks.

During the 1960s, as blacks struggled for equality, many whites raised new questions about the nature and purpose of the Christian churches. The appearance in April, 1963, of Martin Luther King, Jr.'s, "Letter From the Birmingham City Jail" accused the white church for its failure to take a moral stand against racism and injustice. But the black church became a driving force in the civil rights struggle. In the churches, streets, courts, and jails, Negroes and others sang the hymn of revolution:

"We Shall Overcome." Black church leadership tried to bring white Jews, Protestants, and Catholics into the struggle.

Conferences, crusades, protest marches, and prayers were set against discrimination and segregation. In 1963, America's Roman Catholic bishops said, "The first step is to treat all men and women as persons." That step needed both the political authority of the state and the Church's spiritual power. "Without recognition of individual dignity and compassion for suffering," the bishops added, ". . . social justice becomes merely a political matter and we remain as a nation morally tortured by racial injustice."[18]

Ministers and rabbis, black and white, spoke in city councils, church services, and jail cells. Churches, both white and black, became stations for protest against racism, calling for understanding. Many seminary students united—Protestant, Catholic, Jew—in all-night vigils at the nation's capital, standing for justice for all. Many religious printings called the people to "Equality Now!" Biblical faith affirmed it, America's democratic faith required it —all citizens deserved equality, but all did not have it.[19]

Frustration and rage erupted in fire and violence in Detroit and Newark during the summer of 1967. After a "long hot summer," a three-day conference of black leaders convened in the Episcopal Cathedral, with Rev. Nathan Wright as chairman. Their resolution urged a boycott of all churches ignoring the "black revolution." Yet this warning left many dilemmas for those black churchmen who sought to correct the entire American "system" of racial abuse. The black churches faced the question of which road to follow. The white churches met the same issue, reacting to their own laity and clergy demands for special funds and separate societal status.[20]

Given the modern radical revolution, some wondered if the black church hierarchy could stand firmly on already shaky grounds. Sects and cults, with other worldly preoccupations, continued to grow, increasing chaos and mediocrity. Church attendance and membership declined just as they were in the white churches, and more so. The black congregations started from a lower level and dropped at a swifter pace. The crisis worsened as the gap widened between the clergy's educational level and that of the laity.

In 1963 a Harris poll found that regular church attendance (once a week) among blacks was 49 percent. The usual congregation numbered 200, compared to 500 for whites, and 1,000 new ministers were graduated from seminaries. By 1970 a survey of black theological education reported 665 seminarians enrolled for a black membership of 10 million gathered in 40,000 congregations.[21]

Viewing the Church's pietistic, moral message as the true guide to living in the American social and political order, that message best suited the Reformed and Puritan heritage. With pride of race and a concern for social justice, this was the typical theology of most people in the churches' civil rights effort. "We shall overcome" was, and is, its theme song. Yet it draws on both spirituals and traditional preaching for power and effectiveness.

Dr. Martin Luther King, Jr., drew heavily on such evangelical resources. His unique theology was also influenced by idealistic personalism and a Hegelian view of history in doctoral studies at Boston University. Reading Paul Tillich, the existentialists, and the philosophy of Mohandas Ghandi, prompted King to develop a view of black suffering. It related the meaning of historical travail with faith in God's ultimate victory. This standpoint affirmed that Christian love must always be at the heart of the struggle.

At a mass meeting in Montgomery, Ala., Holt Street Baptist Church, King's speech helped launch the bus boycott as well as set the religious tone of his civil rights movement. After declaring that "we are Christian people," King's speech soon reached fervent religious peaks. He cried, "If we are wrong—God Almighty is wrong!" "If we are wrong—Jesus of Nazareth was merely a utopian dreamer and never came down to earth! If we are wrong—justice is a lie!" Citing the prophet Amos (5:24), King resolved, "And we are determined here in Montgomery—to work and fight until justice runs down like water, and righteousness like a mighty stream!"[22]

While rousing emotions, King focused on the dignity of protest and the need for unity. Reinhold Niebuhr's thought shines through as King said it is not enough for us to talk about love. "Love is one of the pinnacle parts of the Christian faith. There is another side called justice. . . . love in calculation . . . is love correcting that which would work against love." God is not just the God of love: He also stands "before the nations and says, 'Be still and know that I am God . . . if you don't obey Me I'm gonna break . . . your power—and cast you out of . . . your international and national relationships," "Standing beside love is always justice."[23]

Yet by April 4, 1968, King meshed these "liberal" views with the Baptist nurture of his youth. Among his final words on the Memphis motel balcony before his assassination was a request that Thomas Dorsey's gospel song, "Precious Jesus, Take My Hand," be a part of that evening's scheduled rally.

Five years earlier a vast throng spread out before the steps of Lincoln Memorial in Washington, D. C. Many then heard King's dream—that "We will be free one day":

> This will be the day when all of God's children will be able to sing with new meaning, "let freedom ring.". . .
>
> When we allow freedom to ring . . . from every city and every hamlet, . . . we will be able to speed up that day when all of God's children, black men and white men, Jews and Gentiles, Protestants and Catholics, will be able to join hands and sing in the words of the old Negro spiritual, "Free at last, Free at last, Great God a-mighty, We are free at last."[24]

Looking back, King's theology helped clarify his bridge-building role as a leader during a crucial decade of American history.

Also in 1968 Rev. Albert B. Cleage, Jr., pastor of Detroit's Shrine of the Black Madonna (associated with the United Church of Christ), published *The Black Messiah*, a series of sermons addressed to black Christians. He became educated at Wayne State University (Detroit) and Oberlin Graduate School of Theology (Ohio). He went to Detroit in 1952 to lead the Central Congregational Church. Cleage worked in the NAACP, but in the 1960s his church joined the black liberation cause. He said Jesus was a "revolutionary black leader." Blacks were not to look to "the resurrection of the physical body of Jesus but the Resurrection of the Black Nation which He started." This message was like Marcus Garvey's African Orthodox church and echoed Black Muslim doctrine.[25]

James H. Cone became more effective in developing a theology that would give Christian substance to black consciousness and provide an ethical base for "Black power." He declared:

> It is not my thesis that all Black Power advocates are Christians or even wish to be so. . . . My concern is, rather, to show that the goal and message of Black Power is consistent with the gospel of Jesus Christ. . . . I have even suggested that if Christ is present among the oppressed, as he promised, he must be working through the activity of Black Power. This alone is my thesis.[26]

Cone poses these urgent questions: "Is there a message from Christ to the countless number of blacks whose lives are smothered under white society? Is it possible to be *really* black and still feel any identity with the biblical tradition expressed in the Old and New Testaments?" Opposing those who would abandon the faith as an opiate of the people, he proposes a theology of revolution that "begins and ends with the man Jesus—his

life, death, and resurrection." He affirms his faith in the One who was sent
"to proclaim release to the captives and recovering of sight to the blind,
to set at liberty those who are oppressed, to proclaim the acceptable year
of the Lord" (Luke 4:18-19, RSV). Without draining the gospel of its
comfort, Cone purposed to prompt faithful social action in both black and
white churches, if they would listen.[27]

However, ex-Black Panther Anthony Bryant recently commented on
Cone's black American theology. Cone supposedly wrote that the whole
social situation should be analyzed in a Marxist context. In response,
Bryant claimed Marxism was a movement with intent to change
capitalism to communism, and communism denies God. Bryant asked:
"How can a Christian support a system that is at war with God?" He
rejected Liberation Theology as the means to correct the American
injustice against blacks. Some injustice will prevail as long as there's a
Satan, and as long as there are imperfect human beings. The black
churches and community accept Christ as a revolutionary—not the
Christ most Christians admit. This Christ of revolution fights against the
rich in defense of the poor. The loving Christ people really need to know
is He who shed His blood and died on the cross for the sins of the
world.[28]

The black church version of Christianity was born in the beliefs forged
by African slaves in the 17th century. After 200 years of struggle, by the
1950s black persons began to see that racism and Christianity were
opposites. In 1972, theologian James Cone wrote to South African readers
that "Black Theology" was quite new to Americans, an event of the 1960s.
He stated:

> . . . it is the religous counterpart of the more secular term "Black
> Power," . . . it is a religious explication of the need for black people
> to define the . . . meaning of black existence in a white racist society.
> While Black Power focuses on the political, social and economic
> condition of black people, seeking to define . . . the meaning of self-
> determination in a society that has placed . . . limits on black
> humanity, Black Theology puts black identity in a theological
> context, showing that Black Power is not only *consistent* with the
> gospel of Jesus Christ,. . . it *is* the gospel of Jesus Christ. . . . [29]

Black theologians challenge racist oppression. Differences within
American Christianity are related to and induced by their historical bond
with color prejudice. The basic issue is the credo of racism in American
Christian culture. Their culture equates the authority and omnipotence of
Euro-American white men with that of God. Black Theology affirms the

converse beliefs that distort the Christian faith to make God fit the culture of white domination.[30]

Neo-orthodox theology's decline after the black revolution of the 1960s brought turmoil and a religious pluralism with theological fads. Such are unlikely to stand the test of time and the vast new challenges of the 21st century. The current revival of conservative evangelicalism, pop religion, and mystic beliefs filling middle class white churches, sparks certain social action without concern for racial justice. So, American Christianity faces racism, and worships a God assumed to prejudge skin color.

According to *National & International Religion Report*, growing numbers of young blacks shun the church. This concerned the 1,000 black evangelical and mainline Protestants who attended the '88 Congress for Evangelizing Black America. The black church community suffers the lack of basic structures, mass media, and financial resources. A dropout increase of black ministers became noted also in some churches. The problems of reaching unchurched black Americans pushes many pastors to the "brink of despair."

The Congress organizer, Matthew Parker, executive of William Tyndale College in Michigan, thought Atlanta '88 would help change things. He saw black Christian unity as a power unchecked by the split between spirituality and social action that afflicts most white churches. Parker, also a consulting editor for *Christianity Today*, sees race relations as the key issue facing this nation, yet white church people are lax. A 1988 *Christianity Today* survey said that many preferred racial integration, but not a priority. A few saw another answer to racial conflict, saying the races must "share bed and board"; integration is "one meaning of 'Choose Life.'"[31]

Such a solution seems faulty. Black Presbyterian Church in America pastor Carl Ellis declares, "If we were to homogenize all the races today, we'd come up with some other way to discriminate against people . . . There's no way around the sinfulness of the human being." He adds, "I don't want integration to mean I have to obliterate my [black] culture . . . That's a price I'm not going to pay."[32] There are no easy ways to build bridges of fellowship and soothe race relations.

Fifty percent of the respondents to the "Race and the Church" survey "strongly agreed" that race relations should be improved. Yet only 20 percent regretted scarce contact with people of other races. Only 10 percent "strongly agreed" that racial integration should be a top national priority. A wise view was, "Integration is best accomplished by individuals rather than forced by the law." William Leslie, pastor of

Chicago's LaSalle Street Church, in a multiracial community, said, "When people of different races find out who each other are, and that we have the same hopes and desires for ourselves and our children, . . . real harmony will come."[33]

Truly, racism—actions and superior attitudes based on distinctions among races—is a rampant evil in the secular world. People without Christ, engrossed in sin and committed to selfish humanity, cannot be expected to act otherwise. However, throughout history till now, racism isn't only a custom of unchurched sinners. Well-meaning church members also practice racism in the name of fear and bias. For supposed good reasons, under strategic guises, the Church continues actions that reflect an evil racist legacy.

To overcome this centuries-old racism, the Church must reject its fears and bigotry. The WASP (White Anglo-Saxon Protestant) concept is not truly Christian. The Church must face generations of biased belief that blacks (and other ethnics) are inferior to whites. The New Testament declares that there are no social, economic, racial, or sexual distinctions before God. The apostle Paul says, "There is neither Jew nor Greek, slave nor free, male nor female, for you are all one in Christ Jesus" (Gal. 3:28). Jews are not the only people who receive the Divine promise. Gentiles are fellow heirs, members, "and sharers together in the promise in Christ Jesus" (Eph. 3:6). No variance is made between "Greek or Jew, circumcised or uncircumcised, barbarian, Scythian, slave or free, but Christ is all, and in all" (Col. 3:11).

These moral principles revealed in Holy Writ show us powerful knowledge that urges us to obey and act accordingly. Even in a Christian setting, both black and white Americans fear sacrifices and risks that true racial harmony demands. This fear becomes the gauge of our racial chasm. The problems from which we run ever pursue us. If we call for courage to counteract fear, racial harmony demands more than courage, it requires relentless moral effort, daily sincere and personal sacrifice of selfish ideas.[34]

By the Bible standard, "we see that from the beginning God has been interested in all the nations of the world, in the human race, as a whole."[35] Basic human likenesses make intercultural communication (though skin-color contrasts) not as difficult as some would infer. Yet, the Church finds it easier to send white missionaries to evangelize in Africa than to promote intercultural fellowship in America. African-Americans have been assigned mostly to the Black churches for conversion. Some church growth strategists advise that churches continue racial distinctions. The concept of "homogeneous units" suggests "Everybody needs to worship with their own kinds of people"—of like culture—whites with whites, blacks with blacks, Asians with Asians, rich with rich, poor with poor.[36]

The "homogeneous units" theory has been a useful evangelistical missionary principle. Yet, as used in American churches, it has often perpetuated racist attitudes and practices. The Church's witness to ethnics in the Western world is weakened because of "respect of persons" given by cultural and skin-color lines. The Church must enact a unique mind-set! The world's distinctions—of skin-color, position, power, possesions, or culture—have no proper place in Christian churches.

Historically, blacks, and others, have lacked education and lived in poverty. Many people see this only as signs of failure. Yet, the Christian "good news" is "the power of God for the salvation of everyone who believes . . ." (Rom. 1:16). This gospel of grace calls Jews and Gentiles, rich and poor, slaves and free into union with God and His Church. Believers from all ethnic and social backgrounds must be welcomed as brothers and sisters in Christ. The stigma of racial inferiority is as wrong in the Church entering the 21st century as it was in the first century when the apostle Peter shunned the Gentiles in Antioch (Gal. 2:11-13).

To face racism honestly also means the Church must admit its fear of excessive social contact with blacks and other ethnics. This fear results from our errors judging value or worth based on skin-color. We, like the Pharisees, set external standards by which to judge. We practice social and spiritual distance. When overt racial discrimination is outlawed, we keep barriers by proud attitudes, racial slurs, and coarse jokes. The goal is to keep "us and them" separate, so they don't live next door, so our children don't play together, grow up together, or marry each other.[37] We may work or go to school together, but we avoid worship together.

Christ never valued a person by mere appearance, but by the internal love of the heart and mind (cf. John 7:24; Rom. 14:17). Parents should strive to instill in their children an ever-growing commitment to live godly in every human relationship. The Church shares in the aspect of racism clouded by deep fear of interracial marriage. Parents want their children to at least marry "equals" on the social ladder. Yet, the Church must resist this natural desire and submit judgments to the standards of the Kingdom. Christians must be careful in choosing their mates. Scripture clearly calls for marriage partners to be believers, but the Bible neither promotes nor bans mixed color skin-marriages. Distinctions based on so-called racial heritage have no biblical defense.[38]

In reality, racism is the practice of power. It is the use of influence or authority of whites over people with other skin colors. It is also the haves over the have-nots. The practice is to subdue and keep someone down to ensure the privileged will remain so. For the Church to curb racism, fellow Christians must look in the same mirror and see, not the visible distinctions, but the person of Christ in every brother and sister. Equal worth is based on "Christ is all, and is in all" (Col. 3:11).

How do evangelical churches speak to racial bigotry stemming from the lengthy legacy into the 21st century? Christians often hold the traditional accent on personal belief over social duty for ethnics. Focus on personal evangelism should not stymie sincere efforts to accept peoples of all skin colors and cultures. A basic church purpose should frankly acknowledge racist attitudes, and prescribe definite corrective measures. Such action could split congregations and cause membership losses like those suffered by liberal Protestants and other churches before the Civil War.

The question, "Will the Church Resolve the Conflict?" concerns a related issue that silently awaits the Church's action. That probing question is: "Will the Church Repent and Be Redeemed From Its Pretense of Innocence in This Racist Legacy?" The redemption needed in churches goes beyond admitting parity of the development of blacks in white society.[39] The redemption that brings true reconciliation is that which accepts all peoples as persons under God, and all believers as brothers and sisters in Christ.

Churches know that racism is a serious moral problem. Too often, the issue is easier identified in other social areas and in other denominations. Approaching the 21st century, Christians of the various white churches have only managed to build the framework of a bridge across the racial chasm. Ventures of Christian organizations, conventions and denominational edicts have not made a floor for communication. Church leaders' statements require the broad support of Christians willing to open the way for reconciliation. Bridge-building requires persons to face the problem, to give equal acceptance of all other ethnics, yielding to God's will over racial pride. Christ's great commission to all His followers means true fellowship of all peoples.

Chapter 12

Reconciliation Constructs Peace

Jesus Christ broke the color barrier. Christ commissioned the Church to enact "rainbow evanglism." Jesus charged His followers, ". . . go and make disciples of all nations . . ." (Matt. 28:19, NIV). This task cannot be achieved just by human efforts. Jesus offers believers an authorizing, empowering experience: "And behold, I send the promise of my Father upon you; but stay in the city, until you are clothed with power from on high" (Luke 24:49).

The evangelization of the Ethiopian eunuch (Acts 8) shows an open racial view within the Early Church. Philip, an evangelist, witnessed to a black man who served Candace, the Ethiopian queen. At the Holy Spirit's bidding, Philip ran to join the Ethiopian in his chariot to explain the prophets, showing the gospel is for all people. Luke cites the apostle Paul's words that God "made from one, every nation of mankind to live on all the face of the earth . . ." (Acts 17:26, NASB). Paul also said that in God's beloved Son "we have redemption, the forgiveness of sins" (Col. 1:14).

The apostle Peter, though, stood averse to mingle with a "God-fearing" Roman centurion (Acts 10:28). Peter held Jesus' earlier training: "Do not go among the Gentiles or enter any town of the Samaritans. Go rather to the lost sheep of Israel" (Matt. 10:5). Peter also kept the custom against a Jew associating with a Gentile, which he called "against our law." God had commanded Israel to keep their worship pure. God now taught Peter that he "should not call any man impure or unclean," as shown in the Old Testament. One should obey Christ's commission. Any person may do what is unclean, but that does not mean one is less than human.

Despite helpful scriptural insights, many Christians neglect equal relations with other peoples. They continue a long legacy of concepts that resist accepting blacks and other ethnic groups as equals. Christ calls His followers to love and accept all peoples into fellowship. Reconciliation requires relation—not resistence. People of other skin colors want to freely worship and associate with whites who often present superior airs to those having colored skin. Many churches show a racial dominance as a community becomes racially mixed. Church leaders must face the prejudice against any people in a multi-racial neighborhood.

Roger Bowman, a friend, with a darker skin than mine, wrote a book titled, *Just Color Us Christian*. He truly states, "Although the terms black and white are frequently used, the issue is *not color*, but CHRISTIAN."[1] The apostle Paul declared, "God does not show favoritism" (Rom. 2:11). A person of any skin color or from any group of people may receive salvation through Jesus Christ. In the last century, John Oxenham caught the vision and wrote the hymn, "In Christ There is No East or West":

> In Christ there is no East or West,
> In Him no South or North;
> But one great fellowship of love
> Thro'out the whole wide earth.

The skin-color labels of racial distinction, such as white, black, yellow, or red "race," are from ideas that view "race" as a sub-species of mankind. Yet, the Bible never uses either the word or the concept of "race." God describes human creation only in terms of "families," "tribes," and "nations." The Scripture first proclaims that God made man in His image (Gen. 1:26-27). All peoples are descendants of that first human pair, depraved, needing redemption and reconciliation. Racial discrimination based on skin color completely misses the case. All peoples live under the love and judgment of God.

Likewise, all peoples are related in the human family. Each person has followed his/her willful way; some have prospered more than others. Amid selfishness and greed, there are broad cultural differences. Yet in nature we are one—one in our sins, requiring a Savior. True faith in Jesus Christ does not routinely expel "racial prejudice" from the hearts and minds of believers, or from their actions. It was not so in New Testament times. An apostle beheld a special vision (Acts 10:7-22) after the great experience of Pentecost. Peter, a chosen Jew, saw Cornelius, a righteous Gentile, also receive the Holy Spirit by faith (Acts 15:9).

Revealing God's view of the world, the Lord Jesus Christ gives the Great Commission. "Go, then, to *panta ta ethne* everywhere and make them many disciples: baptize them in the name of the Father, the Son, and the Holy Spirit, and teach them to obey everything I have commanded you. And I will be with you always, to the end of the age" (Matt. 28:19-20). The words *panta ta ethne* direct us to discern how God sees people and suggest strategies that point to reconcilation and effective evangelism. Commonly, the words *panta ta ethne* have been translated "all nations." Many translators now render these words "to all peoples" or "to all people groups."[2]

Let the Scripture explain itself. The book of Revelation (chap. 5) looks into the future, revealing Christ's return. His Great Commission becomes fulfilled. The writer describes the people before the Lamb singing praises to God. He writes: "You are worthy . . . because you were slain, and with your blood you purchased men for God from every tribe and language and people and nation" (v. 9). Thus God's world view has no geographical, political, or racial bounds, seeing people groups as basic to spreading the gospel and to fulfill the Great Commission. God views the world in diverse people groups, the rainbow of His creation.[3]

Presently, evangelization strategists often confuse the intent of the "people group" tactic in global efforts. Confusion occurs when this access becomes used as an evangelistic method and then as a membership policy. The "people group" approach to world evangelization should not be a membership policy. It only opens a way to reach people within the context of God's creative variety. Another disorder links with a refusal to accept the "people group" move towards world evangelization. This strategy shows that people who do not know the gospel of Jesus Christ still maintain the "wall of hostility" (Eph. 2:14) between people groups. Only as people are evangelized does the gospel enable persons to accept each other as brothers and sisters in Christ, no matter their "people group."[4]

The Church's persistent sin across the centuries includes the biological and cultural differences set in the world. These decide more about how we perceive each other, than the mandate and meaning of the gospel. The problem is complex because skin color and cultural distinctives are viewed as flagrant stereotypes. Such are used as a biased index to judge people—their worth, intelligence, values, and their potential and importance. A color or cultural difference becomes seen as a signal to embrace one and to exclude another. World evangelization stands hampered as the Church coddles this sin, which blocks reconciliation and prevents unity.[5]

Color and culture do have meaning. We must neither deny color nor idolize it with pride. Yet, we cannot dismiss it since God made every human being having some color. In life, color is a tangible factor of personhood—a part of one's total being. Color is not negotiable; one is born with it. This fact of nature is something about which no person should feel any need of apology or have a sense of lack. Color is also a community distinctive that belongs to masses of people. It is one universal factor of meaning in human life.[6] But color is lost in death; it is no longer a part of personhood; spiritual traits become more evident.

Yet, cultures are negotiable and arbitrary. They are not God-derived anthropological givens; they are localized and historical expressions of human development. Color does not relate to sin or salvation. Yet, a culture can block the gospel proclamation or aid its spread and reception. The Christian Church is the social institution most apt to bridge the color concerns and the unwise conventions of culture. The Church should admit the primacy of divine mission, the global need, and the crucial link Jesus Christ came to forge with everyone who believes on Him as Savior. Such efforts avoid doubt and discrimination, to gain reconciliation.

Again, Christ commanded His followers to make disciples of all nations (peoples). The implied purpose is reconciliation, working a global loving fellowship of faith and peace. An obedient, Bible-focused body of believers gathers in bold fellowship to nurture peace through each generation. Jesus prayed that His followers might partake of the Divine unity—to live unselfishly so they are brought "to complete unity to let the world know that you sent me and have loved them even as you have loved me" (John 17:23).

An assurance of truth and faith in progress persists because Jesus Christ authorized the salvation message and commanded the evangelistic mission. It must be carried out so the entire needy world might hear and know the hopeful possibilities of life now and hereafter. This divine message compels not only a sharing with all in knowledge, but sharing in the spirit of *agape* love. Only such a visible unity of believers will inspire our greatest possible impact in a world that must see before it will believe.[7]

The Church has been called individually and corporately to enact the image of peacemaker, "reconciler." Indeed, love is the bond of community. Sebastian de Grazia made this same conclusion in his study of American democracy. He writes:

> The theologian is right. . . . More than anything else, the world needs love . . . a political community exists among men who regard each other as brothers. But they will not think of themselves as a brotherhood until they have and avow filial love and faith for their ruler and for their God. If they have no faith in their rulers or if they allow opposing directions to sway them from the commandment of love, they have no political community; they have *anomie*.[8]

The norm of reconciliation is God-centered love, which makes us responsible to God for our neighbors. *Agape* love sets its model neither from society nor oneself. Christian love embodies the mind of Christ. A development of divine presence best occurs in private lives, returning to society more open to persons and their needs. Such love rejects tyranny, but its freedom takes corporate burden. Despite the racist legacy, Christians with *agape* love can overcome *anomie* (normlessness) to inspire righteous community.

God's Spirit directs Christians to show their faith in both the religious and secular realms of decision and action. Though the democratic institutions and capitalism have granted a receptive background for the progress of the Church, not all democratic values and decisions are compatible with the Christian faith. In some cases, notably slavery and racism, our forefathers fell far short of promoting Christian community. Only as Christians give first loyalty to God in Christ is the moral action produced that alters the orders of culture by Christian moral standards.[9]

In Christian terms, mankind's corporate life submits to the continual sovereign will of God. His love creates, governs, and redeems our lives. The order of creation, in every new birth and new day, shows equality and diversity of creatureliness. The sexual, physical, psychic, and ethnic differences are the shared gifts and limits of common mortality. Our good stewardship to the Creator is grateful acceptance of the unity and diversity of creation, and to cherish and develop this original community.

Yet humanity's corporate life is "in the fall," as people abuse their created freedom and corrupt the order of creation, and all human relations. People striving for power often use the aspect of skin color to measure value. Pride causes trouble as it substitutes the idol of ethnic self-love for the God-centered love of creation. When "whiteness" becomes raised as a mark of worth, the neighbor of different color looks inferior. This disrupts the created community and corrupts the internal springs of action, extending to outer conflict. The peaceful order of creation faces ruin by the warfare of race against race, and clan against clan. Demonic cultural customs issue from striving wills to power, as the "superpersonal forces of evil." These include chattel slavery, racism, segregation, the ghetto, apartheid, which take power separate of the wills of both people who keep such evils and those who are victims. This depicts the racial "fall" of man.[10]

Present customs of American race relations show the tragedies of chattel slavery, the Civil War and Reconstruction, segregation and paternalism. Though people try to erase their memories and build a new base for community, the past haunts them. Our racial history sets a pattern of relations between blacks and whites. What some call paternalism, the *status quo* presumes, and by long usage it seems right and good. These attitudes and customs, laws and institutions, though challenged by civil rights groups, seem normal in both the Southern and Northern ways of life. As the model of good community, the Church embraces such terms.

The inner terms of paternalistic relations posit that the optimum benefits of community become realized when the superior white person provides for the inferior black, and the blacks work for the whites. This relation appears worthy because of the shared economic interdependence, each looking after the other. Familiar biblical virtues seem to sustain this transaction. They enact the words of Christian ethics: love, kindness, concern, obedience, faithfulness, patience, and long-suffering. On paternalism's good moral side, mutual personal concern typifies the arrangement. This in a sense expresses Christian community and reconciliation.

Yet, a paternalistic community has outer walls of segregation, extending inner private walls of pride and power into public custom and legal form. The moral logic of segregation stems from the major premise, (the constitutional principle of the 14th and 15th amendments), the "equal protection of the laws." The minor premise is that separation by skin color is not innately unequal, and that "separate and equal" is a vital axiom for good community to act. Over a century of American experience shows this logic is false.[11]

Separate and equal in theory soon meant separate and unequal, practiced in every sector of common life. This mode became managed only by the powerful white majority. Segregation continues to break community, to increase resentment and distrust that parted neighbors both in spirit and in social space.[12] The Church has historically followed this secular pattern. Though blacks may not wish to worship with whites, the problem occurs from the ignorance of three words: awareness, acceptance, and subordination—to God.

Gunnar Myrdal defined the "American dilemma" as the gap between the moral creed of freedom and equality, and acts of oppression and prejudice. Christians explain this impasse by the variance between God's order of creation, the "original" peaceful community of equality-in-diversity, and the chaos of a broken community of people living in hostility and fear. The acute guilt strains the Divine order of creation by the turmoil of the fall in our souls. Some white Americans claim Christian and democratic ideals put them in conflict with their racially prejudiced actions. This moral self-contradiction needs defenses and reasons.[13]

At various times conscience-stricken people speak to curtail racism. *The Church Woman*, the offical publication of the United Church Women in America, May 1957, carried a summary of 17 major Protestant churches viewing segregation in the public schools, and other problems of race relations. The unity of Christian groups about race appears in the Christian Life Commission report to the Southern Baptist Convention in 1957. That report appeals:

> . . . to our Baptist brethren, white and Negro,. . . other Christian friends to give careful consideration to the . . . truth of the Bible . . . in the spirit of . . . Christian love:

> 1. God created man in his own image. . . . every man possesses infinite worth and should be treated with respect as a person.

> 2. Christ died for all men. Therefore, the Christian view of man, every man, must reflect the spirit of the cross.

> 3. God is no respector of persons. . . . mistreatment of persons on the grounds of race is contrary to the will of God.

> 4. Christ said, "Thou shalt love thy neighbor as thyself." . . . Christians are obligated to manifest . . . goodwill toward all people and to help them achieve . . . as persons.

> 5. Christian love, as exemplified by Christ, is the supreme law for all human relations. . . . such love,. . . practiced, will resolve tensions and bring . . . good will in race relations.

> 6. All true Christians are brothers in Christ and children of God. . . . they are obligated to cultivate prayerful concern . . .

> 7. Every person is accountable to God. . . . individual opinion, tested by the teachings of Christ,. . . freedom to express it, always in . . . Christian love, should be granted to all . . .[14]

Others cite the World Council of Churches for its clear and firm approach about the need for a Christian witness in racial relations. Liberalism and the "Social Gospel" confronted churches in the United States nearly a century ago with the sin of the color line drawn within themselves and in secular society. The council declares that the Christian approach to racial issues must differ from that of a non-Christian. In the mid-1950s they declared:

> . . . God is the Sovereign Creator of all men, and by Him they are sustained . . . But man . . . by his disobedience and pride . . . against his brother—has filled it with division . . .

> What is the Christian hope in this disunity? It is Jesus Christ, who revealed God as Father and who died for all men, reconciling them to God and to each other by His Cross. From

every race and nation as a new people of God is created,. . . the power of the Spirit overcomes racial pride and fear. . . . God's people now as new creatures are co-workers with Him . . .

. . . the final victory is Christ's, we can work actively, continually repentant and continually forgiven, for that reconciliation which we believe to be God's will.

This is the calling of the Church with regard to race, to witness within itself to the Kingship of Christ and the unity of His people, in Him transcending all diversity.[15]

Such statements and religious drives hardly changed the mind-set of white churches toward blacks. The Bible and such decrees bid Christians to obey besides proclaim the salvation and judgment of God. He calls us to holy living, to repent of our personal strife and settle church fellowship. People, races, and nations in conflict with each other must also repent. We should reject ethnic fears and prejudices as neither necessary nor good, and turn, forsaking all racial segregation that comes from color pride.

White people's pride prods them to assign any inferior act by blacks to an innate racial trait. The cultural plight in which blacks must live remains ignored. This ploy shifts the social fault from self-righteous whites to crude blacks. A Christian verdict on the paternalistic terms of community claims that injustice keeps peace. Behind the facade of accord lurks greedy bias and discord. Whatever Christian kindness pervades the system, paternalism and segregation negate Christian community. A *status quo* pursued from this order resists progress toward racial peace.

The terms of peaceful community by reconciliation are freedom, equality, and justice. These moral goods deplore the false peace stemming from a segregated, paternalistic society. Equal justice must be the precondition for real peace in Christian community. Peoples can be truly reconciled only as they are seen as having equal power and worth under God. For "reconciliation" to occur, courageous moves of personal awareness, acceptance, and submission to God must happen. The content and power of what reconciliation means remains ignored by the Church in general.

The word "reconciliation" in the New Testament describes the changed relations between God and mankind through the saving death and resurrection of Jesus Christ. The apostle Paul often used the word when communing with fellow Christians who shared in God's grace, the gospel, and the promise and fruit of the Holy Spirit. Christ's death reconciles humans to God and to each other. Paul declared: "For if, when we were God's enemies, we were reconciled to him through the death of his Son, how much more, having been reconciled, shall we be saved through his life! . . . we also rejoice in God through our Lord Jesus Christ, through whom we have now received reconciliation" (Rom. 5:10-11). The Apostle says: "All this is from God, who reconciled us to himself through Christ and gave us the ministry of reconciliation" (2 Cor. 5:18).

In the 1960s and into the 1970s, Martin Luther King, Jr., not only urged racial integration, but also reconcilation between the races. For him, reconciliation involved repentance and reparation by white society, and forgiveness by black people. Dr. King became convinced that the process of reconciliation could free whites from their oppressing routine and blacks from their fear. Only when persons and groups who differ move to become reconciled with each other—and with God—is real integration possible.

Black theologian J. Deotis Roberts used the reconciliation theme in 1971 to focus on *Liberation and Reconciliation*. His comments reflect the thinking of many of The Methodists who moved to abolish the Central Jurisidiction in 1968. He also expresses the thoughts of other Christians since then. Roberts declared of true Christian reconciliation:

> If we are warned that reconciliation is too futuristic for consideration at this time, we reply to our critics that in the nature of our faith we must always seek reconciliation. Christianity is rooted in the belief that "God was in Christ reconciling the world to himself" (2 Cor. 5:19), and that reconciliation between God and man can only be effected through reconciliation between persons.[16]

Methodist Bishop Charles F. Golden's hope for an "inclusive fellowship in church in our day" faded. Though Methodists scrapped the racist bureaucracy, any day of fellowship also held the fears of both blacks and whites. Blacks feared that by numbering "only one-thirtieth of Methodist members, they would lose many officers if merged into the main body." "They . . . feared that no black bishops would be elected by predominantly white Jurisdictions. Whites . . . feared black participation and black take-over."[17]

The concept of inclusiveness, which generates reconciliation, has not received sufficient acceptance within the various church denominations. God's very gift of life to human beings equips us to perceive inclusiveness. As Jesus lived for all, He died for all. Christ revealed that His followers are united by God's love, with all God loves. The Church must react in faith and love for the persons and "all peoples" God loves and seeks.

With the political and legislative gains of recent decades, a helpful change was the creation of what United Methodist C. Eric Lincoln, black sociologist, called "a new ethnic spirit." Blacks always claimed to be Americans; now they called themselves "black Americans" or "Afro-Americans." Rev. Jesse Jackson said he favored the term "African-American." However, the blacks of the 1970s and '80s tried to tell the world: "Let us find how we can work and play, study and worship together without denying who we are."[18]

The United Methodist General Conference of 1980 realized the church had failed to be inclusive at all levels. It moved to meet that purpose by setting a single missional priority for "Developing and Strengthening the Ethnic Minority Local Church." A goal of $20 million became the focus on ministries supporting "Black, Hispanic, Native American, and Asian and Pacific Islander congregations." It sought the support of every United Methodist local church to give and "study to understand and share in the richness of our ethnic heritage, . . . of our pluralism, the systemic effects of racism and the celebration of the Christian community in the family of God."[19]

The Christian vision includes one human family, one Father of all, one Redeemer, one Lord, one Spirit of God. Persons of every human division—race, nation, culture, and class are called to one lasting fellowship. Racism, nationalism, and denominationalism often become as distorting mirrors which Christ's faulty followers insert before that vision. Yet, some glimmer of that vision inevitably shines through a church that truly senses its mission. It means a quickening faith, greater commitment, and knows this is what Jesus meant the Church to be. Stereotyped attitudes fade away, and Christ's mission becomes humbly engaged.[20]

After shepherding the Salem Lutheran congregation on Chicago's South Side, from the late 1940s to the late '50s, Rev. Philip Johnson gives some helpful suggestions. They specially apply when a church has members of minority groups within its region. Some parishes have, like Abraham, traveled ahead in faith, not knowing the end, but trusted God and obeyed daily. Johnson's shortened points toward reconciliation are:[21]

1. Be clear on the implications of the Gospel: Christ is for all men, without distinction, and so is every local church.

2. The minister . . . must not compromise the Gospel . . . to please the most narrow-minded of his people.

3. Sermons, church school classes, auxiliary organization meetings, exchange visits, . . . larger interracial gatherings . . . can prepare the way. . . .

4. Seek ways of showing interest in and helping people in need, whatever race they may be. . . . help with jobs, educational opportunities, infant care, recreational needs, social problems, legal aid, and health emergiencies . . .

5. Stand for something worthwhile . . . work . . . to improve . . . community life: government, the schools, housing, sanitation, health, welfare,. . . equal opportunities for all. . . .

6. Be just as concerned about offering friendship to your neighbor of a minority group as . . . enlisting him for your congregation. . . .

The Church in true Christian ministry is the only American institution that can heal racism. Racial conflicts will not be won in the courtroom, or by decrees of the Supreme Court. Racism will not be legislated away by Congress, or be eliminated by forced school integration or subsidized housing. The conflicts of racial color will not fade away. The guilt and hurt of racism met by psychology or psychiatry cannot reach the heart of the problem. The Church is like an ailing physician, unable to heal self.

In the United States, a small but growing number of churches try to bridge traditional and cultural barriers. Denominational and interdenominational churches are involved. One is the Atlanta Metropolitan Christian Center in Georgia. This charismatic church began as two lower-middle-class congregations merged, one white and one black. Flynn Johnson, the pastor, became introduced to cross-cultural ministry with his conversion in 1971. Johnson recalls:

> While I was under the influence of the Black Panthers, a white man befriended me and shared the gospel. He was from Alabama and had the worst kind of accent. I was accustomed to intimidating people, but he refused to be put off. He talked to me like I was a brother and led me to Christ.[22]

Pastor Johnson now leads a growing church program of around 300 members that links biblical preaching and teaching with social outreach. This includes literacy programs, food, clothing, shelter assistance, a Christian school, television and radio programming. White members are a minority, but the church is in a racially mixed neighborhood. A cross-cultural ministry ensued not only by merging congregations—by doing God's will. Johnson said they saw "the church as the family of God whose members were related deeply . . . they could minister to one another and the outside community."[23]

"We are one in Christ Jesus" is often defined in the context of one's own homogeneous culture. Our view of the kingdom of God must include any person of any skin color that comes through the church doors. Johnson views the Church's racial rift "as Satan's number-one tool to destroy the body of Christ." We are to be instruments here on earth to unite God's people.[24] Christ's gospel transcends cultural and racial barriers. As Lord of all humanity, His power to save reaches all people regardless of skin color.

An influential segment of the church-growth movement declares homogeneous churches grow best, warning that a cultural mix hinders evangelism. But strict homogeneous concepts halt progress toward racial reconciliation. Pastor Johnson sees "a growing move of God . . . bringing together different cultures within the church . . ." If churches truly evangelize their local communities, congregations will be culturally and racially diverse. Johnson says, "if the power of God is present, and people get their needs met, then they don't really care if the context is black, white, or whatever."[25]

After centuries of Christian preaching and teaching, American churches are the most segregated social institution. Despite the "spiritual awakenings" and Abolition of Slavery movements, with the recent civil rights drives, racism remains. Pastor Johnson states: "Paul says we become false prophets and false people of God when we preach the truth but don't do the truth. In the case of racial reconciliation, I don't believe the gospel has been preached in this country. . . . it certainly hasn't been practiced."[26]

True scriptural knowledge sees reconciliation as a command from God. White evangelicals too easily say let the black churches take care of themselves—let them convert the inner city. Jesus died for all our sins. He also prayed for the Church (John 17), that His followers would be united so the world would know God had sent Him. Many are more intent to see church denominations unite, than acting to see Christians of all skin colors accept each other as brothers and sisters in the family of God.

Like forgiveness, reconciliation requires a price. Jesus Christ paid the price of salvation and redemption to God. The issue is that Christians of various skin colors will come together and say, "We are related."[27] Both blacks and whites face the cost of rejection by their own religious culture. There may also be choices between biological families and the "family of God." Yet, white Christians face paying the most for racial reconciliation, as the burden for repentance and restitution becomes accepted.

To enact reconciliation requires repentance, a turning from certain deeds and attitudes. Restitution, trying to set wrong things right, must follow. As this country's history records, the sin of slavery would not have ensued if white evangelical churches had said *no*. Instead, many wrongly explained Scripture to support it, also desiring power and economic growth. For centuries, people have soothed their conscience by giving millions of dollars to send thousands of missionaries to heathen countries, including Africa. Meanwhile, churches of blacks remain neglected here in America.

According to true Christian community, an integrated society has a design of qualities. First, Christians so view the pluralism that ethnic variations would neither be neglected, nor exalted to privileged rank. Another quality seeks a freedom from limits set on persons because of skin color, nationality, or religion. This freedom should pervade national economic, political, and cultural life. A third quality puts justice on a parity of the power of one group with another. Where these terms become observed as God's will, and where society guards itself against their violation—God's will can be done on earth in human community.[28]

Both an inner change of heart and an outward change of laws and institutions must take place to meet the dual tactic required by responsible love obeying to have a Christian community. An evangelist should not just urge a change of spirit, saying, "Give your heart to Christ, and all social problems will be solved." This ignores the social matrix of the born-again Christian's heart and the new relationships a changed person gains. Both the inner heart and the outer structures must turn from racial bias.

The unique work of *agape* love toward racial reconciliation is the desire to treat any neighbor as equal. Christians must resist the bias and hurdles set by a segregated and racist society. White people need to confess before God the hidden sin of forming a white establishment to rule an integrated society. Christian love's task is to urge forgiveness and reconciliation among equals with social power. That love cherishes others as persons, without thoughts against skin color. This basic interpersonal community must include interracial relations to accomplish reconciliation.

Christian love's public work will alter the outer conditions for African-American lives by environmental changes. These include basics of existence: urban renewal, open-housing, equalization of educational opportunity, integration of the police force, fairness in administering justice, and job opportunity programs in private and public sectors. Some of these proposals have been advanced for decades, but implemented only on a small scale. Yet, these are the firm expressions of the social justice and brotherhood required by the terms of Christian community. Such has been the case for over 10 years in the Liberation Community, started by Director Bryan Stone and his staff in Ft. Worth, Texas.

For years it has been said "Eleven o'clock on Sunday morning is the most segregated hour of the week in America." Though that case is common, it is not always so. There are various role models of racial integration. One is the Minneapolis Park Avenue United Methodist Church. Sunday morning, blacks and whites, young and old, rich and poor gather together to worship God. Co-pastor Art Erickson says, "When we get to heaven, . . . We're all going to be together. We're just practicing for heaven."[29]

Recently, Park Avenue Methodist parish numbered over 1,000, which contained an equal number of blacks and whites. The pastors are white, but many leaders are black. This success was not easy. Pastor Phil Hinerman, minister at Park Avenue for over 35 years, says, "It took 20 years of struggling and losing thousands of white members. Ten years ago we felt like failures. Our membership had dropped to 750. . . . But since it turned around, . . . we've become one of the fastest growing churches in the upper Midwest."[30]

Moving toward integration first required the church board to agree that "anyone who had faith in Christ" could become a member. The church began to reach out to neighborhood children, launching a summer ministry program, with a used-clothing store and a farmers' market. A Soul Liberation Festival, a yearly week-series of evangelistic meetings, from 1973, anchors the church's summer programs. Pastor Hinerman says: "We don't try to be black. We don't even try to be integrated. We just try to be kingdom people."[31]

Then, on the West Side of Chicago, located in the mostly black neighborhood of Austin, is the Rock of Our Salvation Evangelical Free Church. This is the denomination's first mostly black church, and Rev. Raleigh Washington is its first black pastor. The church is not a historic black or a common white congregation. Pastor Washington says, "We're a black church in focus and outreach, . . . But 30 percent of our members are white. . . . We're a hybrid."[32]

Washington, 49, a 1983 Trinity Evangelical Divinity School grad, began "to reach out and embrace whites, to be a bridge builder," to have a multiracial church. The Rock of Our Salvation Church held its first service in October, 1983. Washington's vision of a church where blacks and whites met together took shape when he met a white man who shared that vision. This was Glen Kehrein, 39, executive director of Circle Urban Ministries, a multifaceted ministry whose complex houses the Rock Church.[33]

Glen Kehrein thinks some churches err in racial reconciliation efforts because they miss that persons must be reconciled, one on one, to each other. Pastor Washington and he use their personal commitment as a model—that blacks and whites can build reconciliation and serve God together. Kehrein says, "If your commitment is to a philosophy, an idea, or a dream, rather than a person, you won't make it through the difficult times."[34]

Kehrein claims that churches that are intentionally "racially pure hinder the power of the gospel." At its core, the gospel is the message of reconciliation: persons being reconciled to God and to each other. "We don't have vehicles within our society to act on that reconciliation. . . . Present church-growth models stress homogeneity as the easy path to church growth—as if church growth were the goal of the kingdom of God."[35]

Pastor Raleigh Washington agrees. He declares: "Homogeneous churches may be easier, but I don't think they are God's intent. The first New Testament church at Antioch had elders who were from different races and cultures. That's our model church. . . . When we get to heaven, it's not going to be homogeneous. Where better for us to start than right here?"[36] The effort is in response to the "Lord's Prayer": "Thy will be done on Earth as it is in heaven."

Reconciliation and peace must occur on the personal and local church levels, and involve denominations. The United Methodist Church and Baptist churches have long tried. Other groups also have made random reconciliation attempts. At its 1973 convention, the Resolutions Committee of the Christian Holiness Association adopted a report: "Racism and Poverty and Christian Example." The CHA churches are: Brethren in Christ, Churches of Christ in Christian Union, Church of God (Anderson, Ind.), Church of the Nazarene, Evangelical Church, Evangelical Methodist, Free Methodist, Salvation Army, and the Wesleyan Church. Their report states:

> The Bible indicates the church is the community of Christ on earth. . . . the model of loving, caring, . . . human relations . . . a loving, obedient relationship to God in Christ.
>
> . . . The world will listen to our pronouncements on racism, poverty and morality when we demonstrate to them what life can be when Christ's tenets are followed.

> For Jesus compressed all that matters most into one word . . .
> LOVE—Love to God and Love to Man.
>
> . . . that word demonstrated in Christ's cross put an end to
> artificial, separating, sinful barriers in human relations.
>
> . . . let those who profess perfect love reaffirm their belief in
> the . . . value of every person for whom Christ died, regardless of
> race or color, . . . divest . . . every . . . trace of racism . . . and
> abandon any . . . form as light comes to them.
>
> . . . the time has come for the proponents of Christian
> holiness to demonstrate perfect love in every . . . relationship . . .
> to recover the compassion for . . . the poverty-stricken,. . . the
> Wesleyan heritage . . . eroded by . . . confusion of true Christian
> compassion with the so-called "Social Gospel". . . .[37]

For decades, various church organizations have expressed such
concern for the problems of racism. Yet, often the Christian Church is
only a "conspiracy of silence," failing to put righteous words into general
action. The real world has an urgent need for a holistic approach to the
American dilemma. Though a "heavenly view" of all peoples' need of
God's salvation is essential, a "world view" of humanity must converge.
That broad focus must include American ethnic minorities with the needy
around the world.

The International Consultation on Racism and Racial Justice met in
Los Angeles January 17-21, 1988. The World Council of Churches'
Program to Combat Racism urged U. S. church groups to resume
leadership in that struggle. Racial injustice continued to rise world-wide.
The meeting was the most racially inclusive gathering the council has
held in America, but it found little progress in eradicating racism. This
became viewed as a failure of Christians to sustain commitment to the
struggle.[38]

Rev. Joan Campbell, a Christian Church (Disciples of Christ)
minister who heads the World Council's U.S. office in New York,
confessed, "We came in pain, knowing our churches no longer play the
role they once did in securing racial justice." She challenged white
Christians, saying: "People of color have continued to press the churches
on the issue. It's the Whites who have stopped."[39] The *status quo*
syndrome still prevails, bypassing inclusiveness.

In the spring of 1989, during the 15th anniversary celebration of the
Lamb's Church in New York City, a Racism and Reconciliation
Workshop was held. Dr. Tom Nees, pastor of the Community of Hope

Church in Washington, D.C., and several members of his congregation joined with Pastor David Best and the Lamb's group in the workshop to discuss racism and the proper Christian response. America experiences a tense rise in racism. News services and police officials report a steady increase in racially motivated attacks.

Yet, as Tom Nees declared, it's not simply "a black-white issue." The awareness of the problem was clarified:

> It's a right-wrong issue, isn't it? And if it is an issue of right and wrong—of justice and injustice—why is it that, in this sense, the people speaking out for justice are almost always black and even the white folks who claim to be allies are embarrassingly silent? If it is a justice issue, we all ought to be speaking together about it.[40]

Both of the churches involved in this unique workshop, the Lamb's and the Community of Hope, are cross-cultural congregations of the Church of the Nazarene. However, the focus is on total ministry, that the good news of salvation is for every person, every place, and in any condition, without respect of persons.

Many churches across the nation have found that survival came as they achieved the community racial mix in their congregation. Denominational loyalty or doctrinal preference become secondary to the critical points of ministry. For example, in Kansas City, some churches face a harsh choice: change or close the doors. In urban areas where whites flee to the suburbs, churches with aging congregations survive only if they can gather new members from the community or somehow attract young families that need a church.[41]

For churches to be bodies of reconciliation it often means adapting to the changing neighborhoods. All denominations become caught up in changes within the cities. A crucial factor in the survival of urban churches is to know their problems and work to solve them. Often, churches simply maintain the *status quo*, satisfying current parishoners who want only a normal message every Sunday. Bridges of understanding are not built from the ground of *status quo*, to have reconciliation that helps to construct peace among peoples. Self-pleasure must be rejected to become aware of community problems. We must accept community people, acknowledging that God has made us all brothers and sisters before Him[42]

The past racist legacy which churches have at times ignored, requires current repentance. This means a turning from racism by individual Christians and by the Church as a whole. It can begin with you and me, in our places of worship, and in our daily contacts. Our awareness of the lingering dilemma can transform previous neglect to useful flesh-and-blood friendship. God's Word draws each of us from racial bias to brotherhood: "He made from one, every nation of mankind to live on all the face of the earth . . ." (Acts 17:26, NASB). When individuals and groups become fully reconciled to God, they become reconciled to each other.

Actual Christian concern compels us to put aside the false racial barriers. We must then persist in actions toward resolving the Civil War conflict, the current racial conflict, and the personal conflict within. Such peace must become more than a hazy dream, but a reality in the making—by reconciliation. The crucial question is: To what extent will the Church humble herself in paying the price for peace? That price includes giving ourselves to the ongoing task of resolving the racist conflict. True holy actions must at last support the oft repeated scriptural edicts.

Epilogue

How harshly, yet subtly, the heinous concept and practice of slavery surged from the past to entice our nation's fathers! Such grim knowledge reveals that this vile practice spawned racism in "the land of the free." Despite many a troubled moral conscience and abolition attempts, slavery thrived for over 200 years, and the outgrowth of racism remains entrenched. Political approval and usage, social desire, and economic utility lured even religious Americans to concur with *laissez-faire*. Daily problems of racism continue to confront the various social, economical, educational, political, and religious arenas of our nation.

Historically, Christian churches ranged from the Apostolic beginnings, to Roman Catholic, and to Protestant. All condoned the custom and practice of slavery. Scripture provided seeming points to accept slavery, but no definite grounds to avoid or challenge it. However, Christians received repeated admonitions to handle slaves humanely—to care for their physical needs, and to teach them about spiritual salvation through Jesus Christ. Yet, upon conversion and baptism, were black Christians to remain enslaved? Most American slaveowners decided, "Yes."

Our racist legacy, traced from the first colonial settlement in Jamestown, resultantly indicts present day Americans. That bitter-sweet juncture, from the introduction of slavery, continues to afflict black-white relationships. The hostile white attitudes against the Africans flourished because of racist beliefs that perceived blacks as having inferior traits and capacities. Our guilt now does not persist because of previous misdeeds in history; it issues from present mind-sets, attitudes, and acts. The whites' prejudice that once seemed so politically wise, socially elevating, and religiously acceptable, remains a noxious human ingredient that stifles justice, love, and reconciliation.

Sociologically, black slaves faced annihilation—no identification as persons—until Lincoln's Emmancipation Proclamation that freed the slaves after the Civil War. Though gaining freedom and personal identity, the blacks' social standing merely moved to a low strata. This status included the concept of group segregation, which prevented the normal mix of human relationships between blacks and whites. Blacks endured a stratified segregation until the 1960s. During that decade, with the peaceful protests under the leadership of Dr. Martin Luther King, society began to accept an assimilative integration of blacks. The passage of civil rights laws guaranteed it. Yet, for the blacks, this also meant a loss of identity, a blurring of esteem as individual persons. Since the '70s, Rev. Jesse Jackson has urged a social assimilative pluralism, seeking personal identity for blacks along with acceptance and equal social relationships.

The cost of providing equal opportunities and acceptance for blacks remains an economic stumbling block, foiling both religious and political views. A similar hurdle blocked the colonization movement to transport freed slaves back to Africa, both before and after the Civil War. Churches boosted this project as a missionary effort; politicians saw it as getting rid of a malignant problem. Even now, some people say all blacks should be returned to Africa. The overall cost was and is beyond computation—nor is it the right or Christian thing to do.

The Southern section of our country must not be blamed for all the racism woven into the fabric of our nation's society. The vast majority of Northerners also believed in white supremacy. From its start, slavery became condoned by both Northern and Southern churches. Nor did the Northern abolition of slavery cancel racist feelings about the race indelibly marked by that bondage. Though slavery eventually divided the churches as well as the regions, concepts of white supremacy prevailed in both Northern and Southern churches. Similar attitudes today stem from the Civil War views.

Recent reminders reveal some startling passions that linger from that bitter racist conflict. Only in 1993 did the Senate reject the renewal of the patent on the insignia of the United Daughters of the Confederacy. Their insignia includes the seven-starred Confederate flag, a stirring symbol that continues to divide blacks from whites in the South. That same year, the New Orleans City Council voted to dismantle the Liberty Monument, a granite obelisk built to white supremacy.

Economic historian and Nobel Prize winner Robert Fogel disputed the accepted view that slavery became unprofitable in the United States and thus could only fail. His findings show that slavery became economically efficient and it faced ruin only because of the Civil War. But Fogel refused to endorse slavery, which he viewed as inhumane, whatever its economic worth to any society. In all of these passionate currents, the Church remained a silent factor, clinging to the social *status quo.*

One main sociological focus views the extent that whites will allow freed blacks to take part in American politics and common society. Such set limits also pollute churches with racism—one very persistent evil result of slavery. In dealing with blacks, most white churches subtly keep them subdued in terms of Christian fellowship as well as social equality. The Church generally kept silent through the black pilgrimage, from slavery to freed persons, trying to find social standing. By so doing, the Church blandly heeded the *status quo*, ignoring the ongoing social conflict from the Civil War. White Christians abandoned the great task of evangelizing blacks to struggling efforts by the black churches.

Someone prophesied generations ago, in 1870, "Negro" problems would be "upon us in 1970." Sadly, and shamefully, the words rang true, reaching the century mark—and beyond. Presently, related issues plague our nation, our society, and our churches. Nearing the 21st century, the saying, "And the beat goes on," is apropos. The daily news shows mounting evidence how most Americans mark time or allow the ongoing cadence of social conflict to persist.

The past and present concerns of blacks yet await the equal treatment of justice. Can caring Christians remain quiet about the injustice swamping this people? Can loving Christians refrain from attempts to build bridges of fellowship? Every professing Christian should treat any person, no matter the skin color, as he or she would want to be treated. God is not merely the white people's deity; His Son, Jesus Christ died to be everyone's Savior. His Great Commission sends His followers out to give the gospel to peoples of every tribe and nation. Yet, adversely, His Church has often culturized the gospel and pronounced some restrictions and definitions that God's Word never specified.

What genre of the Christian gospel really meets the challenge of centuries-old racism? Throughout its history, our nation has experienced several widespread "spiritual awakenings." Revivalism remains an occasional strong force in society. Yet, such spiritual prods have never produced the needed framework for racial reconciliation. Many Christians joined the efforts to abolish slavery. Those crusades, coupled with the evangelical movements, raised the level of national conscience about bondage over "God's creatures." Today, the churches and religious organizations most committed to spiritual and social ministry make the greatest impact against racism and injustice.

As the previous spiritual awakenings ignored slavery and the outgrowth of racism, the impact of science also offered support instead of opposing racist tenets. The free-thinking effect of Social Darwinianism on Christianity encouraged the *laissez-faire* stance and upheld the *status quo* white treatment of blacks. The theory of evolution expected the triumphant survival of the dominant white race. Why evangelize black people, the fading race? Such subconscious thought stifled the so-called "social gospel" that appealed for more concern about people's daily affairs, and faced the rampant racial issues with no hope of reconciliation.

Over a century and a quarter from the Civil War era, we may stand in judgment over faulty decisions, wrongful explanations of Scripture, and the misappropriation of divine grace. Despite the various attempts of Christians in churches to form the Body of Christ in our time, their efforts often reflect the prominent bias of the secular mind-set. Something remains lacking. Christians are to be new creations in Christ Jesus, being Christlike and doing as He would do (2 Corinthians 5:17).

From the Reconstruction years on, white society, North as well as South, moved to segregate blacks and withhold any "undeserved" privileges. Even good church members carried their social strata concepts through the church door, to bias the congregation. In the most recent decades one readily observes that the attitudes of Christian congregations generally coincide with the racial views of secular society. Yet, some people, transformed by Jesus' love, reach beyond the socially accepted *status quo.*

The Billy Graham evangelistic crusades, and other inter-denominational efforts have offered "neutral" ground for some bridge-building and reconciliation of peoples. Such allowances may be called tokenism, but they become a base for further progress. However, reconciliation must extend to neighborhood churches, to personal relationships, from the urban and inner city, to rural areas. As previously noted, churches that engage in holistic ministry make steady attempts to deal with racism. Both the physical and spiritual needs of people, of any skin color or culture, becomes confronted with gospel truth. Such ministry becomes the main focus rather than promoting denominational tags.

The cross of Jesus Christ is the proven crossroads where all peoples may meet on equal terms in true reconciliation, love, and peace. It opens the Church's hope to resolve the conflict flaring from our racist legacy. Any individual or group of believers may "take up his cross daily" (Luke 9:23, RSV), and follow Christ. True followers of Jesus Christ know first-hand about forgiveness and redemption. Christ's witnesses obeying His Great Commission also know the necessity and power of divine love that must work in their lives. God's Holy Spirit and the eternal truth of His

Holy Word ever repeat the message pointing to the vital ministry of reconciliation in all people.

Throughout American history, churches, other Christian groups, and individuals have sought an acceptable way to curtail the racist legacy. Radical measures that split denominations, valiant efforts to pass laws, and sincere calls for a remedy to racism have never met the need. The true answer for quelling feelings of racism and to bring peace to racial conflict resides plainly in Jesus' words. Yet statements affirming human equality, and commissions set to organize groups to properly receive all peoples, do not ease the conflict. Committed Christian individuals must live out scriptural truth and begin bridge-building to reconciliation where they are.

Perhaps various denominations of the Christian Church will never really seek to build bridges of reconciliation to accept people of other cultures and skin colors. Most American Christians often seem more concerned about standing by the safe *status quo*, with a prosperous social position. But fulfilling Christ's Great Commission in meeting the complex problems of racism is the only true catalyst for transforming their communities.

Hopefully, more local churches, and denominations as a whole, will faithfully engage the need to resolve the conflict of racism. We must acknowledge that no secular program based on human effort alone will ever settle racism. In obedience to Jesus' command to love and to His Great Commission, like the apostle Paul, we must freely accept all peoples as brothers—equals. This forsakes the historical safety of the *status quo* of white supremacy, the favored position of religious leadership, and economic strength.

Once the future rested with the theorem, "the survival of the fittest," and white churches persistently ignored the black people marked with slavery. From the present sociological stance of assimilative pluralism, the best expected progression in the future is accommodation that permits personal identity. But not even social accommodation can resolve bitter racial conflict. It becomes, at best, a seething inner turmoil.

July, 1991, Bill McCartney founded the first men's conference called Promise Keepers, which drew 4,200 men to Boulder, Colorado. By summer in 1994, Promise Keepers had expanded men's conferences to seven cities around the nation. Over 280,000 men became moved to join this ministry. The summer of 1995 committed Promise Keepers to 13 nationwide men's conferences, with over 500,000 men participating. One of the seven promises every Promise Keeper makes is: "A Promise Keeper is committed to reaching beyond any racial and denominational barriers to demonstrate the power of biblical unity." There does seem to be an increasing number of men with other than white skin color who attend the conferences. To make such a promise moves one in the right direction, but true fulfillment awaits honest acceptance and caring relationships.

In 1993, Edith Guffey, secretary of the 1.6 million-member United Church of Christ, saw racial divisions as increasing. She said that the denomination recognized the need to make progress to become a multiracial, multicultural church. The church adopted a statement outlining this goal at its 1993 General Synod in St. Louis. The urgency remains that the church become more inclusive, nationally, regionally, and locally.

June 20, 1995, the mostly white Southern Baptist Convention, stemming from the North and South split over slavery, apologized to black people for condoning racism. The resolution received a standing ovation from 20,000 members of the nation's largest Protestant denomination gathered in Atlanta for their annual convention. The decree reproves racism, repudiates "historic acts of evil such as slavery" and asks for forgiveness. It commits the 15.6 million-member church to remove the vestiges of racism and to make changes that build bridges for racial harmony.

The best future hope remains with those Christian groups and congregations working to resolve the racial conflict within their own minds and relationships. Paying the price of self-sacrifice, they strive to bring reconciliation through Christ's compelling love. Salvation and reconciliation will never be purchased by political maneuvers, economic ploys, or led by legal guides. It awaits the increased and faithful effort of Christians truly following Christ, taking up the cross of self-sacrifice, to learn, to accept, and to love as He would have them do. Facing our racist legacy, only the future holds the complete answer to the question: "Will the Church Resolve the Conflict?"

You and I begin the answer by our personal caring response to this gut-wrenching issue. This will happen only as the love of Christ compels us to risk moving beyond the social *status quo*. As bridge builders aroused by Christ's accepting love, our persistent work and patience will help resolve the racial conflict.

Notes

Chapter 1.Notes—Slavery and the Watersheds of Religion in America

1 Edwin Scott Gaustad, *A Religious History of America*, (New York: Harper & Row, 1966), 37.

2 Ibid, 38.

3 Sydney Ahlstrom, *A Religious History of the American People*, (New Haven, Conn.: Yale University Press, 1972), 185; *Eerdman's Handbook to Christianity in America*, (Grand Rapids, Mich.: Wm B. Eerdmans Publishing Co., 1983), 23.

4 Ahlstrom, loc. cit., 187.

5 Benjamin Quarles, *The Negro in the Making of America*, (New York: Macmillan Publishers, Inc., 1969), 36.

6 Cited in Saunders Redding, *They Came in Chains*, (Philadelphia: J. B. Lippincott Co., 1973), 34.

7 See Winthrop D. Jordan, *White Over Black*, (University of North Carolina Press, 1968), chap. 5, "The Souls of Men."

8 Redding, loc. cit.

9 Cited in Gaustad, loc. cit., 47.

10 Ahlstrom, loc. cit., 137-8.

11 Ibid, 138.

12 Gaustad, loc. cit., 50.

13 Ibid, 51.

14 Joanne Grant, *Black Protest History, Documents and Analyses* (New York: Fawcett Premier, 1968), 26; from *The Friend*, IV, Seventh Day, English Month, 1831, No. 46, 363.

15 William Katz, *Eyewitness*, (New York: Pitman Publishing Co., 1967), 22.

16 Ibid.

17 Cited in Quarles, loc. cit., 42.

18 Cf. Gaustad, loc. cit., 76; Quarles, loc. cit., 43.

19 Ibid.

20 *Eerdman's Handbook*, 91.

21 David B. Davis, *The Problem of Slavery in Western Culture*, (Ithica, N.Y.: Cornell University Press, 1966), 307.

22 Cited in Gaustad, loc. cit., 91.

23 Cf. Katz, loc. cit., 23; Quarles, loc. cit., 43.

24 Ahlstrom, loc. cit., 650.

25 Lewis V. Baldwin and Horace L. Wallace, *Touched By Grace*, (Nashville: Graded Press, 1986), 13.

26 Ibid, 20.

27 From W. J. Wells, *The African Methodist Episcopal Zion Church* (A.M.E. Zion Publishing House, 1974), 41.

28 Gaustad, loc. cit., 44.

29 Cited in *Eerdman's Handbook*, 146.

30 Ibid.

31 Ibid.

32 Cf. J. Wesley Bready, *This Freedom—Whence?* (New York: American Tract Society, 1942), 238; Davis, loc. cit., 148.

33 David Christy, *Pulpit Politics*, (New York: Negro Universities Press, reprint, 1969), 38.

34 Cf. Helmut Thielicke, trans. and ed. by John W. Doberstein. *Man in God's World*, (New York: Harper & Row Publishers, 1963), 51-53.

Chapter 2. Notes—Scriptural Pespectives of Slavery and Racism

1 Cited in Eugene D. Genovese, *The Political Economy of Slavery*, 198; in *Journal of Southern History*, XI (Aug. 1945), 422.

2 Cited in Ibid.; *De Bow's Review* (Jan. 1861), 103.

3 Howell Cobb, *A Scriptural Examination of the Institution of Slavery in the United States with Its Objects and Purposes*, (Georgia, 1856), 121.

4 William A. Smith, *The Philosophy and Practice of Slavery* (New York: Negro Universities Press, reprint, 1969), 135.

5 Ibid., 139.

6 Ibid., 139-40.

7 Ibid., 143.

8 Ibid., 144.

9 Cf. Smith, loc. cit., 208-9.

10 Ibid., 172-74.

11 Cited in David B. Davis, *The Problem of Slavery*, 451.

12 Cited in Ibid., 451-52.

13 Cf. Ibid., 453; Morgan Godwyn, *The Negro's and Indian's Advocate, Suing for Their Admission into the Church* . . . (London, 1680), 12, 19-23.

14 John Wesley, *Journal*, standard ed., Nehemiah Curnock, ed. (1906-16), V, 458; cf. Davis, *The Problem of Slavery*, 458-59; Margaret T. Hodgen, "The Negro in the Anthropology of John Wesley," *Journal of Negro History*, XIX (July, 1934), 308-23; James Ramsay, *An Essay on the Treatment and Conversion of African Slaves in the British Sugar Colonies* (London, 1784), 198-245.

15 Cf. David B. Davis, *Slavery and Human Progress*, (New York: Oxford University Press, 1984), 131; James Beattie, *Elements of Moral Science* (Edinburgh, 1793), II, 164.

16 Cited in Ibid., 137.

17 Cited in Ibid., 139.

18 Cited in Ibid., 142.

19 Cf. Ibid., 146.

20 Cited in Ibid.; Weld to Garrison, January 2, 1833, *Weld-Grimke Letters*, I, 48.

21 Newell G. Bringhurst, *Saints, Slaves, and Blacks* (Westport, Conn.: Greenwood

Press, 1981), 4; cf. Fawn M. Brodie, *No Man Knows My History*, 2nd ed. (New York, 1971), 34-61; Donna Hill, *Joseph Smith: The First Mormon* (New York, 1977), 70-89.

22 Cf. *Book of Mormon*, Alma 22:28; 2 Nephi 5:20.

23 Cf. Ibid, 2 Nephi 5:21-24; 1 Nephi 12:33; Alma 3:13-19.

24 Cf. Bringhurst, loc. cit, 10; *Book of Mormon*, Jacob 3:5, 9-10; Alma 3:6; Mormon 5:15.

25 Brigham Young, *Journal of Discourses*, VII, 290.

26 Ibid, X, 110.

27 Joseph Fielding Smith, *The Way to Perfection* (Salt Lake City, 1931), 102.

28 Cf. William Goodell, *Slavery and Anti-Slavery: A History of the Great Struggle in Both Hemispheres, With a View to the Slavery Question in the United States* (New York, 1853), 143-219; Davis, *Slavery and Human Progress*, 152.

29 Winthrop Jordan, *White Over Black*, 72.

30 Cf. *The Annals*, "Blacks and the Law," Richard D. Lambert, ed. (Philadelphia: The American Academy of Political and Social Science, 1973), 6-7; George M. Stroud, *Sketch of the Laws Relating to Slavery*, (Philadelphia: Henry Longstreth, 1856), 34.

31 Charles Darwin, *Life and Letters*, I, (letter to W. Graham, July 3, 1881), 316; cited in Gertrude Himmelfarb, *Darwin and the Darwinian Revolution* (London: Chatto and Windus, 1959), 343.

32 Henry M. Morris, *The Troubled Waters of Evolution* (San Diego: Creation-Life Publishers, 1975), 164.

33 Thomas Huxley, *Lay Sermons, Addresses, and Reviews* (New York: Appleton, 1871), 20.

34 Cf. *Southern Magazine*, XVI, (1875), 320; *Sunny South*, November 6, 1875; November 13 and December 9, 1875; October 12, 1889; Claude H. Nolen, *The Negro's Image in the South* (Lexington: University of Kentucky Press, 1967), 7.

35 Cited in Nolen, loc. cit.; cf. James H. Croushore and David Morris Potter, eds., *A Union Officer in the Reconstruction* (New Haven, Conn., 1948), 192.

36 Buckner H. Payne, *Ariel's Reply to the Rev. John A. Seiss, D.D., of Philadelphia;* also, *His Reply to the Scientific Geologist and Other Learned Men in Their Attacks on the Credibility of the Mosaic Account of the Creation and of the Flood* (Nashville, 1876), 5-94; cf. Nolen, loc. cit., 9.

37 Cf. Nolen, loc. cit., xvi.

38 *The Devil's Inkwell: A Story of Humanity Embracing Biblical Evidence Establishing Irrefutable and Utter Supremacy of the White Man on the Earth Since the Beginning of Historical Time* (Houston, 1923), passim 32-46.

39 Cited in "Monthly Record of Events," *Harper's Magazine*, XXXIV (1867), 398; cf. James G. Blaine, *Twenty Years in Congress*, 2 vols. (Norwich, Conn., 1884), I, 505.

40 *Carrolton West Alabamian*, March 9, 1870; cited in Nolen, loc. cit., 17-18.

41 George Gaylord Simpson, "The Biological Nature of Man," *Science*, vol. 152, April 22, 1964, 474; cited in Morris, *The Troubled Waters of Evolution*, 162.

Chapter 3. Notes —Revolution, Religion, and Slavery in a Free Country

1 Cited in William Katz, *Eyewitness*, 35; George H. Moore, *Notes on the History of Slavery in Massachusetts*, (New York, 1866), 75-77.

2 Terry Bilhartz, *Francis Asbury's America*, (Grand Rapids, MI: Francis Asbury Press, 1984), 23.

3 Saul K. Padover, ed., *Thomas Jefferson on Democracy*, (New York: New Amican Library, 1967), 1.

4 Cited in Louis H. Pollack, *The Constitution and the Supreme Court: A Documentary History*, (New York: World Pub. Co., Meridian Books, 1968), I, 9.

5 Thomas Jefferson, *Autobiography*, I, 68-9.

6 Cited in John Hope Franklin, *From Slavery to Freedom*, (New York: Alfred A. Knopf, 1980), 91.

7 Katz, loc. cit., 27.

8 Ibid., 46.

9 Ibid., 48.

10 Cited in Ibid., 41; John C. Fitzpatrick, ed., *The Writings of George Washington from the Original Manuscript Sources 1754-1799*, (Washington, 1938), vol. 28, 407-8.

11 Cf. Benjamin Quarles, *The Negro in the Making of America*, 58.

12 Cited in Bilhartz, loc. cit., 26.

13 Cited in Sydney Ahlstrom, *A Religious History of the American People*, 371.

14 Cited in Ibid.

15 Noted in Ibid., 374.

16 Cf. Ibid., 375.

17 Cited in Ibid., 383.

18 Quoted in Carter Woodson, *The History of the Negro Church*, 2nd ed. (Washington D.C.: Associated Publishers, 1921), 97-8.

19 Katz, loc. cit., 50.

20 Franklin, loc. cit., 95.

21 Ibid., 95-6.

Chapter 4. Notes—Christians and Abolitionist Action

1 Cf. Gilbert H. Barnes, *Antislavery Impulse, 1830-1844*, (New York: D. Appleton-Century Co., 1933), 3-4.

2 Cf. Ibid.

3 Timothy L. Smith, *Revivalism and Social Reform* (Gloucester, Mass.: Peter Smith, reprint, 1976), 180-1.

4 Cf. L. C. Matlack, *The History of American Slavery and Methodism from 1788 to 1849*, 32.

5 Kenneth Katz, *Eyewitness*, 165.

6 Cited in J. Wesley Bready, *This Freedom—Whence?* 239.

7 *Liberator*, April 14, 1832

8 Cf. George Fredrickson, *The Black Image in the White Mind*, 39; Aileen S. Kraditor, *Means and Ends in America Abolitionism: Garrison and His Critics on Tactics and Strategy*, 1834-1850 (New York, 1969), 242-3.

9 Cf. Ibid, 54; Theodore Weld to William Lloyd Garrison, January 2, 1833, *Letters of Theodore Weld, Angelian Grimke Weld, and Sarah Weld*, 1822-1844, ed. Gilbert H. Barnes and Dwight L. Dumond (New York, 1934), I, 98.

10 Cited in Willis D. Weatherford and Charles S. Johnson, *Race Relations*, (New York: Negro Universities Press, reprint 1969), 111.

11 Cited in Edwin Gaustad, *A Religious History of America*, 189.

12 Peter Cartwright, *Autobiography*, ed. W. P. Strickland, (Cincinnati: Cranston and Curts, 1856), 128.

13 Ibid, 129.

14 Gaustad, loc. cit., 186.

15 John Hope Franklin, *From Slavery to Freedom*, 129.

16 Cited in Gaustad, loc. cit., 187.

17 Bready, loc. cit., 238-9.

18 Arnold M. Rose, ed., *Assuring Freedom to the Free* (Detroit: Wayne State University Press, 1964), 77.

19 Cf. Barnes, loc. cit., 9.

20 Charles G. Finney, *Lectures to Professing Christians* (New York: Fleming H. Revell Co., 1878), 18.

21 Ibid., 56.

22 Ibid., 71.

23 Cited in Franklin, loc. cit., 183.

24 Cited in Gaustad, loc. cit., 182.

25 Cf. Smith, *Revivalism and Social Reform*, 180-1; Lucius C. Matlack, *The Life of Rev. Orange Scott* . . . (New York, 1847), 33-4; Matthew Simpson, ed. *Cyclopedia of Methodism* . . . (Philadelphia, 1878), 191.

26 Melvin E. Dieter, *The Holiness Revival of the Nineteenth Century* (Metuchen, N.J.: The Scarecrow Press, 1980), 24-5; S.B. Shaw, *Michigan Holiness Record*, II (June, 1884), 21. "An Unkind Insinuation," *Advocate of Bible Holiness*, XIII (September, 1882), 263; cf. *Christian Standard and Home Journal*, XIX (February 21, 1885), 5.

27 George Hughes, "An Awful Drift," *Guide, CII* (March 1898), 82-3.

28 Timothy L. Smith, *Called Unto Holiness* (Kansas City: Nazarene Publishing House, 1962), 28.

29 Cf. Smith, *Revivalism and Social Reform*, 182; May, *Some Reflections of Our Antislavery Conflict*, 233-237; 239-40, (pro-Garrison). *Appeal of Clerical Abolitionists on Anti-Slavery Measures* (Boston, 1838), and Massachusetts Abolition Society, *The True History of the Late Division in the Anti-Slavery Societies* . . . (Boston, 1841), 1-12.

30 Cited in Ibid., 187; Anon., "The Vital Forces of the Age," *The Christian Review*, XXVI (1861), 566.

31 Cited in Ibid, 184; James G. Birney to the Christian Antislavery Society April 2, 1850, quoted in Dwight L. Dumond, ed., *Letters of James Gillespie Birney, 1831-1857* (New York, 1935), II, 1134.

32 Gaustad, loc. cit., 187.

33 Cf. Smith, loc. cit., 184; Matlack, loc. cit., 33-5, 38, gives Orange Scott's own account.

34 Cited in Baldwin and Wallace, *Touched by Grace,* 41; from William Barclay, *History of Methodist Missions*, III, 85.

35 Cf. Ibid.

36 Cf. Smith, *Revivalism and Social Reform*, 184; Matlack, loc. cit., 39-40, 130-39; Abel Stevens, *Life and Times of Nathan Bangs, D.D.* (New York, 1863), 313-23.

37 Noted in Smith, *Revivalism and Social Reform*, 186; cf. C. Bruce Staiger, "Abolitionism and the Presbyterian Schism of 1837-1838, *"The Mississippi Valley Historical Review*, XXVI (1949-50), 395, 399-400.

38 Ibid.

39 Cited in Gaustad, loc. cit., 189-90.

40 Henry C. Vedder, *A Short History of the Baptists* (Philadelphia: American Baptist Publication Society, 1897), 233-4.

41 Ibid, 235.

42 Ibid.

43 Ibid, 236.

44 Cf. J. B. Phillips, *The Church Under the Cross*, (New York: The Macmillan Co., 1956), 48.

45 Cartwright, loc. cit., 157.

46 Gaustad, loc. cit., 188.

47 Cited in Ibid, 189.

48 Cited in Ibid.

49 Cited in Ibid., 190.

50 Cited in Ibid.

51 Cited in Ibid.

52 Cited in Ibid., 191.

Chapter 5. Notes—Some Problems That Faced Evangelical Antislavery

1 Cited in David B. Davis, *Slavery and Human Progress*, 146; Lewis C. Perry, *Childhood, Marriage, and Reform: Henry Clarke Wright, 1797-1870* (Chicago, 1980), 21-2.

2 Sydney Ahlstrom, *A Religious History of the American People,* 657.

3 Timothy Smith, *Revivalism and Social Reform*, 188.

4 Cited in Ibid.

5 Cited in Ibid.

6 Cited in David Christy, *Pulpit Politics*, 99-100.

7 Cited in Ibid, 100.

8 Cf. Smith, loc. cit., 189; Abel Stevens, *Nathan Bangs*, 316; Stevens, *Slavery—the Times*, 260, 445, 448, 454; *The Watchman and Reflector* (March 16, 1854), 2.

9 Cited in Ibid, 190; *The Watchman and Reflector* (October 29, 1857), 2.

10 Cf. Ibid, 191.

11 Ahlstrom, loc. cit., 661.

12 Ibid, 662.

13 Christy, loc. cit., 392.

14 Peter Cartwright, *Autobiography*, 416.

15 Ibid, 416-17.

16 Cited in Ahlstrom, loc. cit., 662.

17 Ibid, 663.

18 Cf. Ibid.

19 Smith, loc. cit., 191; *Zion's Herald*, (September 15, 1852), 2; (September 22, 1852), 2; cf. (July 28, 1852), 1; and (August 11, 1852), 2.

20 Ibid; *Zion's Herald* (October 6, 1852), 2; cf. Plainfield, Vt. letter from reader (October 13, 1852), 4.

21 Cited in Ibid, 192.

22 Cf. Ibid; Letters to the editor, *Zion's Herald* (January 21, 1852), 4: (March 3, 1852), 2; Charles K. Whipple, *The Methodist Church and Slavery* (New York, 1859), 13-15, 19-21.

23 Cited in Ibid, 193; Stephen Olin, London, 1846, to Abel Stevens, in Julia M. Olin, ed., *The Life and Letters of Stephen Olin* (New York, 1853), II, 318-19; American and Foreign Antislavery Society, *Remonstrance Against the Course Pursued by the Evangelical Alliance on the Subject of American Slavery* (New York, 1847), 1-9.

24 Cf. Ibid; Charles Howard Hopkins, *History of the Y.M.C.A. . . .* (New York, 1951), 60, 64, 77, 80.

25 Cf. Ibid, 194; *The Independent* (January 28, 1858), 4; editorials in September 20 and November 22, 1885 issues.

26 James Russell Lowell, "The American Tract Society," *The Atlantic Monthly,* II (1857-58), 246-51; cf. Ibid.

27 Cf. Ahlstrom, loc. cit., 678; Edwin Gaustad, *A Religious History of America,* 184.

28 Smith, loc. cit., 195; cf. George Prentice, *Wilbur Fisk,* 211-12; Albert Barnes, *The Church and Slavery,* 2nd ed. (Philadelphia, 1857), 150-1, 164-5.

29 Ahlstrom, loc. cit., 664.

30 Cf. Ibid.

31 Ibid, 665.

32 Cf. Smith, loc. cit., 196; A. Barnes, loc. cit., 76-8.

33 Cf. Ibid, 197-8; E. H. Gilbert, *Presbyterian Church,* II, 555-8.

34 Ibid; Prentice, *Wilbur Fisk,* 207-8, 211-12; George Barrell Cheever, *God Against Slavery, and the Freedom and Duty of the Pulpit to Rebuke It, As a Sin Against God* (New York, 1857), 94-5, 100-1.

35 Ibid, 199-200; *The Watchman and Reflector* (October 1, 1857), 2.

36 Harriet Beecher Stowe, *Uncle Tom's Cabin* (Boston: Houghton, Mifflin and Co., 1891), 499-500.

37 Cited in William Katz, *Eyewitness,* 189.

38 Christy, loc. cit., 224.

39 Cited in Ibid, 598-9.

40 Ibid, 604.

41 Smith, loc. cit., 196.

42 Cited in *The Squire* (published in Prairie Village, Kansas), vol. II., No. 9, September 15, 1988, "Saint or Sinner?" 8A.

43 From Kansas State Historical Society as noted in Ibid.

44 Cited in Gaustad, *A Religious History of America,* 193.

45 Cited in *The Annals,* 2; Dred Scott v. Sanford, 60 U.S. 393, 412 (1857).

46 Davis, loc. cit., 263; Frederick Frothingham, *Significance of the Struggle between Liberty and Slavery in America* (New York, 1857), 19-20.

47 Cited in Gaustad, loc. cit., 192.

48 Ibid., 194.

Chapter 6. Notes—The Faltering Church Crusade Against Slavery

1 Timothy Smith, *Revivalism and Social Reform,* 200; *The American Missionary,* V (1861), 268, quoted and commented upon the *Christian Advocate* statement; cf. David C. Mears, *Life of Edward Norris Kirk, D.D.* (Boston, 1877), 283, 291.

2 Ibid; Abel Stevens, *Nathan Bangs*, 322; Julian M. Sturtevant, *The Lessons of Our National Conflict. Address to the Alumni of Yale College* . . . (New Haven, 1861), 18-20; *The Watchman and Reflector*, (January 1, 1863), 1.

3 Cf. Smith, loc. cit., 200-1; Lincoln's Second Inaugural (March 4, 1865), cited in Edwin Gaustad, *A Religious History of America*, 196-7.

4 Cited in Ephraim Douglas Adams, *The Power of Ideals in American History* (New Haven: Yale University Press, 1924), 11-12.

5 *Complete Works of Abraham Lincoln*, ed. by John G. Nicolay and John Hay (New York: The Century Co., 1920), I, 186, 199.

6 Cf. Smith, loc. cit., 201; Albert J. Beveridge, *Abraham Lincoln, 1809-1858* (Boston, 1928), II, 30-2; 151-2; 218-22; 238-9; 244-54; 358-61; 500-13.

7 Cited in David Christy, *Pulpit Politics*, 533; from letter to John Holmes, April 2, 1820.

8 Clarence B. Carson, *A Basic History of the United States*, vol. 3, *The Sections and the Civil War* (Wadley, Ala.: American Textbook Com., 1985), 134.

9 William R. Moody, *The Life of D. L. Moody* (Fleming H. Revell Co., 1900), 81-2, 567.

10 Cited in Smith, loc. cit., 205; *Zion's Herald*, July 7, 1852, 2; August 11, 1852, 2; cf. "Civilization and Slavery," the same, August 19, 1852, 4.

11 Cf. Ibid; Frank L. Mott, *A History of American Magazines, 1850-1865*, (Cambridge, Mass., 1938), 67-8.

12 Cited in Ibid, 206; William Hosmer, *The Higher Law in Its Relation to Civil Government, with Particular Reference to Slavery and the Fugitive Slave Law* (Auburn, N.Y., 1852), 175-6, 178.

13 Cf. Ibid; Hosmer, *Slavery and the Church* (Auburn, N.Y., 1853), 129-30; 155-7; 164.

14 Cited in Christy, loc. cit., 100.

15 Cf. Smith, loc. cit.,m 207; *Zion's Herald*, October 20 and December 22, 1852; November 12, 1852, 4.

16 Cited in Ibid; Edward Thomson, "Slavery," *The Methodist Quarterly Review*, XXXIX (1857), 533, 539-40.

17 Cf. Ibid, 208; *The Independent*, January 4, 1849, 1; December 19, 1850, 2.

18 Cited in Wesley Norton, *Religious Newspapers in the Old Northwest to 1861* (Athens, Ohio: University of Ohio Press, 1977), 131; *Cincinnati Journal*, October 5, 1832.

19 Cf. Smith, loc. cit., 208; *The Independent*, October 10, 1850, 2; January 3, 1850, 2; March 21, 1850 supplement.

20 Cited in Christy, loc. cit., 173-4.

21 Cited in Smith, loc. cit., *The Independent*, January 18, 1855, 1.

22 Noted in Ibid; Cf. Cheever's editorials, *The Independent*, "The Sure Aggressive Tyranny of Slave Legislation," March 8, 1855; and "The Sphere of Conscience as the Judge and Interpreter of the Law," May 31, 1855; George I. Rockwood, *Cheever, Lincoln and Causes of the Civil War* (Worcester, Mass.: 1936), 40-55.

23 Cf. Ibid; Rockwood, *Cheever, Lincoln* . . ., 14, 19, 73-6, 79-81; Frederick A. Ross, *Slavery Ordained of God* (Philadelphia, 1859), contains speeches made at the New School General Assemblies in 1853 and 1856.

24 Cf. Ibid, 211; *The Watchman and Reflector*, March 30, 1854, 49-50; Henry C. Fish, *Freedom or Despotism. The Voice of Our Brothers' Blood* . . . (Newark, 1856), 12.

25 Cited in Ibid; cf. *The Guide to Holiness*, XXX (July-December, 1856), 127; Richard Wheatley, . . . Phoebe Palmer (New York, 1876), 218, 315, 552, 599-601.

26 Cf. Charles Edward White, *The Beauty of Holiness* (Grand Rapids: Francis Asbury Press, 1986), 228; Phoebe Palmer, *A Mother's Gift; or A Wreath for My Darlings* (New York: Walter C. Palmer, 1875), 208-9.

27 Cf. Smith, loc. cit., 130-1.

28 Cf. Ibid, 212; Phoebe Palmer, *Four Years in the Old World* . . . (New York, 1864), 647.

29 Ibid; Lucius C. Matlack, *Orange Scott*, 245, 248, 251; cf. 252-261.

30 Cf. Ibid, 214; "The National Crisis," *The Christian Review*, XXVI (1861), 491-5, 507-8; Charles William Heathcote, *The Lutheran Church and the Civil War* (New York, 1919), 54-65; Robert Fortenbaugh, "American Lutheran Synods and Slavery," 1830-1860, *The Journal of Religion*, XIII (1933), 72, 74, 91.

31 Cf. Ibid; William W. Manross, *A History of the American Episcopal Church* (2nd ed. rev., New York, 1950), 290-2, 150-1; Madeleine Hooke Rice, *American Catholic Opinion in the Slavery Controversy* (New York, 1944), 155-7, 275, 96.

32 Cf. Sydney E. Ahlstrom, *A Religious History of the American People*, 667-8.

33 Cited in Smith, loc. cit., 214; *The Watchman and Reflector*, March 26, 1857, 2; Albert Barnes, *The Church and Slavery* (2nd ed., Philadelphia, 1857), 151.

34 Charles G. Finney, *Memoirs*, (New York: Fleming H. Revell Co., 1908), 444.

35 Cited in Smith, loc. cit., 215; *The American Missionary* (Magazine), III, 6 (June, 1859), 131; II (November, 1859), 251.

36 Christy, loc. cit., 102; cf. Adam Clarke, *Commentary*.

37 Cited in Smith, loc. cit., 216; cf. "Slavery and the Bible," *The New Englander*, XV (1857), 129-30; Barnes, *Church and Slavery*, 10-11.

38 Ibid, 216-7; cf. Cheever, *Guilt of Slavery*, iv, ix-xx; and *God Against Slavery*, 9-15; Albert Barnes, *An Inquiry into the Scriptural Views of Slavery* (Philadelphia, 1846).

39 Cf. Ibid, 217; Joseph P. Thompson, *Teachings of the New Testament on Slavery*, (New York, 1856), quoted from review in *The New Englander*, XV (1857), 110, 113.

40 Cf. Ibid; Charles Elliott, *The Bible and Slavery* . . . (Cincinnati, 1857), 336-54.

41 Cf. Ibid; Gasparin, *Uprising* . . ., 93-4, 99-100; Fisch, *Nine Months* . . ., 130-1.

42 Cf. Ibid; Barnes, *The Church and Slavery*, 159-60; "Higher Law and Divorces," *The Independent*, July 5, 1855, 212; *The American Missionary* (Magazine) IV, 7 (July, 1860), 149 and 8 (August, 1860), 181, condemned tobacco with slavery.

43 Cf. Ibid, 220; George Prentice, *The Life of Gilbert Haven* . . . (New York, 1883), 107, 137, 292; Gilbert Haven, *National Sermons* . . . (Boston, 1869), 109-10.

44 Cf. Ibid; Haven, loc. cit., 137, 142-8.

45 Cf. Ibid, 222; Haven, loc. cit., 359.

46 George M. Fredrickson, *The Black Image in the White Mind*, 102.

47 Ibid, 100; Theodore Parker, "The Nebraska Question" sermon of February 12, 1854, *Collected Works*, ed. Frances P. Cobbe (London, 1863-1870), V, 250.

48 Norton, loc. cit., 126.

49 Christy, loc. cit., 421.

50 Ahlstrom, loc. cit., 702; cf. Gross Alexander, *History of the Methodist Episcopal Church, South*, ACHS, vol. 11 (New York, 1894), 117.

51 Christy, loc. cit., 240-1.

52 Ibid, 241.

53 Ibid, 206-7.

54 Ibid, 209-10.

55 Ibid, 210.

Chapter 7. Notes—Churches, Clergy, and President Lincoln

1 D. D. Thompson, *Abraham Lincoln, the First American* (New York: Hunt & Eaton, 1894), 10, 11.

2 *Eerdman's Handbook to Christianity in America,* 266.

3 Ibid.

4 Thompson, loc. cit., 43.

5 John G. Nicoly and John Hay (eds.), *Complete Works of Abraham Lincoln* (New York: The Century Co.,1920), I, 203.

6 Ibid, 215-6.

7 *Eerdman's Handbook*, loc. cit., 267.

8 Cited in Edwin S. Gaustad, *A Religious History of America*, 193-4.

9 Cited in Thompson, loc. cit., 69; cf. J. G. Holland, *Life of Lincoln,* 544.

10 Ibid, 70.

11 Cited in David Donald, *Lincoln's Herndon* (New York: Alfred A. Knopf, 1948), 214.

12 Nicolay and Hay, *Works*, I, 637.

13 V. Jacque Voegeli, *Free But Not Equal*, 13; cf. *Congressional Globe*, 37 Cong., 2 sess., 5, 6, 18-9.

14 Ibid, 16; cf. loc. cit., 76, 194-5, 327-32, 348-9, 858-9, 1816.

15 Ibid, 22-3; cf. "Annual Message to Congress," December 3, 1861, in Roy P. Basler (ed.) *The Collected Works of Abraham Lincoln*, 9 vols. (New Brunswick, N. J.: Rutgers University Press, 1953), V, 48.

16 Cf. Ibid, 23; Doolittle to Mary Doolittle, April 19, 1862, Doolittle Papers.

17 Cf. Timothy Smith, *Revivalism and Social Reform*, 232; *The American Missionary* (Magazine), 1862, IV, 10: see examples of appeals, Levi Sternberg, "Revivals," *The Evangelical Quarterly Review*, 1864, XV, 286-7.

18 Cf. Voegeli, loc. cit., 28; *Congressional Globe,* loc. cit., 1491.

19 Cited in Ibid; *Illinois State Journal* (Springfield), March 22, 1862.

20 Cf. Ibid, 39; "Annual Message to Congress," April 16, 1862, in Basler, (ed.), loc. cit., V, 48; Richard N. Current, *The Lincoln Nobody Knows* (New York: McGraw-Hill, 1958), 221-2.

21 Cf. Ibid, 40; Current, loc. cit., 71-5.

22 Nicoly and Hay, loc. cit., II, 227.

23 Basler, (ed.), loc. cit., V, 419-25, "Reply to Emancipation Memorial Presented by Chicago Christians of All Denominations," September 13, 1862.

24 Ibid, 433-6; "Preliminary Emancipation Proclamation," September 22, 1862.

25 Cited in Voegeli, loc. cit., 47; cf. Basler, (ed.), loc. cit., 425; Beale, (ed.), loc. cit., I, 143; *Diary and Correspondence of Salmon P. Chase*, 88.

26 Basler, (ed.), loc. cit., V, 28-30, "Emancipation Proclamation," January 1, 1863.

27 Cited in Ibid, 79-80; cf. Council Bluffs, Iowa *Nonpareil,* January 10, 31, 1863; Chicago *Tribune,* January 1, 3, 1863.

28 Cited in Ibid, 85; cf. *Ohio State Journal* (Columbus), March 16, April 14, June 1, 1863; Chicago *Tribune,* April 12, 21, 1863; *Nonpareil,* January 23, 1863; Dubuque, Iowa *Times,* April 21, May 6, 1863.

29 Cited in Ibid, 96; cf. Bell Irvin Wiley, *Southern Negroes, 1861-1865,* (2nd ed.), (New York: Rinehart, 1953), 175 ff.; Basler, (ed.), loc. cit., V, 535-6.

30 Cited in Ibid, 102; cf. Kirkwood to Henry W. Halleck, August 5, 1862, in U. S. War Dept., Adjutant General's Office, Record Group 94 (National Archives, Washington, D.C.); Dan Elbert Clark, *Samuel J. Kirkwood* (Iowa City: State Historical Society of Iowa, 1917), 294.

31 Cited in Ibid; cf. John Lynch to A. Kitchell (1863), *Richard Yates Papers* (Springfield: Illinois State Historical Society).

32 Cited in Ibid, 121; cf. Davis W. Clark, "The Editor's Table-Development of Treason in the North," *Ladies Repository,* XXIII, (March, 1863), 192; Chicago *Times,* October 12, December 31, 1863.

33 Cf. Ibid; Chicago *Times,* loc. cit.; *Western Christian Advocate* (Cincinnati), October 7, 1863; *Catholic Telegraph* (Cincinnati), February 18, April 8, 15, 23, May 6, 13, 20, June 10, 24, July 8, 15, August 26, October 7, November 11, 18, December 2, 1863.

34 Cited in Ibid, 131; cf. *Catholic Telegraph,* July 8, 15, 1863.

35 Basler (ed.), loc. cit., VII, 281-2, "To Albert G. Hodges," April 4, 1864.

36 Cited in Voegeli, loc. cit., 139; cf. *Congressional Globe,* 38 Cong. 1 sess., 444, 1203, 2038, 2955.

37 Cited in Thompson, *Abraham Lincoln,* 116.

38 Cited in Ibid, 117-8.

39 Smith, loc. cit., 231-2.

40 Cf. Ibid, 232; *Christ in the Army: A Selection of Sketches of the Work of the U.S. Christian Commission* (Philadelphia, 1865), 135, 139-41.

41 Cited in Voegeli, loc. cit., 163; cf. Chicago *Tribune,* November 19, 26, 1864; January 5, 1865; Robert B. Warden, *An Account of the Private Life and Public Services of Salmon Portland Chase* (Cincinnati: Wilstock Baldwin, 1874), 595; *Western Christian Advocate,* December 14, 1864).

42 Cf. *Congressional Globe,* 38 Cong., 1 sess., 1072.

43 Cited in Ibid, 180; New York *Tribune,* May 7, 1864.

44 Cf. Ibid; John G. Sproat, "Blueprint for Radical Reconstruciton," *Journal of Southern History,* XXIII (February, 1957), 25-44; "Final Report of the American Freedmen's Inquiry Commission to the Secretary of War," (May 15, 1864) , *Official Records,* 3rd ser., IV, 370-82.

45 Cf. Ibid, 180-1; *Official Records,* IV, 378-9.

46 Cited in William Katz, *Eyewitness,* 248; *The liberator,* December 29, 1865.

47 Cited in Voegeli, loc. cit., 154; Dubuque, Iowa *Democratic Herald,* February 2, 1865.

48 Cited in Ibid, 154-5; Springfield *Illinois State Journal,* February 1, 1865; Indianapolis *State Journal,* February 7, 14, 1865; Chicago *Tribune,* February 1, 1865.

49 Cited in Gaustad, loc. cit., 194-5.

50   Cited in Ibid, 196-7.

51   Cited in Ibid, 197.

52   Cf. Smith, loc. cit., 223-4; *The Nation*, I, 520-1.

Chapter 8. Notes—The Church and Biased Reconstruction

1 William W. Sweet, *The Story of Religion in America* (New York: Harper & Brothers, 1950), 312.

2 From an interview reported in the *Presbyterian Herald*, Louisville, Ky.; quoted in Chester F. Dunham, *The Attitude of the Northern Clergy Toward the South, 1860-65* (Toledo, Ohio: Gray Co., 1942), 2.

3 Cf. Sydney Ahlstrom, *A Religious History of the American People*, 673.

4 James W. Silver, *Confederate Morale and Church Propaganda* (Tuscaloosa, Ala.: Confederate Publishing Co., 1957), 101.

5 Cited in Ahlstrom, loc. cit., 671; A. V. G. Allen, *Life and Letters of Phillips Brooks*, I, 531.

6 Cited in Ibid, 682.

7 Kansas City *Times*, "A Flag of Bitter Insult," Carl T. Rowan, (Feb. 5, 1988); cf. Ibid, 682-3.

8 Robert W. Winston, *Andrew Johnson: Plebian and Patriot* (New York, 1928), 40.

9 Cited in Ahlstrom, loc. cit., 695-6.

10 Cf. Claude Nolen, *The Negro's Image in the South*, 53; John Preston McConnell, *Negroes and Their Treatment in Virginia from 1865 to 1867* (Pulaski, Va., 1910), 87; Paul Lewinson, *Race, Class, and Party: A History of Negro Suffrage and White Politics in the South* (New York, 1932), 37-42; Charleston, S.C. *Courier*, July 27, Aug. 31, Sept. 1, 1865.

11 Cf. Ibid; New Orleans *Crescent*, Dec. 5, 1865, Mar. 22, 1866, Nov. 20, 1867.

12 William Katz, *Eyewitness*, 249; Freedmen's Bureau Files (Washington, D.C., National Archives), R.G., 92.

13 Cf. Nolen, loc. cit., 55; Lewinson, loc. cit., 36.

14 Cf. Claude G. Bowers, *The Tragic Era* (Cambridge, Mass.: Riverside Press, 1929), 193; S. S. Cox, *Three Decades of Federal Legislation* (Providence, R.I., 1888), 591-3.

15 Benjamin Quarles, *The Negro in the Making of America*, 137-8.

16 Cited in Bowers, loc. cit., 139.

17 Cited in Ahlstrom, loc. cit., 684; from *A Defence of Virginia* (1867), quoted by William A. Clebsch, "Christian Interpretations of the Civil War," *Church History*, 30 (1961), 4.

18 Quoted in Ibid. From an address delivered in Charleston, S.C., Feb. 14, 1865, when the Stars and Stripes were restored to Ft. Sumter. General Robert J. Anderson presided at the ceremony; he as a major surrendered the fort in 1861.

19 Cited in Ibid, 685; Theodore Munger refers to Elisha Mulford's, *The Nation* (1870) as a supreme contribution to political science. Mulford said, "The war was not primarily between freedom and slavery. It was the war of a nation and the Confederacy."

20 Cf. Ibid, 685-6; Horace Bushnell's "Our Obligations to the Dead," delivered at Yale to a gathering in honor of those who had fallen; *Building Eras in Religion* (New York, 1881), 319-56.

21 Frederick A. Norwood, ed., *Sourcebook of American Methodism* (Nashville: Abingdon Press, 1982), 356; Baldwin and Wallace, *Touched By Grace*, 51.

22 Cf. Baldwin and Wallace, loc. cit.

23 Cf. Lewis G. Jordan, *Negro Baptist History, U.S.A.*, 84.

24 Ibid.

25 Ibid, 87.

26 Cited in Leon Litwack, *Been So Long in the Storm* (London: The Athlone Press, 1979), 489-90; *American Freedman*, I (April 1866), 5-6, (May 1866), 23-4; H. S. Beals to Rev. E. P. Smith, Feb. 15, 1867.

27 Cf. Nolen, loc. cit., 102; cited in Henry Lee Swint, *The Northern Teacher in the South* (Nashville, 1941), 43.

28 Cf. Ibid, 103; Henrietta Stratton Jaquette, ed., *The South After Gettysburg: Letters of Cornelia Hancock, 1863-1868*, (New York, 1956), 195-210.

29 Cf. Ibid, 104; Swint, loc. cit., 109.

30 Cf. Ibid, 104-5; Maria Waterbury, *Seven Years Among the Freedmen* (Chicago, 1890), 50-4, 116, 130-5; "Report of the State Superintendent of Public Education to the United States Bureau of Education, Oct. 28, 1871," in Frederick Eby, ed., *Education in Texas Source Materials* (Austin, Tex., 1918), 543-5.

31 Cf. W. E. B. DuBois, *Black Reconstruction: An Essay Toward a History of the Past Which Black Folk Played in the Attempt to Reconstruct Democracy in America, 1860-1880* (New York, 1935), 648.

32 Cf. Nolen, loc. cit., notes, 113.

33 Cf. Baldwin and Wallace, loc. cit., 55; William Barclay, *History of Methodist Missions*, III, 149.

34 Cited in Ibid; from Barclay, loc. cit., 151.

35 Cited in Ahlstrom, loc. cit., 692; *Independent*, vol. 17, no. 871 (Aug. 1865), 4; quoted in Chester F. Dunham, *The Attitude of the Northern Clergy*, 234.

36 Kenneth M. Stampp, *The Era of Reconstruction, 1865-1877* (New York: Random House, Vintage Books, 1965), 19; cf. Ahlstrom, loc. cit., 691.

37 Katz, loc. cit., 267.

38 Cf. Ahlstrom, loc. cit., 691.

39 Cited in Ahlstrom, loc. cit., 695; cf. John S. Brubacher and Willis Rudy, *Higher Education in Transition* (New York: Harper & Brothers, 1958), 75.

40 Cf. Taylor Branch, *Parting the Waters*, (New York: Simon and Schuster, 1988), 2.

41 Cited in Gaustad, loc. cit., 201; written by an unknown Negro slave in Guilford County, North Carolina, around 1825.

Chapter 9. Notes—Postwar Churches: Religion, Science, and Racism

1 Cited in Claude H. Nolen, *The Negro's Image in the South*, 39; *Century Magazine*, VIII (1885), 273-5.

2 Sydney Ahlstrom, *A Religious History of the American People*, 607.

3 Cf. Ibid, 765.

4 Cited in Richard Hofstadter, *Social Darwinism in American Thought* (Boston: Beacon Press, 1955), 28; *Independent*, Feb. 23, April 12, July 16, 1868.

5 Cf. Ibid; "Scientific Teaching in the Colleges," *Popular Science Monthly* XVI, (1880), 558-9.

6 Cf. Ibid; Bert J. Loewenberg, in "Darwinianism Comes to America 1859-1900," *Mississippi Valley Historical Review*, XXVIII (1841), 339-68, sees the period 1859-1880

as one of probation for Darwinianism, and the 1880-1900 period as one that witnessed the conversion of vocal American sentiment.

7 Cited in Ibid; Rev. J. M. Whiton, "Darwin and Darwinianism," *New Englander* XLII, (1883), 63.

8 Cited in Ahlstrom, loc. cit., 789, quoted by Sidney E. Mead, *The Lively Experiment: The Sharing of Christianity in America* (New York: Harper & Row, 1963), 160.

9 Gunnar Myrdal, *An American Dilemma* (New York: Harper & Brothers Publisher, 1944), 1048.

10 Ibid, 1049.

11 Cited in Hofstadter, loc. cit., 51; cf. 66.

12 Cited in Ray Ginger, *Age of Excess* (New York: MacMillan Co., 1965), 280.

13 Cited in Ahlstrom, loc. cit., 789-90.

14 Cited in Hofstadter, loc. cit.; Henry Ward Beecher, *Evolution and Religion* (New York, 1885), 52, 115.

15 Cf. Ibid, 29-30; Lyman Abbott, *The Theology of an Evolutionist* (Boston, 1897), 31ff.; Beecher, loc. cit., 90ff.

16 Ahlstrom, loc. cit., 771.

17 Cf. Hofstadter, loc. cit., 30; Daniel Dorchester, *Christianity in the United States*, (New York, 1888), 650.

18 Cited in Ibid; A. V. G. Allen, *Phillips Brooks, 1835-1893* (New York, 1907), 309.

19 Cited in Ibid; Beecher, loc. cit., 18.

20 Ahlstorm, loc. cit., 744-5.

21 Edwin Gaustad, *A religious History of America*, 230.

22 Cited in Ginger, loc. cit., 284.

23 Laura Jones, *The Life and Sayings of Sam P. Jones* (by His Wife), (Atlanta: Franklin-Turner Publishers, 1907), 64.

24 Ibid, 292.

25 Ibid, 293.

26 Cited in Gausted, loc. cit., 231.

27 Cited in Ahlstrom, loc. cit., 733-4.

28 Cf. Ibid, 848-9.

29 Cf. Nolen, loc. cit., 26.

30 Cited in Ibid, 17; from "Monthly Record of Events," *Harpers' Magazine* XXXIV (1867), 398.

31 Cited in Ibid, 17-8; Carrolton *West Alabamian*, March 9, 1870.

32 Edgar Gardner Murphy, *The White Man and the Negro at the South* (Philadelphia, 1900), 22-3.

33 Cited in Weatherford and Johnson, *Race Relations*, 217; from Thomas Pearce Bailey, *Race Orthodoxy in the South and Other Aspects of the Negro Question* (New York: Neale Publishing Co., 1914), 93.

34 Cf. Ginger, loc. cit., 187; Josiah Strong, *Our Country: Its Possible Future and Its Present Crisis* (New York: the American Home Missionary Society, 1885), 174-5.

35 Cited in Ibid, 282.

36 Cited in Gaustad, loc. cit., 243.

37 Cited in Hofstadter, loc. cit., 108; Walter Rauschenbush, *Christianizing the Social Order* (New York: The MacMillan Co., 1912), 90.

38 Charles M. Sheldon, *In His Steps* (New York: Grosset & Dunlap, 1935), 15.

39 Cited in Hofstadter, loc. cit., 108; A. J. F. Behrends, *Socialism and Christianity* (New York: Baker and Taylor, 1886), 6; cf. Washington Gladden, *Social Facts and Forces* (New York, 1897), 2; Josiah Strong, *The Next Great Awakening* (New York, 1893), 16-17.

40 Cited in Ibid, 109-10; cf. George Herron, *The Christian Society* (New York, 1894), 103, 108-9; *The Christian State* (New York, 1895), 88; *The New Redemption* (New York, 1893), 16-7.

41 Cited in Ibid, 110; Herron, *The New Redemption*, 30.

42 Cited in Ginger, loc. cit., 206.

43 Cited in Ibid, 207.

44 Rowland Berthoff, *An Unsettled People: Social Order and Disorder in American History*, (New York: Harper & Row Publishers, 1971), 415; Paul A. Carter, *The Decline and Revival of the Social Gospel: Social and Political Liberalism in American Protestant Churches, 1920-1940* (Ithica, N.Y., 1956), 56-7.

45 Cited in Ahlstrom, loc. cit., 728; David M. Reimers, *White Protestantism and the Negro* (New York: Oxford University Press, 1965), 29.

46 Cited in Ibid; Rufus B. Spain, *At Ease in Zion: Social History of Southern Baptists* (Nashville: Vanderbilt University Press, 1967), 214; cf. 184-5, 190-2.

47 C. Vann Woodward, *The Strange Career of Jim Crow* (New York: Oxford University Press, 1974), 72.

Chapter 10. Notes—How the Church Befriended Jim Crow

1 Cited in Claude Nolen, *The Negro's Image in the South*, 16; "Strivings of the Negro Race," *Atlantic Monthly*, LXXX (1897), 197.

2 Cf. Ibid, 24; Chevereux Gris, "The Negro in His Religious Aspect," *Southern Magazine*, XVII (1879), 501-2; Noah K. Davis, "The Negro in the South," *Forum*, I (1886), 130; Robert F. Campbell, *Some Aspects of the Race Problem in the South*, 23.

3 Cf. Ibid; Thomas M. Norwood, *Address on the Negro* (Savannah, Ga.; 1908), 12.

4 Cf. Ibid, 24-5; "How shall We Help the Negro?" *Century Magazine*, XVIII (1885), 279-80.

5 Cf. Ibid, 31; Fort Smith, Ark. *Herald*, May 2, 1868.

6 Cited in Ibid; Hillary A. Herbert, ed., *Why the Solid South? or, Reconstruction and Its Results*, 330-40.

7 Cf. Rowland Berthoff, *An Unsettled People*, 365; Constitutional Amendments XIV and XV.

8 Cf. Ibid, 366; C. Vann Woodward, *Origins of the New South, 1887-1913*, 211.

9 As quoted in Rayford W. Logan, *The Betrayal of the Negro* (London: Colliers, 1965), 9-10.

10 Cited in Nolen, loc. cit., 57; Honeyville, Ala., *Examiner*, clipped in Carrolton *West Alabamian*, March 16, 1870.

11 Cited in Ibid; *Banner of the South*, Sept. 25, 1869.

12 Cited in Ibid; Ft. Smith, Ark., *Herald*, April 9, 1870; Carrolton *West Alabamian*, Aug. 9, 1871.

13 Cited in Helen M. Ludlow, *Harper's Magazine*, XLVIII (1873), 672.

14 Cf. Walter Hines Page, *Forum*, XVI (1893), 303-41; Atticus G. Haygood, "The Black Shadow in the South," *Forum*, XVI (1893), 167-75; William P. Trent, "Tendencies of Higher Life in the South," *Atlantic Monthly*, LXXIX (1897), 769; Edgar G. Murphy, *The White Man and the Negro at the South*, 19-20.

15 Cf. Weatherford and Johnson, *Race Relations*, 509; Atticus G. Haygood, *Our Brother in Black, His Freedom and His Future* (Nashville: Publishing House of the Methodist Episcopal Church, South, 1881), 40, 100, 118ff., 183.

16 Cited by the National Association for the Advancement of Colored People, in *Thirty Years of Lynching in the United States, 1889-1918*, (New York, 1919), 8.

17 Cf. Ibid, 20-5.

18 163 U.S. 537 (1896).

19 Cited in "Blacks and the Law," *The Annals*, 15; 163 U.S. at 548.

20 Cited in Benjamin Quarles, *The Negro in the Making of America*, 73.

21 Cited in Kenneth Katz, *Eyewitness*, 340.

22 Ibid, 342.

23 Cited in Berthoff, loc. cit., 412; Arthur Meier Schlesinger, *The Rise of the City, 1878-1898*, (New York, 1933), 332.

24 Ibid; Aaron Ignatius Abell, *The Urban Impact on American Protestantism* (Cambridge, Mass., 1943), 64.

25 Ibid; Henry F. May, *Protestant Churches and Industrial America* (New York, 1949), 51.

26 Cf. Sydney Ahlstrom, *A Religious History of the American People*, 709.

27 Jno. J. Tigert, ed., *The Doctrines and Discipline of the Methodist Church, South* (Nashville: Publishing House of the M. E. Church, South, 1894), 295.

28 Cf. Quarles, loc. cit., 160.

29 Cited in Ibid, 161.

30 W. E. Burghard DuBois, *The Souls of Black Folk* (Greenwich, Conn.; Fawcett Publications, Inc., 1961), 143-4.

31 Cited in Nolen, loc. cit., 89; Mississippi Constitutional Convention, 1890, *Journal of the Convention* (Jackson, Miss., 1890), 9-10.

32 Ibid; *Journal of the Convention*, 676.

33 Ibid, 90; cited in Paul Lewison, *Race, Class, and Party: A History of Negro Suffrage and White Politics in the South* (New York, 1932), 86; *Virginia Convention Debates, 1901-1902*, 3076-7.

34 Cited in Ibid, 91-2; *Christian Advocate* (Nashville), Feb. 17, 1898; cf. Nov. 3, Dec. 1, 1898.

35 Cited in Katz, loc cit., 357-9; Booker T. Washington, *Up From Slavery* (New York, 1901), 218-25.

36 DuBois, loc. cit., 53-4.

37 Nolen, loc. cit., 92.

38 Loren Miller, *The Petitioners* (New York: Pantheon, 1956), 170, 178, 180.

39 Cited in Nolen, loc. cit., 182-3; "Address," in Southern Society, *Race Problems of the South*, 54-6.

40 Cited in Ibid, 184; Carter G. Woodson, *A Century of Negro Migration* (Washington, D.C., 1918), 125, 138-9.

41 Cf. Ibid, 186; *Christian Advocate* (Nashville), April 4, 1891.

42 Cf. Ibid; Charles B. Galloway, *The South and the Negro* (New York, 1904), 5-7.

43 Cited in C. Vann Woodward, *The Strange Career of Jim Crow*, (New York: Oxford University Press, 1974), 108.

44 Ibid, 91-2.

45 Rayford W. Logan and Irving S. Cohen, *The American Negro*, (Boston: Houghton-Mifflin Co., 1970), 156.

46 Cf. Ibid, 156-7; John Hope Franklin, *From Slavery to Freedom*, 314-5.

47 Ibid, 157.

48 Cited in Katz, loc. cit., 366; William E. Walling, "The Race War in the North," *The Independent*, vol. 65 (Sept. 3, 1908), 529-34.

49 Quarles, loc. cit., 174-5.

50 Cited in Ginger, *Age of Excess*, 289-90.

51 Cf. Ahlstrom, loc cit., 852-3.

52 Cf. Weatherford and Johnson, loc. cit., 515; *Christian Century*, "Will the Church Remove the Color Line?" (Dec. 9, 1931), 1554-56.

Chapter 11. Notes—Racism and the Burden of Bridge-Building

1 *World Evanglization*, "Ten Major Trends in World Missions," (May-June, 1988), 14.

2 Ibid.

3 *The Christian Index*, "Modern Challenges to the American Black Church," (Vol. 120, No. 14, July 15, 1987), 10.

4 Ibid.

5 Ibid.

6 James W. Sells (ed.), *An Informed Church and Other Messages from the Methodist Hour* (Atlanta: Joint Radio Committee, The Methodist Church, 1947), 49-54.

7 Ibid., 54.

8 Ibid., 56-7.

9 Benjamin Quarles, *The Negro in the Making of America*, 227.

10 Edward McKinley, *Marching to Glory*, 196; Sallie Chesham, *Born to Battle: The Salvation Army in America* (Chicago, 1965), 254; Herbert Whisbey, *Dissertation*, 129; *Soldiers*, 62; *Testament to Youth*, 37-8.

11 Ibid., 197.

12 Ibid.; cf. "A Position Statement: The Salvation Army and Intergroup Relations," approved by the Commissioners' Conference, May 1964; Chesham, loc. cit., 253-4.

13 Ibid., 198.

14 Cited in Baldwin and Wallace, *Touched By Grace*, 280; Harry Richardson, *Dark Salvation*, loc. cit., 278.

15 Cited in Ibid.; *Daily Christian Advocate* (The Methodist Church, May 3, 1956), 363.

16 Cited in R. W. Hurn, *Black Evangelism—Which Way from Here?* (Kansas City: Nazarene Publishing House, 1974), 30.

17 Ibid.; William B. McClain, *Black People in The Methodist Church: Whither Thou Goest?* (Schenkman Publishing Co., 1984), 91.

18 Cited in Edwin Gaustad, *A Religious History of America*, 341.

19 Ibid.

20 Sydney Ahlstrom, *A Religious History of the American People*, 1074.

21 Noted in Ibid.; *Theological Education* 4 (Spring 1970) with supplement, 5-10.

22 Taylor Branch, *Parting the Waters*, 140-1.

23 Ibid.

24 Ahlstrom, loc. cit., 1076; Martin Luther King, Jr., *I Have A Dream* (Los Angeles: John Henry and Mary Louise Dunn Bryant Foundation, 1963).

25 Noted in Ibid.

26 Ibid.; James H. Cone, *Black Theology and Black Power* (New York: Seabury Press, 1969), 48; cf. 32-5.

27 Ibid, 1077-8.

28 *Family Protection Scoreboard*, "Liberation Theology Special Edition," "Black American Looks at Liberation Theology," Anthony B. Bryant (1989), 9.

29 Cited in *Theology Today*, "Ritual, Drama, and God in Black Religion" (January 1985), 440; B. Moore (ed.), *The Challenge of Black Theology in South Africa* (Atlanta: John Knox Press, 1974), 48, 56-7.

30 Gerald H. Anderson and Thomas F. Strnasky, C.S.P. (eds.) *Mission Trends No. 4* (New York: Paulist Press and Grand Rapids: Wm. B. Eerdmans Publishing Co., 1979), 116; *Occasional Bulletin of Missionary Research*, "The New Context of Black Theology in the United States," Gayraud S. Wilmore (Oct. 1978).

31 *Christianity Today*, "Race and the Church: A Progress Report," (March 4, 1988), 16.

32 Ibid.

33 Ibid., 17.

34 Shelby Steele, *The Content of Our Character*, (New York: St. Martin's Press, 1990), 20.

35 Stephen Neill, *Call to Mission* (Philadelphia: Fortress Press, 1970), 15.

36 *Moody Monthly*, "In the Name of Fear and Prejudice," (January 1987), 18.

37 Ibid.

38 Ibid., 19.

39 Cf. Steele, loc. cit., 79-80.

Chapter 12. Notes—Reconciliation Constructs Peace

1 Roger E. Bowman, *Color Us Christian* (Kansas City: Nazarene Publishing House, 1975), 9.

2 *World Evangelization*, "Rainbow Evangelism," Kent R. Hunter (Sept.-Oct. 1988), 22-3.

3 Ibid, 23.

4 Ibid.

5 *American Festival Manuscript*, "The Theology of Evangelism: With Culture But Without Color," James Earl Massey (July 1981).

6 Ibid.

7 Ibid.

8 Noted in Waldo Beach, *Christian Community and American Society* (Philadelphia: Westminster Press, 1959), 146; cf. Sebastian deGrazia, *The Political Community: A Study in Anomie*, 187, 189.

9 Ibid, 128.

10 Ibid, 151.

11 Ibid, 154.

12 Cf Ibid; *Brown VS Board of Education*. Opinion of the United States Supreme Court, May 17, 1954.

13 Cf. Ibid, 155; Gordon Allport, *The Nature of Prejudice* (abridged, Doubleday & Co., Inc., 1958).

14 Cited in Harold A. Bosley, *Doing What Is Christian* (Nashville: Graded Press, 1960), 65-6.

15 Ibid; 68; W. A. Visser 't Hooft, (ed.), *The Evanston Report* (New York: Harper & Row Brothers, 1959), 152-3.

16 Baldwin and Wallace, *Touched by Grace*, 87; J. Deotis Roberts, *Liberation and Reconciliation: A Black Theology* (Philadelphia: Westminster Press, 1971), 28-9.

17 Cf. Ibid, 91; Harry Richardson, *Black Salvation*, 62.

18 Ibid, 90.

19 Ibid, 91; *Daily Christian Advocate* (April 26, 1980), 4.

20 Philip A. Johnson, *Call Me Neighbor, Call Me Friend* (Garden City, N.Y.: Doubleday & Co., Inc., 1965), 163-4.

21 Ibid, 164-6.

22 *Christianity Today*, "The Gospel in Black & White," Barbara Thompson (March 4, 1988), 18.

23 Ibid.

24 Ibid.

25 Ibid, 19.

26 Ibid.

27 Ibid.

28 Beach, loc. cit., 165-6.

29 *Moody Monthly*, "Church's Integration Didn't Come Easily," Doug Trouten (January 1987), 40.

30 Ibid.

31 Ibid.

32 *Christianity Today*, "Fudge Ripple at the Rock," Robert M. Kaucher (March 4, 1988), 21.

33 Ibid.

34 Ibid, 21, 23.

35 Ibid.

36 Ibid.

37 Cited in R. W. Hurn, (compiler), *Black Evangelism—Which Way from Here?* "Christ Makes Men Brothers," Roger E. Bowman, (Kansas City: Nazarene Publishing House, 1974), 20-1; *Christian Holiness Association Bulletin* (Indianapolis, summer issue, 1973).

38 *The Interpreter* (May-June 1988), 7.

39 Ibid.

40 *Lamb's Newletter*, Vol. 2, No. 2 (Spring 1989), 3.

41 *The Kansas City-Jackson County Star*, "Keeping the Faith Means Keeping Up with the Times," Calvin Wilson (April 19, 1989), 1, 8-9.

42 R. W. Hurn (compiler), *Black Evangelism*, "Three Indispensable Words," Sergio Franco, 59-68.

Expanded Bibliography

Lyman Abbott. *The Theology of an Evolutionist*. Boston, 1897.

Aaron Abell. *The Urban Impact on American Protestantism*. Cambridge, Mass., 1943.

Massachusetts Abolition Society, Second Annual Report . . . 1841. Boston, 1841.

Massachusetts Abolition Society. *The True History of the Late Division in the Anti-Slavery Societies* . . . Boston, 1841.

Ephraim Adams. *The Power of Ideals in American History*. New Haven: Yale University Press, 1924.

Christian Advocate (Nashville). April 4, 1891; May 2, 1891; Aug. 4, 1892; Feb. 17, 1898.

Northwestern Advocate. March 12, 1853.

Western Advocate. December 4, 1835; November 28, 1860.

Sydney Ahlstrom. *A Religious History of the American People*. New Haven, Conn.: Yale University Press, 1972.

Honeyville, Ala. *Examiner*, clipped in Carrolton *West Alabamian*. March 16, 1870.

Octavia Albert. *The House of Bondage, or Charlotte Brooks and Other Slaves*. New York, 1891.

Gross Alexander. *History of the Methodist Episcopal Church, South*. ACHS, vol. 11, New York, 1894.

Richard Allen. *The Life, Experience, and Gospel Labors of the Rt. Reverend Richard Allen*. Nashville: Abingdon Press, 1960.

A. Allen. *Phillips Brooks, 1835-1893*. New York, 1907.

Don Allen. "Symbolic Color in the Literature of the English Renaissance," *Philosophical Quarterly*, XV. January, 1936.

Gordon Allport. *The Nature of Prejudice*. Garden City, N. Y.: abridged, Doubleday & Co., Inc., 1958.

The American and Foreign Antislavery Society. *Remonstrance Against the Course Pursued by the Evangelical Alliance on the Subject of American Slavery*. New York, 1847.

North American Review. CXXXIX, 1884.

The American Missionary. III, June, 1859; IV, July and August, 1860, issues condemned tobacco with slavery.

The American Missionary. V, 1861 and 1862.

Gerald Anderson and Thomas F. Strnasky, C.S.P. eds. *Mission Trends No. 4*. New York: Paulist Press; and Grand Rapids: Wm. B. Eerdmans Publishing Co., 1979.

Elizabeth Andrews. *War-Time Journal of a Georgia Girl*.

The Annals. "Blacks and the Law." Philadelphia: American Academy of Political and Social Science, 1973.

"Race Antagonism in the South," *Forum*. VI, 1888.

"Our Apostle to the Colored People," *The Conqueror*. V, Oct. 1896.

Memphis *Appeal*. Feb. 26, 1867.

The *Appeal of Clerical Abolitionists on Anti-Slavery Measures*. Boston, 1838.

Herbert Aptheker. *American Negro Slave Revolts*. New York: Columbia University Press, 1943.

Nazarene Archives. *Pentecostal Advocate*. "Evangelistic Work Among the Colored," April 30, 1911.

Nazarene Archives. *Pentecostal Advocate*. "Evanglizing Among the Colored People," Dec. 31, 1911.

Nazarene Archives. *Journal of the Seventh General Assembly*. Columbus, Ohio, June 13-25, 1928.

Nazarene Archives. *Journal of the Tenth General Assembly*. Oklahoma City, June 16-24, 1940.

Nazarene Archives. Report by Warren Rogers, August, 1972.

Isaac Arnold. *Life of Lincoln*. Chicago: A. C. McClurg & Co., n.d.

The Ascetic Works of Saint Basil. tr. W. K. L. Clarke, London, 1925.

The *Assembly of God Heritage*. "'Jesus Only,' The Ministry of Charles Price Jones," Edith L. Blumhofer (Spring 1987, vol. 7, No. 1).

National Association for the Advancement of Colored People, in *Thirty Years of Lynching in the United States, 1889-1918*. New York, 1919.

Saint Augustine. *City of God*, iv, iii; *Confessions*, vi, xv.

Leonard Bacon. *Slavery Discussed in Occasional Essays, from 1833 to 1846*. New York, 1846.

Clarence Bacote. *Journal of Southern History*. XXV, 1957.

Thomas Bailey. *Race Orthodoxy in the South and Other Aspects of the Negro Question*. New York: Neale Publishing Co., 1914.

Lewis Baldwin and Horace L. Wallace. *Touched By Grace*. Nashville: Graded Press, 1986.

The Banner of the South. Mar. 28, April 24, Sept. 25, 1869.

Dover Baptist Association Minutes. 1862, 1863, and 1864 (all published together in 1866).

Southwestern Baptist. Sept. 18, 1862.

William Barclay, ed. *The Bible and History*. Nashville: Abingdon Press, 1968.

Ernest Barker. *From Alexander to Constantine: Passages and Documents Illustrating the History of Social and Political Ideas*, 336 B.C.-A.D. 337. Oxford, 1956.

Albert Barnes. *An Inquiry into the Scriptural Views of Slavery*. Philadelphia, 1846.

Albert Barnes. *The Church and Slavery*. 2nd ed. Philadelphia, 1857.

Albert Barnes. "Revivals of Religion in Cities and Large Towns," *The American National Preacher*. XV, 1841.

Roy Basler, ed. *The Collected Works of Abraham Lincoln*. 9 vols. New Brunswick, N. J.: Rutgers University Press, 1953.

Waldo Beach. *Christian Community and American Society*. Philadelphia: Westminster Press, 1959.

Howard Beale, ed. *Diary of Gideon Welles: Secretary of the Navy Under Lincoln and Johnson*. 3 vols. New York: W. W. Norton, 1960.

James Beattie. *Elements of Moral Science*. Edinburgh, 1793.

Henry Beecher. *Evolution and Religion*. New York, 1885.

A. Behrends. *Socialism and Christianity*. New York: Baker and Taylor, 1886.

David Benedict. *A General History of the Baptist Denomination in America and Other Parts of the World*. New York: Lewis Colby and Co., 1848.

Anthony Benezet. *Some Historical Account of Guinea*. London: J. Phillips, 1788.

Lerone Bennett, Jr. *Before the Mayflower*. New York: Penguin Books, 1985.

Rowland Berthoff. *An Unsettled People: Social Order and Disorder in American History*. New York: Harper & Row Publishers, 1971.

Albert Beveridge. *Abraham Lincoln, 1809-1858.* Boston, 1928.

Terry Bilhartz. *Francis Asbury's America.* Grand Rapids, Mich.: Francis Asbury Press, 1984.

James Birney to the Christian Antislavery Society April 2, 1850, quoted in Dwight L. Dumond, ed. *Letters of James Gillespie Birney, 1831-1857.* New York, 1935.

James Blaine. *Twenty Years in Congress.* 2 vols. Norwich, Conn., 1884.

Council Bluffs, Iowa *Nonpareil.* January 10, 31, 1863.

The *Book of Mormon.*

Harold Bosley. *Doing What Is Christian.* Nashville: Graded Press, 1960.

Edward Bourne, ed. "The Voyages of Columbus and of John Cabot," in *The Northmen, Columbus, and Cabot, 985-1530.* New York: Charles Scribner's Sons, 1906.

Claude Bowers. *The Tragic Era.* Cambridge, Mass.: Riverside Press, 1929.

Roger Bowman. *Color Us Christian.* Kansas City: Nazarene Publishing House, 1975.

Jeffrey Brackett. *The Negroes in Maryland, A Study of the Institution of Slavery.* Baltimore, 1889.

George Braden, "Ku Klux Klan, an Apology," *Southern Bivoac.* IV, 1885.

Taylor Branch. *Parting the Waters.* New York: Simon and Schuster, 1988.

James Brawley. *Two Centuries of Methodist Concern.* Vantage Press, 1974.

Wesley Bready. *This Freedom—Whence?* New York: American Tract Society, 1942.

William Brewer. *Lifting the Veil; or Acts of the Salvationists.* Boston, 1895.

The "Brief on Ohio, Pittsburgh & Southern Province, 1908, Colonel R. E. Holz, P.O."

Newell Bringhurst. *Saints, Slaves, and Blacks.* Westport, Conn.: Greenwood Press, 1981.

Fawn Brodie. *No Man Knows My History.* 2nd ed. New York, 1971.

Charles Brown. *When the Trumpet Sounded.* Anderson, Ind.: Gospel Trumpet Co., 1951.

John Brubacher and Willis Rudy. *Higher Education in Transition.* New York: Harper & Brothers, 1958.

Philip Bruce. *The Plantation Negro as a Freeman: Observations on His Character, Condition, and Prospects in Virginia.* New York, 1889.

William Buckland. *The Roman Law of Slavery: The Condition of the Slave in Private Law from Augustus to Justinian.* Cambridge, England, 1908.

James Buckley. *Constitutional and Parliamentary History of the Methodist Episcopal Church.* New York, 1912.

Occasional Bulletin of Missionary Research. "The New Context of Black Theology in the United States," Gayraud S. Wilmore. Oct., 1978.

Freedmen's Bureau Files. Washington, D.C., National Archives.

John Burnham. *Science.* vol. 175, February 4, 1972.

Richard Bushman. *From Puritan to Yankee: Character and the Social Order in Connecticut, 1690-1765.* Cambridge, Mass., 1967.

John Calhoun, *The Works of John C. Calhoun.* New York, 1854.

William Calhoun. *The Caucasian and the Negro in the United States. They Must Separate. If Not, Then Extermination; A Proposed Solution: Colonization.* Columbia, S.C., 1902.

Robert Campbell. *Some Aspects of the Race Problem in the South.* 2nd ed. Ashville, N. C., 1899.

Charles Carroll. *The Negro a Beast or in the Image of God.* St. Louis, 1900.

Clarence Carson. *A Basic History of the United States.* vol. 3, *The Sections and the Civil War.* Wadley, Ala.: American Textbook Com., 1985.

Paul Carter. *The Decline and Revival of the Social Gospel: Social and Political Liberalism in American Protestant Churches, 1920-1940.* Ithica, N.Y., 1956.

Peter Cartwright. *Autobiography,* ed. W. P. Strickland, Cincinnati: Cranston and Curts, 1856.

Helen Catterall. *Judicial Cases Concerning American Slavery and the Negro.* Washington, D.C.: Carnegie Institution of Washington, 1926.

Christian Century. "Will the Church Remove the Color Line?" Dec. 9, 1931.

George Cheever. *God Against Slavery: and the Freedom and Duty of the Pulpit to Rebuke It, as a Sin Against God.* New York, 1857. Also his *Fire and Hammer of God's Word Against the Sin of Slavery.* Boston, 1858. And *The Guilt of Slavery and Crimes of Slaveholding, Demonstrated from the Hebrew and Greek Scriptures.* Boston, 1860.

Sallie Chesham. *Born to Battle: The Salvation Army in America.* Chicago, 1965.

The *Christ in the Army: A Selection of Sketches of the Work of the U.S. Christian Commission.* Philadelphia, 1865.

Central Christian Herald. January 10, March 21, April 4, October 3, November 7, 1850.

Daily Christian Advocate (Central Jurisdiction, The Methodist Church). May 3, 1956; June 19, 1964; Oct. 16, 1967.

Michigan Christian Herald. February 9, 1852.

Western Christian Advocate. April 10, Dec. 11, 1846; Nov. 15, 1848; Oct. 9, 1850; Oct. 1, 1862; June 24, Oct. 7, 1863.

The Christian Index. "Modern Challenges to the American Black Church," Vol. 120, No. 14. July 15, 1987.

The Christian Review. "Does the Bible Sanction Slavery?" XXVII, 1862.

The Christian Advocate and Journal. January 18, 1855.

Vital Christianity. "The Brothers and Sisters of Love," Feb. 14, 1988.

Vital Christianity. "Wherever There's a Soul to Save," Feb. 14, 1988.

David Christy, *Pulpit Politics: or, Ecclesiastical Legislation of Slavery, in its Disturbing Influences on the American Union.* New York: Negro Universities Press, 1969, reprint.

Dio Chrysostom, *Fourteenth Discourse,* 18; *Fifteenth Discourse*

John Chrysostom, *Commentary on Saint John the Apostle and Evangelist.* Homily 54 tr. Sister Thomas Aquinas Goggin, New York, 1960.

Southern Churchman. Jan. 31 and Nov. 21, 1862; Feb. 20, 1863.

The Cincinnati *Morning Herald.* May 21, 1845.

Kansas City *Times*, March 1, 1988.

Elmer Clark, ed. *The Journal and Letters of Francis Asbury.* Nashville: Abingdon Press, 1958.

Davis Clark. "The Editor's Table," *Ladies Repository*, XXII. December, 1862.

Dan Clark. *Samuel J. Kirkwood.* Iowa City: State Historical Society of Iowa, 1917.

Davis Clark. "The Editor's Table-Development of Treason in the North," *Ladies Repository.* XXIII, March, 1863.

Adam Clarke, *Commentary.*

William Clebsch. "Christian Intrpretations of the Civil War," *Church History.* 30, 1961.

Titus Clement of Alexandria. *Christ the Educator.* tr. Simon P. Wood, New York, 1954.

Catherine Cleveland, *The Great Revival in the West.* Chicago, 1916.

Howell Cobb. *A Scriptural Examination of the Institution of Slavery in the United States with Its Objects and Purposes.* Georgia, 1856.

O. Cobbins, ed. *History of the Church of Christ* (Holiness) U.S.A.

James Cone. *Black Theology and Black Power.* New York: Seabury Press, 1969.

Virginia Convention Debates, 1901-1902.

Archibald Coody, *The Race Question from the White Chief.* Vicksburg, Miss., 1944.

Richard Cook. *The Story of the Baptists in All Ages and Countries.* Baltimore: R. H. Woodward and Co., 1889.

Reginald Coupland. *Wilberforce: A Narrative.* Oxford, 1923.

LaWanda Cox and John H. Cox, *Politics, Principle & Prejudice*, 1865-66. Glencoe, Ill., 1963.

S. Cox. *Three Decades of Federal Legislation*. Providence, R.I., 1888.

Avery Craven. *The Growth of Southern Nationalism, 1840-1860*. Baton Rouge, La., 1953.

The Crisis. VIII. May, 1914.

The *Cross and Journal*. November 27, 1846.

James Croushore and David Morris Potter, eds. *A Union Officer in the Reconstruction*. New Haven, Conn., 1948.

War Cry (Central ed.). June 11, 1921.

War Cry (Pacific Coast edition). Nov. 1884.

War Cry (Eastern ed.). Nov. 17, 1923 (pictoral section). Brig. Hester Dammes, comp., "The Salvation Army Eastern Territory, Opening Dates of Women's Social Institutions," Salvation Army Archives, interview, Brig, Emma Ellegard.

Richard Current. *The Lincoln Nobody Knows*. New York: McGraw-Hill, 1958.

Edmund D'Auvergne. *Human Livestock*. 1933.

Charlotte *Daily Observer*. "Our Women in the War Supplement," narrative of Mrs. F. C. Roberts; Mrs. Elizabeth Allston Pringle, *Chronicles of Chicora Wood*.

Richmond *Daily Dispatch*. Jan. 30, 1865.

Charleston *Daily Courier*. Aug. 6, 1864.

Charles Darwin. *Life and Letters*. I, (letter to W. Graham, July 3, 1881).

Basil Davidson. *Black Mother: The Years of the African Slave Trade*. Boston, 1961.

Murice Davie. *Negroes in American Society*. New York: Whittlesey, 1949.

David Davis, *The Problem of Slavery in Western Culture*. Ithica, N.Y.: Cornell University Press, 1966.

David Davis. *Slavery and Human Progress*. New York: Oxford University Press, 1984.

Harry Davis and Robert C. Good, eds. *Reinhold Neibuhr on Politics*. Charles Scribner's Sons, 1960.

Noah Davis. "The Negro in the South," *Forum*. I, 1886.

Gomes deAzurara. *The Chronicle of the Discovery and Conquest of Guinea*. tr. by C. Raymond Beazley and Edgar Prestage.

Austen deBlois. *Fighters for Freedom*. Philadelphia: The Judson Press, 1929.

Agenor deGasparin. *The Uprising of a Great People*. trans., Mary L. Booth. 4th ed., New York, 1861.

J. DeGraft-Johnson. *African Glory*. New York: Walker & Co., 1954.

Sebastian deGrazia. *The Political Community: A Study in Anomie*.

The Development of State Legislation Concerning the Free Negro. New York: n.p., 1918.

The Devil's Inkwell: A Story of Humanity Embracing Biblical Evidence Establishing Irrefutable and Utter Supremacy of the White Man on the Earth Since the Beginning of Historical Time. Houston, 1923.

Melvin Dieter. *The Holiness Revival of the Nineteenth Century*. Metuchen, N.J.: The Scarecrow Press, 1980.

Classified Digest of the Records of the Society for the Propagation of the Gospel in Foreign Parts. London, 1893.

David Donald. *Lincoln's Herndon*. New York: Alfred A. Knopf, 1948.

Elizabeth Donnan, ed. *Documents Illustrative of the History of the Slave Trade to America*. Carnegie Institution of Washington, 1930-33, I.

Daniel Dorchester. *Christianity in the United States*. New York, 1888.

Thomas Drake. *Quakers and Slavery in America*. New Haven, Conn., 1950.

W. DuBois, ed. *Efforts for Social Betterment among Negro Americans*. Atlanta: Atlanta University Press, 1909.

W. DuBois. *Black Reconstruction: An Essay Toward a History of the Past Which Black Folk Played in the Attempt to Reconstruct Democracy in America, 1860-1880.* New York, 1935.

W. DuBois. *The Souls of Black Folk.* Greenwich, Conn.; Fawcett Publications, Inc., 1961.

Chester Dunham, *The Attitude of the Northern Clergy Toward the South, 1860-1865.* Toledo, Ohio: Gray Co., 1942.

Frederick Eby, ed. *Education in Texas Source Materials.* Austin, Tex., 1918.

Sherwood Eddy. *Pathfinders of the World Missionary Crusade.* New York: Abingdon-Cokesbury Press, 1945.

Cheever's editorials. *The Independent.* "The Sure Aggressive Tyranny of Slave Legislation," March 8, 1855; and "The Sphere of conscience as the Judge and Interpreter of the Law," May 31, 1855.

Theological Education. 4 (Spring 1970) with supplement.

Walther Eichrodt. *Theology of the Old Testament.* trans. J. A. Baker. Philadelphia: The Westminster Press, 1975, II.

Stanley Elkins. *Slavery a Problem in American Institutional and Individual Life.* Chicago, 1959.

Charles Elliott. *The Bible and Slavery* . . . Cincinnati, 1857.

Oberlin Evangelist. February 13, 1839; March 15, 1843.

World Evangelization. "Rainbow Evangelism," Kent R. Hunter. Sept.-Oct. 1988.

World Evanglization. "Ten Major Trends in World Missions," May-June, 1988.

Religious Experiences and Journal of Mrs. Jarena Lee, by Jarena Lee. Philadelphia, 1849.

Wabash Express. Terre Haute, Ind. September 16, 1862.

Andrew Fairbairn. *The Philosophy of the Christian Religion.* New York: The MacMillan Co., 1902.

Max Farrand. *The Records of the Federal Convention of 1787.* rev. ed., New Haven, Conn.: Yale University Press, 1966.

American Festival Manuscript. "The Theology of Evangelism: With Culture But Without Color," James Earl Massey. July 1981.

Charles Finney. *Lectures to Professing Christians.* New York: Fleming H. Revell Co., 1878.

Charles Finney. *Memoirs.* New York: Fleming H. Revell Co., 1908.

Georges Fisch. *Nine Months in the United States* . . . London, 1863.

Henry Fish. *Freedom or Despotism. The Voice of Our Brothers' Blood* . . . Newark, 1856.

Miles Fisher. *Crisis.* XLV, July, 1938.

George Fisher. *The Christian Religion.* New York: The Chautauqua Press, 1887.

Charles Fisher. "The Development of Morgan Memorial as a Social Institution," Ph.D. diss., Boston University, 1949.

John Fitzpatrick, ed. *The Writings of George Washington from the Original Manuscript Sources 1754-1799.* Washington, 1938.

Walter Fleming. *Documentary History of Reconstruction.* Cleveland, 1906.

Robert Fogel and Stanley L. Engerman. *Time on the Cross: The Economics of Negro Slavery.* Boston, 1974.

Robert Fortenbaugh. "American Lutheran Synods and Slavery," 1830-1860, *The Journal of Religion.* XIII, 1933.

John Franklin. *From Slavery to Freedom, A History of Negro Americans.* 3rd ed. New York: Random House, 1969.

John Franklin. *The Militant South.* Boston: Beacon Press, 1968.

Franklin Frazier. *The Negro Church in America.* New York: Schocken Books, 1964.

Franklin Frazier. *The Negro in the United States.* New York: Macmillan Co., 1949.

George Fredrickson. *The Black Image in the White Mind.* New York: Harper Torchbooks, 1972.

American Freedman. I, April, 1866.

Edward Freeman. *The Epoch of Negro Baptists and the Foreign Mission Board.* Kansas City, Kans.: The Central Seminary Press, 1953.

The Friend. IV, Seventh Day, English Month, 1831, No. 46.

Philip Froner, ed. *The Life and Writings of Frederick Douglass.* 4 vols. New York: International Publishers, 1950-55.

Frederick Frothingham. *Significance of the Struggle between Liberty and Slavery in America.* New York, 1857.

Octavius Frothingham. *The Religion of Humanity.* New York, 1873.

Charles Galloway. *The South and the Negro.* New York, 1904.

Charles Gardiner and others. *North American Review.* CXXXIX, 1884.

Edwin Gaustad. *A Religious History of America.* New York: Harper & Row, 1966.

Eugene Genovese. *The Political Economy of Slavery.* New York: Vintage Books, 1967.

Loyal Georgian. Mar. 3, 1866.

Wesley Gewehr. *The Great Awakening in Virginia, 1740-1790.* Duke University Press, 1930.

Ray Ginger. *Age of Excess.* New York: MacMillan Co., 1965.

E. Girvin, *Phineas F. Bresee: A Prince in Israel.* Kansas City: Pentecostal Nazarene Publishing House, 1916.

Washington Gladden. *Social Facts and Forces.* New York, 1897.

Washington Gladden. *Applied Christianity.* Boston: Houghton-Mifflin & Co., 1886.

Congressional Globe, 37 Cong., 2 sess.

Congressional Globe, 38 Cong. 1 sess.

Morgan Godwyn. *The Negro's and Indian's Advocate, Suing for Their Admission into the Church . . .* London, 1680.

C. Goen. *Revivalism and Separatism in New England, 1740-1800: Congregationalists and Separate Baptists in the Great Awakening.* New Haven, 1962.

William Goodell. *Slavery and Anti-Slavery: A History of the Great Struggle in Both Hemispheres, With a View to the Slavery Question in the United States.* New York, 1853.

William Goodell. *The American Slave Code.* 1853, reprint ed., New York: New American Library, 1968.

Henry Grady. "In Plain Black and White; A Reply to Mr. Cable," *Century Magazine Alabamian.* March 16, 1870.

Joanne Grant. *Black Protest History, Documents and Analyses.* New York: Fawcett Premier, 1968.

Robert Grant. *The Letter and the Spirit.* London: 1957.

Asa Gray. *Darwiniana.* New York: D. Appleton & Co., 1876.

Eugene Gressman, "The Unhappy History of Civil Rights Legislation," *Michigan Law Review.* 50, 1952.

Chevereux Gris. "The Negro in His Religious Aspect," *Southern Magazine.* XVII, 1879.

The Guide to Holiness. XXX, July-December, 1856.

J. Hamilton, ed. *The Papers of Thomas Ruffin.* Raleigh: North Carolina Historical Commission, 1920.

J. Hamilton, "The Many-Sided Lincoln," *American Mercury*, V.

Holman Hamilton. *Prologue to Conflict.* Lexington, Ky., 1964.

Eerdman's Handbook to *Christianity in America.* Grand Rapids, Mich.: Wm. B. Eerdman Publishing Co., 1983.

Gilbert Haven. *National Sermons . . .* Boston, 1869.

Laura Haviland. *A Woman's Life Work.* Cincinnati: Walden and Stowe, 1881.

Atticus Haygood. "The Black Shadow in the South," *Forum.* XVI, 1893.

Atticus Haygood. *Our Brother in Black, His Freedom and His Future.* Nashville: Publishing House of the Methodist Episcopal Church, South, 1881.

B. Haynes. *Tempest-tossed on Methodist Seas.* Louisville, Ky.: Pentecostal Publishing Co., 1921.

Charles Heathcote. *The Lutheran Church and the Civil War.* New York, 1919.

P. Heather. "Color Symbolism," *Folk Lore,* LIX. 1948.

James Hedges. *The Browns of Providence Plantation: Colonial Years.* Cambridge, Mass., 1952.

Edgar Helms. *Pioneering in Modern City Missions.* Boston: Morgan Memorial, 1927.

Josiah Henson. Father *Henson's Story of His Own Life.* J. H. Jowett & Co., 1858.

The *Herald of Holiness.* "Our Church and the American Negro," Aug, 9, 1922.

Religious Herald (Richmond, Baptist organ for Virginia). July 2, 1863.

Zion's Herald. Letters to the Editor. January 21, 1852.

Zion's Herald. September 15 and September 22, 1852.

Hillary Herbert, ed. *Why the Solid South? or Reconstruction and Its Results.* Baltimore, 1890.

George Herron. *The Christian State.* New York, 1895.

George Herron. *The New Redemption.* New York, 1893.

George Herron. *The Christian Society.* New York, 1894.

Melville Herskovits. *The Myth of the Negro Past.* Boston: Beacon Press, 1958.

Donna Hill *Joseph Smith: The First Mormon.* New York, 1977.

Gertrude Himmelfarb. *Darwin and the Darwinian Revolution.* London: Chatto and Windus, 1959.

Glenn Hinson. *The Early Church Fathers.* Christian Classics, Nashville: Broadman Press, 1980.

F. Hirst. *Life and Letters of Thomas Jefferson.* New York: The MacMillan Co., 1926.

Thomas Hobbes. *De Cive* (The Citizen). ed. w/intro., Sterling P. Laprecht, New York, 1949.

Margaret Hodgen, "The Negro in the Anthropology of John Wesley," *Journal of Negro History,* XIX. July, 1934.

Frederick Hoffman. *Race Traits and Tendencies of the American Negro.* New York, 1896.

Richard Hofstadter. *Social Darwinism in American Thought.* Boston: Beacon Press, 1955.

Christian Holiness Association Bulletin. Indianapolis, summer issue, 1973.

Edwin Holland. *A Refutation of the Calumnies Circulated Against the Southern and Western States Respecting the Institution and Existence of Slavery Among Them.* Charleston, 1822.

"Colonel Holland: An Interview," *The Conqueror.* VI, Jan. 1897.

Richard Holz. "The Salvation Army and the Negroes of the Southern States of North America," *The Officer.* XXII, July 1914.

Visser't Hooft, ed. *The Evanston Report.* New York: Harper & Row Brothers, 1959.

Charles Hopkins. *The Rise of the Social Gospel in American Protestantism, 1865-1916.* New Haven, Conn., 1940.

Charles Hopkins. *History of the Y.M.C.A. . . .* New York, 1951.

William Hosmer. *The Higher Law in Its Relation to Civil Government, with Particular Reference to Slavery and the Fugitive Slave Law.* Auburn, N.Y., 1852.

William Hosmer. *Slavery and the Church.* Auburn, N.Y., 1853.

Julia Howe. *Reminiscences, 1819-1899.* Boston, 1899.

George Hughes. "An Awful Drift," *Guide, CII.* March ,1898.

David Hume. *Essays Moral, Political, and Literary.* ed. by T. H. Greene and T. H. Grose, London, 1889.

John Hurd. *The Law of Freedom and Bondage.* New York, 1858.

R. Hurn, comp. *Black Evangelism.* "Three Indispensable Words," Sergio Franco.

R. Hurn, comp. *Black Evangelism—Which Way from Here?* "Christ Makes Men Brothers," Roger E. Bowman. Kansas City: Nazarene Publishing House, 1974.

Thomas Huxley. *Lay Sermons, Addresses, and Reviews.* New York: Appleton, 1871.

The *Hymnal of the Methodist Episcopal Church.* New York: Nelson & Phillips, 1878.

The *Illinois State Journal* (Springfield). March 22, 1862.

The Independent. Jan. 4, 1849; Oct. 10, 1850; Jan. 28, 1858.

The *Indiana True Republican* (Centerville). December 8, 1864.

The Indianapolis *State Journal.* February 7, 14, 1865.

Christian Intelligencer. January, 1829.

The Interpreter. May-June 1988.

Dubuque, Iowa *Democratic Herald.* February 2, 1865.

Dubuque, Iowa *Times.* April 21, May 6, 1863.

Henry Jacobs. *A History of the Evangelical Lutheran Church in the United States.* ACHS, vol. 4. New York, 1893.

Henrietta Jaquette, ed. *The South After Gettysburg: Letters of Cornelia Hancock, 1863-1868.* New York, 1956.

William Jay. *A Review of the Causes and Consequences of the Mexican War.* Boston, 1849.

Thomas Jefferson. *Autobiography*, I.

Thomas Jefferson. *Writings*, IX.

Thomas Jefferson. *Notes on the State of Virginia.* Chapel Hill: University of North Carolina Press, 1954.

Thomas Johnson, *History of the Southern Presbyterian Church.* New York, 1894.

Clifton Johnson, ed. *God Struck Me Dead: Religious Conversion Experiences and Autobiographies of Ex-Slaves.* Philadelphia: Pilgrim Press, 1969.

Philip Johnson. *Call Me Neighbor, Call Me Friend.* Garden City, N.Y.: Doubleday & Co., Inc., 1965.

Harry Johnston. *A History of the Colonization of Africa.* 1899.

Charles Jones *The Religious Instruction of the Negros in the United States.* Savannah, Ga.: Thomas Purse Publisher, 1842.

Laura Jones. *The Life and Sayings of Sam P. Jones* (by His Wife). Atlanta: Franklin-Turner Publishers, 1907.

Lewis Jordan. *Negro Baptist History, U.S.A.* Nashville: The Sunday School Publishing Board of the National Baptist Convention, 1930.

Winthrop Jordan. *White Over Black.* University of North Carolina Press, 1968.

Flavius Josephus. *Works.* trans., William Whiston. New York: A.L. Burt Co., n.d.

Cincinnati Journal, Jan. 26, Feb. 2, 1830; Oct. 5, 1832; June 6, 1834; June 4, 1838.

The "Journal of the Proceedings of the Thirty-Second Annual Council of the Protestant Episcopal Church in the Diocese of Alabama," Bishop Wilmer address. 1863.

The *Journal of Southern History*, XI. Aug. 1945.

Philo Judaeus. *Quad Omnis Probus.* 24 Loeb classical Library, ed. tr. by F. W. Colson, London, 1941.

The Kansas City *Times.* "A Flag of Bitter Insult," Carl T. Rowan. Feb. 5, 1988.

The Kansas City-Jackson County Star. "Keeping the Faith Means Keeping Up with the Times," Calvin Wilson. April 19, 1989.

William Katz. *Eyewitness: The Negro in American History.* New York: Pitman Publishing Co., 1967.

Ralph Keeker. *Reclamation of Men and Things: The Goodwill Industries.* Philadelphia: Board of Home Missions, M. E. Church, c. 1921.

Alfred Kelly and Winfred Harbison. *The American Constitution: Its Origins and Development.* New York, 1948.

Klaud Kendrick. *The Promise Fulfilled: A History of the American Pentecostal Movement.* Springfield, Mo.: Gospel Publishing House, 1961.

The Kerner Commission Report. Bantam Books, 1968.

J. Killebrew. "How to Deal with the Negro," *Southern States Farm Magazine.* V, 1898.

Martin King, Jr. *Stride Toward Freedom.* Harper & Row Brothers, 1958.

Martin King, Jr. *I Have A Dream.* Los Angeles: John Henry and Mary Louise Dunn Bryant Foundation, 1963.

Martin King, Jr. *Strength to Love.* Harper & Row Publishers, 1963.

Caroline Kirkland. *Glimpses of Western Life.* New York, 1850.

Adrienne Koch. *The Philosophy of Thomas Jefferson.* Glouster, Mass.: reprint ed., 1957.

Aileen Kraditor, *Means and Ends in American Abolitionism: Garrison and His Critics on Tactics and Strategy,* 1834-1850. New York, 1969.

John Krout and Dixon Ryan Fox. *The Completion of Independence, 1790-1830.* New York, 1944.

The Lamb's Newsletter. Vol. 2, No. 2. Spring 1989.

"Lynch Law in the South," *North American Review.* CLV, 1892.

"Higher Law and Divorces," *The Independent.* July 5, 1855.

The *Leader* (Cleveland). January 3, 1863.

Joseph LeConte. *Religion and Science.* New York, 1873.

Louis LeFevre. *Liberty and Restraint.* New York: Albert A. Knopf, 1931.

Julius Lester. *To Be a Slave.* New York: Dell Publishing Co., 1975.

"A Letter From George Liele," in *Rippon's Register.*

Weld-Grimke Letters, I. Weld to Garrison, January 2, 1833.

Harry Levin. *The Power of Blackness.* New York, 1958.

John Lewis. *Goodwill—For the Love of People.* Washington, D.C.: Goodwill Industries of America, Inc., 1977.

Paul Lewison. *Race, Class, and Party: A History of Negro Suffrage and White Politics in the South.* New York, 1932.

The *Liberator.* April 14, 1832.

The *Liberia.* Bulletin no. 10, Feb., 1897.

The Library of the University of Richmond, Church Book of Upper King and Queen Baptist Church, *Minutes of Rappahannock Baptist Association for 1863.*

Eric Lincoln. *The Negro Pilgrimage in America.* New York: Bantam Books, revised 1969.

Leon Litwack. *Been in the Storm So Long.* London: The Athlone Press, 1979.

John Locke. *Two Treatises of Government,* a critical edition with an introduction and Apparatus Criticus, by Peter Laslett. Cambridge, England, 1960.

Bert Loewenberg. "Darwinianism Comes to America 1859-1900," *Mississippi Valley Historical Review,* XXVIII, 1841.

Rayford Logan and Irving S. Cohen. *The American Negro.* Boston: Houghton-Mifflin Co., 1970.

Rayford Logan. *The Betrayal of the Negro.* London: Colliers, 1965.

J. Loguen. *As a Slave and As a Freeman.* Syracuse, 1859.

Arthur Lovejoy. *The Great Chain of Being; A Study of the History of an Idea.* New York: Torchbook ed., 1960.

James Lowell, "The American Tract Society," *The Atlantic Monthly*. II, 1857-58.

Helen Ludlow. *Harper's Magazine*. XLVIII, 1873.

Martin Luther. *Werke*. XVIII. Weimar, 1908.

Letter, Lyon to Clark. Jan. 17, 1865, Miss. Archives, Ser. E, no. 68; Feb. 10, 1865.

Century Magazine. "How shall We Help the Negro?" XVIII, 1885.

Time Magazine, "Taking the Measure of American Racism," November 12, 1990.

Southern Magazine. XVI, 1875.

William Manross. *A History of the American Episcopal Church*. 2nd ed. rev., New York, 1950.

Charles Marshall. *The Exodus*: Its Effects upon the People of the South. Washington, D.C., 1880.

James Massey. "The Church of God and the Negro," *National Association of the Church of God Historical Report*, 1974.

Cotton Mather. "Diary," Massachusetts Historical Society *Collections*, seventh series, I.

Cotton Mather. *A Good Master Well Served*. Boston, 1696.

Lucius Matlack. *The Life of Rev. Orange Scott . . .* New York, 1847.

Henry May. *Protestant Churches and Industrial America*. New York, 1949.

Samuel May. *Some Recollections of Our Antislavery Conflict*. Boston, 1869.

William McClain. *Black People in The Methodist Church: Whither Thou Goest?* Schenkman Publishing Co., 1984.

John McClintock. "Stephen Olin," *The Methodist Quarterly Review*. XXXVI, 1854.

Robert McColley. *Slavery and Jeffersonian Virginia*. Urbana: University of Illinois Press, 1964.

John McConnell. *Negroes and Their Treatment in Virginia from 1865 to 1867*. Pulaski, Va., 1910.

Col. McIntrye. *Twenty Years Housing the Salvation Army*. New York, 1920.

Edward McKinley. *Marching to Glory*. San Francisco: Harper and Row Publishers, 1980.

James McPherson, ed. *The Negroe's Civil War: How American Negroes Felt and Acted During the War for the Union*. New York, 1965.

Edward McPherson. *The Political History of the United States of America During the Period of Reconstruction, From April 15, 1865 to July 15, 1870*. Washington, D.C., 1880.

H. McTyeire. "Plantation Life—Duties and Responsibilities," *De Bow's Review*. XXIX (September, 1860).

Sidney Mead. *The Lively Experiment: The Sharing of Christianity in America*. New York: Harper & Row, 1963.

David Mears. *Life of Edward Norris Kirk, D.D*. Boston, 1877.

Charleston *Mercury*. Nov. 29, 1862.

The *Messenger*. "Being Black and Brethren," June, 1988.

The Methodist Quarterly Review. XXV, 1853.

Loren Miller. *The Petitioners*. New York: Pantheon, 1956.

Kelly Miller. "The Industrial Condition of the Negro in the North," *The Annals*. XXVII, May 1906.

Perry Miller. *Jonathan Edwards*. New York, 1949.

Ethnic Minorities in the United Methodist Church. Discipleship Resources, 1976.

The *Minutes of the Western Yearly Meeting of Friends, 1862*.

Jackson, Miss. *Clarion*. Sept. 8, 1870; June 28, 1888.

The Mississippi Constitutional Convention, 1890. *Journal of the Convention*. Jackson, Miss., 1890.

Douglass' Monthly. "What Shall Be Done with the Freed Slaves?" November, 1862.

Moody Monthly. "In the Name of Fear and Prejudice," January 1987.

The *Moody Monthly.* "Church's Integration Didn't Come Easily," Doug Trouten. January, 1987.

William Moody. *The Life of D. L. Moody.* Fleming H. Revell Co., 1900.

B. Moore, ed. *The Challenge of Black Theology in South Africa.* Atlanta: John Knox Press, 1974.

George Moore, *Notes on the History of Slavery in Massachusetts.* New York, 1866.

George Moore. *Notes on the History of Slavery.* New York, 1866.

George Moore. *History of Religions.* New York: Charles Scribner's Sons, 1919, II.

Henry Morgan. *Shadowy Hand, or Life Struggles.* c. 1874.

Edmund Morgan. *The Puritan Family.* New York: Harper & Row, 1966.

Henry Morris. *The Troubled Waters of Evolution.* San Diego: Creation-Life Publishers, 1975.

Lemuel Moss. *Annals of the United States Christian Commission.* Philadelphia, 1868.

Frank Mott. *A History of American Magazines, 1850-1865.* Cambridge, Mass., 1938.

Edgar Murphy. *The White Man and the Negro at the South.* Philadelphia, 1900.

Gunnar Myrdal. *An American Dilemma.* New York: Harper & Brothers Publisher, 1944.

"The National Crisis," *The Christian Review.* XXVI, 1861.

"Shall Negro Majorities Rule," *Forum.* VI, 1888.

"The Negro American Artisan," *Atlanta University Publications.* No. 17. Atlanta, 1912.

The "Negro", in *Encyclopaedia Britannica: or A Dictionary of Arts, Sciences, and Miscellaneous Literature.* 3rd ed. Edinburgh, 1797, XII.

"Wealthy Negroes," The New York *Times.* July 14, 1895.

Stephen Neill. *Call to Mission.* Philadelphia: Fortress Press, 1970.

The New York Freeman. July 11, 1887.

James Nichols and W. R. Bagnall, trans. *The Writings of James Arminius.* Grands Rapids, Mich.: Baker Book House, 1956, I.

John Nicoly and John Hay, eds. *Complete Works of Abraham Lincoln.* New York: The Century Co., 1920.

Claude Nolen. *The Negro's Image in the South.* Lexington: University of Kentucky Press, 1967.

W. Northen. "The Negro at the South:" An Address before the Congregational Club, Boston, May 22, 1869.

Wesley Norton. *Religious Newspapers in the Old Northwest to 1861.* Athens, Ohio: Ohio Univ. Press, 1977.

Frederick Norwood, ed. *Sourcebook of American Methodism.* Nashville: Abingdon Press, 1982.

Thomas Norwood. *Address on the Negro.* Savannah, Ga.; 1908.

Julia Olin, ed. *The Life and Letters of Stephen Olin.* New York, 1853.

Frederick Olmstead. *A Journey in the Seaboard Slave States.* New York, 1856.

New Orleans *Picayune.* May 16, 30, 1876; July 18, 1887.

New Orleans *Crescent.* Dec. 5, 1865, Mar. 22, 1866, Nov. 20, 1867.

Gilbert Osofsky. *Harlem: The Making of a Ghetto.* New York: Harper Torchbook, 1971.

Saul Padover, ed. *Thomas Jefferson on Democracy.* New York: New American Library, 1967.

Walter Page. *Forum.* XVI, 1893.

Thomas Page. *The Negro: The Southerner's Problem.* New York, 1904.

Phoebe Palmer. *A Mother's Gift; or A Wreath for My Darlings.* New York: Walter C. Palmer, 1875.

Phoebe Palmer. *Four Years in the Old World . . .* New York, 1864.

Theodore Parker to Salmon P. Chase, March 9, 1858, *Diary and Correspondence of Salmon P. Chase*. Washington D.C.: Government Printing Office, 1903.

Theodore Parker. "The Nebraska Question," sermon of February 12, 1854, *Collected Works*. ed. Frances P. Cobbe. London, 1863-1870, V.

C. Pascoe. *Two Hundred Years of the Society for the Publication of the Gospel*. London, 1901.

Daniel Payne. *Recollection of Seventy Years*. A.M.E. Sunday School Union, 1888.

Buckner Payne. *Ariel's Reply to the Rev. John A. Seiss, D.D., of Philadelphia; also, His Reply to the Scientific Geologist and Other Learned Men in Their Attacks on the Credibility of the Mosaic Account of the Creation and of the Flood*. Nashville, 1876.

Theodore Pease and James G. Randall, eds. *The Diary of Orville Hickman Browning*. 2 vols. Springfield, Ill.: Illinois State Historical Library, 1927-33.

Lewis Perry. *Childhood, Marriage, and Reform: Henry Clarke Wright, 1797-1870*. Chicago, 1980.

The *Philanthropist*. October 17, 1817; August 23, 1820.

Ulrich Phillips. *American Negro Slavery*. Baton Rouge: Louisiana State University Press, 1966.

The "Plantations with Slave Labor and Free," *American Historical Review*.

William Polk. *Leonidas Polk: Bishop and General*. 2 vols. New York, 1893.

Louis Pollack. *The Constitution and the Supreme Court: A Documentary History*. New York: World Pub. Co., Meridian Books, 1968.

Richard Popkin. "The Philosophical Basis of Eighteenth Century Racism," in *Racism in the Eighteenth Century Culture*. vol. 3, Cleveland and London, 1973.

Anthony Porter. *Led On; Step by Step: Scenes from Clerical, Military, Educational and Plantation Life in the South, 1828-1898*. New York, 1898.

"A Position Statement: The Salvation Army and Intergroup Relations," approved by the Commissioners' Conference, May 1964.

George Prentice. *The Life of Gilbert Haven . . .* New York, 1883.

Southern Presbyterian. XVI, July, 1863.

John Price. *The Negro: Past, Present and Future*. New York, 1907.

The *Proceedings of the Meetings in Charleston, South Carolina, May 13-15, 1845, on the Religious Instruction of the Negroes*. Charleston, 1845.

The Proceedings of the Fifth General Assembly. Kansas City, Sept. 25-Oct. 6, 1919.

Family Protection Scoreboard, "Liberation Theology Special Edition," "Black American Looks at Liberation Theology," Anthony B. Bryant. 1989.

Major Purser. *Report on the Meeting of Active Black Officers Serving in the Eastern Territory, The Salvation Army Territorial Congress, June 1969*. New York, 1969.

Mary Putnam. *The Baptists and Slavery, 1840-1845*. Ann Arbor, Mich.: 1913.

Benjamin Quarles. *Lincoln and the Negro*. New York: Oxford University Press, 1962.

Benjamin Quarles. *The Negro in the Making of America*. New York: Macmillan Publishers, Inc., 1969.

Johannes Quasten. *Patrology*, III. Utrecht and Westminster, Md., 1960.

George Railton in a letter to William Booth, quoted in Eileen Douglas and Mildred Duff. *Commissioner Railton*. London, 1920.

George Railton. *Twenty-One Years Salvation Army*. London, 1888.

James Ramsay. *An Essay on the Treatment and Conversion of African Slaves in the British Sugar Colonies*. London, 1784.

Walter Rauschenbush. *Christianizing the Social Order*. New York: The MacMillan Co., 1912.

George Rawick, ed. *The American Slave: A Composite Autobiography.* Westport, Conn., 1972.

George Rawick ed. *Mississippi Narratives.* Greenwood Press, 1977.

"Monthly Record of Events," *Harper's Magazine.* XXXIV, 1867.

"Monthly Record of Events," *Harper's Magazine.* XXXII, 1866.

Chicago Record. Dec. 15, 1860.

Weekly Recorder. Dec. 23, 1819; Feb. 9, 1820.

Southern Recorder. Nov. 4, 1862, quoting the *Confederate Union; Southwestern Baptist.* Sept. 18, 1862.

Official Records of the Union and Confederate Armies, Ser. 1, XIV.

Saunders Redding. *They Came in Chains.* Philadelphia: J. B. Lippincott Co., 1973.

Niles Register. LXVIII.

Ira Reid. *In A Minor Key.* Washington, D.C.; American Council on Education, 1940.

David Reimers. *White Protestantism and the Negro.* New York: Oxford University Press, 1965.

The Report of the Industrial Commission on Agriculture and Agriculture Labor. . ..Washington, D.C., 1901.

"Final Report of the American Freedmen's Inquiry Commission to the Secretary of War," (May 15, 1864) , *Official Records*, 3rd ser., IV.

Grattan Report. Virginia, VII.

The "Report of the Majority Committee," Charleston, S. C. *News and Courier.* May 13, 1876.

The *Reports of Committees of the House of Representatives*, No. 148, 37 Cong., 2 sess.

African Repository, IV. June 1829.

DeBow's Review. Jan. 1861.

Madeline Rice. *American Catholic Opinion in the Slavery Controversy.* New York, 1944.

Harry Richardson. *Dark Salvation.* Anchor Press/Doubleday, 1976.

Deotis Roberts. *Liberation and Reconciliation: A Black Theology.* Philadelphia: Westminster Press, 1971.

Benson Roberts. *Holiness Teachings Compiled from the Editorial Writings for the Late Rev. Benjamin Titus Roberts.* North Chili, N.Y.: The Earnest Christian Publishing House, 1893; reprint, Salem, Ohio: Schmul, 1983.

George Rockwood. *Cheever, Lincoln and Causes of the Civil War.* Worcester, Mass.: 1936.

Arnold Rose, ed. *Assuring Freedom to the Free.* Detroit: Wayne State Univ. Press, 1964.

Eugene Roseboom. *The Civil War Era, 1850-1873.* Columbus: Ohio State Archeological and Historical Society, 1944.

Frederick Ross. *Slavery Ordained of God.* Philadelphia, 1859.

Baton Rouge, La. *Capitolian-Advocate.* Sept. 19, Nov. 31, 1881.

Ronald Sanders. *Lost Tribes and Promised Lands: The Origins of American Racism.* Boston, 1978.

Sherman Savage. *The Controversy Over the Distribution of Abolition Literature 1830-1860.* New York: Negro Universities Press, 1938.

Arthur Schlesinger. *The Rise of the City, 1878-1898.* New York, 1933.

Herbert Schneider. *Religion in 20th Century America.* Cambridge, Mass., 1952.

"The Schools of the People," *Journal of the Proceedings of the National Education Association, 1903.* Chicago, 1903.

The *Selections From the Letters and Speeches of the Hon. James H. Hammond of South Carolina.* New York, 1866.

James Sells, ed. *An Informed Church and Other Messages from the Methodist Hour.* Atlanta: Joint Radio Committee, The Methodist Church, 1947.

Robert Semple. *History of the Baptists in Virginia.* Richmond: Pitt and Dickenson, 1894.

Robert Service. *The Harpy.* st. 12, Ryerson Press.

N. Shaler. "An Ex-Southerner in South Carolina," *Atlantic Monthly.* XXVI, 1870.

S. Shaw. *Michigan Holiness Record.* II, June, 1884.

Charles Sheldon. *In His Steps.* New York: Grosset & Dunlap, 1935.

James Silver. *Confederate Morale and Church Propaganda.* Tuscaloosa, Ala.: Confederate Publishing Co., 1957.

Francis Simpkins. *Pitchfork Ben Tillman: South Carolinian.* Baton Rouge, La. 1944.

Matthew Simpson, ed. *Cyclopedia of Methodism* . . . Philadelphia, 1878.

George Simpson. "The Biological Nature of Man," *Science.* vol. 152, April 22, 1964.

In "Slavery and the Bible," *The New Englander.* XV, 1857.

Frank Smith. *The Salvation War in America, 1885.* New York, 1886.

Ft. Smith, Ark., *Herald.* Aug. 24, 1867; April 9, 1870.

Joseph Smith (Fielding). *The Way to Perfection.* Salt Lake City, 1931.

Joseph Smith, Jr. *Views on the Government and Policies of the United States.* Nauvoo, Ill., 1844.

Powis Smith. *The Prophets and Their Times.* Chicago: University of Chicago Press, 1965.

Timothy Smith. *Called Unto Holiness.* Kansas City: Nazarene Publishing House, 1962.

Timothy Smith. *Revivalism and Social Reform.* Gloucester, Mass.: Peter Smith, reprint, 1976.

Whitefoord Smith. *God the Refuge of His People.* Columbia, 1850.

William Smith. *The Philosophy and Practice of Slavery.* New York: Negro Universities Press, reprint, 1969.

The "Strivings of the Negro Race," *Atlantic Monthly.* LXXX, 1897.

Sunny South. Nov. 6, Nov. 13, Dec. 9, 1875; Dec. 9, 1876; Jan. 28, 1888; Oct. 12, 1889.

The *Southern Disposition of Forces.* Feb. 1927, listed Washington No. 2 Corps in Potomac Division as "colored," as was the Servicemen's Hotel, Seventh and P streets.

Editorial, *Southern Bivoac.* IX, 1887.

"The Southern Question," *North American Review.* CXXV, 1877.

The *Southern Field and Fireside.* Jan. 8, 1862.

Rufus Spain. *At Ease in Zion: Social History of Southern Baptists.* Nashville: Vanderbilt University Press, 1967.

John Sproat. "Blueprint for Radical Reconstruction," *Journal of Southern History.* XXIII, February, 1957.

The Squire (published in Prairie Village, Kansas). vol. II., No. 9, September 15, 1988, "Saint or Sinner?"

Bruce Staiger "Abolitionism and the Presbyterian Schism of 1837-8," *Mississippi Valley Historical Review.* 36 (1949-50).

Kenneth Stampp. *The Era of Reconstruction, 1865-1877.* New York: Random House, Vintage Books, 1965.

Christian Standard and Home Journal. XIX, February 21, 1885.

Ohio State Journal (Columbus). March 16, April 14, June 1, 1863.

United States Commission on Civil Rights. "Freedom to the Free." Washington, D.C., US GPO, 19.

Shelby Steele. *The Content of Our Character.* New York: St. Martin's Press, 1990.

Levi Sternberg. "Revivals," *The Evangelical Quarterly Review.* XV, 1864.

Abel Stevens. "American Slavery—Its Progress and Prospects," *The Methodist Review.* XXXIX, 1857.

Abel Stevens. *Life and Times of Nathan Bangs, D.D.* New York, 1863.

Moorfield Storey. *Negro Suffrage Is Not a Failure: An Address before the New England Suffrage Conference,* March 30, 1903. Boston, 1903.

Harriet Stowe. *Uncle Tom's Cabin*. Boston: Houghton, Mifflin and Co., 1891.

Josiah Strong. *The Next Great Awakening*. New York, 1893.

Josiah Strong. *Our Country: Its Possible Future and Its Present Crisis*. New York: the American Home Missionary Society, 1885.

George Stroud. *Sketch of the Laws Relating to Slavery*. Philadelphia: Henry Longstreth, 1856.

Julian Sturtevant. *The Lessons of Our National Conflict. Address to the Alumni of Yale College . . .* New Haven, 1861.

William Sweet. *The Story of Religion in America*. New York: Harper & Brothers, 1950.

Samuel Swell. "Diary," Massachusetts Historical Society, *Collections*, fifth series, II.

Henry Swint. *The Northern Teacher in the South*. Nashville, 1941.

Gabriel Tarde. *The Laws of Imitation*. trans. Elsie Claws Parsons. New York, 1903.

A. Taylor. *The Negro in Tennessee, 1865-1880*. Washington, D.C., 1941.

"Scientific Teaching in the Colleges," *Popular Science Monthly*. XVI, 1880.

Catholic Telegraph (Cincinnati). Jan. 7, Feb. 18, April 8, 15, 23, May 6, 13, 20, June 10, 24, July 8, 15, Aug. 26, Oct. 7, Nov. 11, 18, Dec. 2, 1863.

Joseph Thompson. *Teachings of the New Testament on Slavery*. New York, 1856.

D. Thompson. *Abraham Lincoln, the First American*. New York: Hunt & Eaton, 1894.

Edward Thomson. "Slavery," *The Methodist Quarterly Review*. XXXIX, 1857.

Jno. Tigert, ed. *The Doctrines and Discipline of the Methodist Church, South*. Nashville: Publishing House of the M. E. Church, South, 1894.

Miriam's Timbrel. . .. 2nd ed. Mansfield, Ohio, 1853.

Christian Times. October 20, 1853.

Christianity Today, "Race and the Church: A Progress Report," March 4, 1988

Christianity Today. "Fudge Ripple at the Rock," Robert M. Kaucher. March 4, 1988.

Christianity Today. "Race and the Church: A Progress Report," March 4, 1988.

Christianity Today. "The Gospel in Black & White," Barbara Thompson. March 4, 1988.

Theology Today. "Ritual, Drama, and God in Black Religion," January, 1985.

Joseph Tracy. *A History of the Great Awakening*. Boston: Tappan and Dennet, 1842.

William Trent. "Tendencies of Higher Life in the South," *Atlantic Monthly*. LXXIX, 1897.

William Trent. "Dominant Forces in Southern Life," *Atlantic Monthly*. LXXIX, 1897.

Chicago *Tribune*. Jan. 1, 3, 1863.

Leonard Trinterud. *The Forming of an American Tradition: A Re-examination of Colonial Presbyterianism*. Philadelphia, 1949.

Ernst Troeltsch. *Die Soziallehern der Christlichen Kirchen and Gruppen*. Gesammelte Schriften, Erster Band, n.p., 1961.

Mark Twain. *Adventures of Huckleberry Finn*. New York: Harper & Brothers, 1884.

Alice Tyler. *Freedom's Ferment: Phases of American Social History to 1860*. Minneapolis: University of Minnesota Press, 1944.

The U.S. Department of Commerce, *Negro Population: 1790-1915*. Washington D.C., Government Printing Office, 1918.

"An Unkind Insinuation," *Advocate of Bible Holiness*. XIII, September, 1882.

Henry Vedder. *A Short History of the Baptists*. Philadelphia: American Baptist Publication Society, 1897.

"The Vital Forces of the Age," *The Christian Review*. XXVI, 1861.

Jacque Voegeli. *Free But Not Equal*. Chicago: University of Chicago Press, 1969.

William Walling. "The Race War in the North," *The Independent*. Vol. 65. Sept. 3, 1908.

American War Cry. July 18, 1885.

Robert Warden, *An Account of the Private Life and Public Services of Salmon Portland Chase*. Cincinnati: Wilstock Baldwin, 1874.

Joseph Washington, Jr. *Black Religion: The Negro and Christianity in the United States.* Boston: Beacon Press, 1964.

Booker Washington, to Maj. T. C. Marshall, Tuskegee, Ala., July 28, 1896. *The Conquerer.* I, Oct., 1896.

Booker Washington. *Up From Slavery.* New York: Doubleday, Page & Co., 1901.

The Watchman and Reflector. March 16, 1854; July 16, Oct. 1, 1857; Jan. 1, 1863.

The *Watchmen of the Valley.* Jan. 21, July 1, 1847.

Maria Waterbury. *Seven Years Among the Freedmen.* Chicago, 1890.

Major Watson. *Report: Services to Minorities and the Inner City. The Salvation Army Eastern Territory, July 1973,* New York, 1973.

Henry Watterson. *North American Review.* CXXVIII, 1879.

Willis Weatherford and Charles S. Johnson. *Race Relations.* New York: Negro Universities Press, reprint, 1969.

Willis Weatherford. *Race Relations.* New York: Negro Universities Press, 1969.

Willis Weatherford. *American Churches and the Negro.* Christopher Publishing House, 1957.

A. Weinstein and F. Gatell, eds. *American Negro Slavery, A Modern Reader.* New York: Oxford University Press, 1968.

Theodore Weld to William Lloyd Garrison, January 2, 1833, *Letters of Theodore Weld, Angelian Grimke Weld, and Sarah Weld,* 1822-1844. ed. Gilbert H. Barnes and Dwight L. Dumond. New York, 1934.

David Wells and John A. Woodbridge, eds. *The Evangelicals.* Grand Rapids, Mich.; Baker Book House, 1977.

Herbert Wells. *The Outline of History.* Garden City, N.Y.: Garden City Publishing Co., Inc., 1930, reprint.

Ida Wells. *A Red Record.* Chicago, 1894.

W. Wells. *The African Methodist Episcopal Zion Church.* A.M.E. Zion Publishing House, 1974.

John Wesley. *Works.* Reprint, Kansas City: Beacon Hill Press, n.d., "Thoughts Upon Slavery," XI.

John Wesley. *Journal.* standard ed., Nehemiah Curnock, ed. 1906-16.

Carrolton *West Alabamian.* March 9, 1870.

George Weston. *The Progress of Slavery in the United States.* Washington, D.C., 1857.

Charles Whipple. *The Methodist Church and Slavery.* New York, 1859.

Herbert Whisbey. *Dissertation,* 129; *Soldiers,* 62; *Testament of Youth,* 37-8.

Charles White. *The Beauty of Holiness.* Grand Rapids: Francis Asbury Press, 1986.

Rev. Whiton. "Darwin and Darwinianism," *New Englander.* XLII, 1883.

Calvin Wiley to Vance. Jan. 24, 1865, Vance Papers.

Bell Wiley. *Southern Negroes, 1861-1865.* New Haven, Conn.: Yale University Press, 1965.

Samuel Willard. *A Compleat Body of Divinity.* Boston, 1736.

George Willison. *Saints and Strangers.* New York: Regnal and Hitchcock, 1945.

Charles Wiltsie. *John C. Calhoun Sectionalist, 1840-1850.* Indianapolis: The Bobs-Merrill Co., Inc., 1951.

Robert Winston. *Andrew Johnson: Plebian and Patriot.* New York, 1928.

James Woodburn. "Party Politics in Indiana During the Civil War," *American Historical Association Report for the Year 1902.* I, 1903.

Carter Woodson. *A Century of Negro Migration.* Washington, D. C., 1918.

Carter Woodson. *The History of the Negro Church.* 2nd ed. Washington D.C.: Associated Publishers, 1921.

Vann Woodward. *The Strange Career of Jim Crow*. New York: Oxford University Press, 1974.

Federal Writer's Project. *The Negro in Virginia*. New York: Hastings House, 1940.

Richard Yates Papers. Springfield: Illinois State Historical Society.

New York Age. April 1, 1909.

New York *Independent*. Oct. 17, 1861.

New York World. Aug. 2, 1865.

Brigham Young. *Journal of Discourses*, VII.